Booze and the Private Eye

Booze and the Private Eye

Alcohol in the Hard-Boiled Novel

RITA ELIZABETH RIPPETOE

McFarland & Company, Inc., Publishers

Jefferson, North Carolina, and London

Library of Congress Cataloguing-in-Publication Data

Rippetoe, Rita Elizabeth, 1948–
    Booze and the private eye : alcohol in the hard-boiled novel /
Rita Elizabeth Rippetoe.
        p.   cm.
    Includes bibliographical references and index.

    ISBN 0-7864-1899-0 (softcover : 50# alkaline paper)

    1. Detective and mystery stories, American—History and
criticism.   2. American fiction—20th century—History and
criticism.   3. Noir fiction, American—History and criticism.
4. Drinking of alcoholic beverages in literature.   5. Private
investigators in literature.   6. Drinking customs in literature.
7. Alcoholism in literature.   8. Alcoholics in literature.   I. Title.
PS374.D4R57   2004
813'.0872093561—dc22   2004009592

British Library cataloguing data are available

Cover photograph ©2004 Photospin

Manufactured in the United States of America

McFarland & Company, Inc., Publishers
  Box 611, Jefferson, North Carolina 28640
  www.mcfarlandpub.com

To my grandmother,
Mabel Maryland Robins Teague, who,
despite having formal schooling only through the eighth grade,
taught me to read and to love reading and writing

Table of Contents

Preface

This book had its genesis in a graduate seminar on the hard-boiled detective novel taught by Dr. Robert Merrill at the University of Nevada, Reno. For that seminar I wrote a paper on the role of alcohol in Chandler's *The Big Sleep* and *The Long Goodbye*. The fact that these works came at the beginning and near the end of his writing career, yet seemed to reflect a similar sensitivity to the nuances of drinking behavior, suggested to me that drinking behavior was a major issue for Chandler.

When the time came to choose a topic for my dissertation, I was drawn back to this subject, feeling that there was much more material to be explored, both in the works of Chandler and in the works of other writers categorized as hard-boiled. My dissertation, "*...sober and I didn't care who knew it*": *Alcohol in the Hard-Boiled Detective's Code*, was completed in January of 2003. The title, with its quotation from the first page of *The Big Sleep* and references to the code of the detective, indicates both the genesis of my research and the theme I explored.

Although the original seminar paper dealt only with Chandler, the project expanded both backward in time to Dashiell Hammett and forward to contemporary writers such as Lawrence Block. Hammett could hardly be excluded, especially since Chandler lauded him as the founder of the new genre and his Prohibition-era novels set the stage for the concept of drinking as a problematic area of behavior for the detective. Beyond these founding fathers of the genre the choices multiplied, and in some instances came down to personal preference or familiarity with an author.

Although Chandler may not have originated the idea that the private detective lives by a code, his definition, in "The Simple Art of Murder," of the detective as "the best man in his world" became a classic.

1

This theme seemed closely related to Marlowe's personal rules for drinking and my goal became to trace this relationship in Chandler's works and to determine whether similar connections existed in the works of other major writers in the genre. The idea that there might be such a connection was supported by the enduring stereotype of the PI as a hard-drinking man, an image so enduring that it has become the subject both of beer ads and of satiric sketches.

The mystery genre includes many types: the amateur detective of the Golden Age and beyond, the hard-boiled PI novel, the police procedural, the comic mystery, the crime caper, and historical mystery, as well as marginal genres such as thrillers, spy fiction and gothics. However, as I explain in the Introduction, the PI novel is the only variety in which the personal ethic of the detective, conceptualized as a code, is central to the definition. With hundreds of series available, both classic and current, my selection of authors to examine was influenced by several factors, including the popularity of a writer, the writer's critical reputation, the amount of critical attention the writer has received, and the degree to which alcohol seemed to be an important concern. My dissertation dealt with Hammett, Chandler, Spillane, Parker and Block. The time constraints of my degree program prevented me from working with any women writers and their female protagonists. I have filled that gap in the current work, adding Marcia Muller, Sue Grafton, and Karen Kijewski to the authors examined.

My study of the genre has been aided by a number of works. George Grella's essay on the hard-boiled novel and John Cawelti's extended study of genre fiction, *Adventure, Mystery, and Romance: Formula Stories as Art and Popular Culture*, are classics of criticism, although I have not always agreed with their conclusions or their analyses of particular works. A more contemporary reference work is Rosemary Herbert's *Oxford Companion to Crime and Mystery Writing*, useful for succinct articles on writers, characters and themes of the genre, and Willetta Heising's *Detecting Men* and *Detecting Women* are valuable for basic background and lists of works by contemporary writers. All students of the genre are in debt to Allan Hubin for founding *The Armchair Detective* and to Pat Browne for editing *Clues: A Journal of Detection*. Several of the articles I consulted, especially on more recent authors, were published in these journals. Both ceased publication, but *Clues* is now being revived.

Three works outside the field of detective fiction criticism have been especially helpful to me. *Drink: A Social History of America* by Andrew Barr and *Drinking in America: A History* by Martin Lender and James Martin provided historical information on the drinking habits and customs of America and the Temperance Movement, as well as contrasting views on the origin and effects of Prohibition. *An Aesthetics of Junk Fiction*, by John Roberts, furnished the useful critical concepts of "newspaper reality" as well as the formulation of a genre as an ongoing interaction between readers and practitioners, an interaction which is not critically accessible to those who read only the exceptional works in a given genre.

Booze and the Private Eye is, in one sense, a historical study, since it spans the hard-boiled genre from Hammett's first efforts to the current writers, examining changes in the nature of the detective protagonist and developments such as the introduction of female detectives. However, it is not intended as a comprehensive history, given the focus on alcohol as a determinant of moral character. For many authors within the genre, even well known and critically appraised authors such as Ross Macdonald, depictions of alcohol use function as part of the newspaper reality of their work rather than as contributions to the theme of the man with a code.

Other works, notably *The Thirsty Muse: Alcohol and the American Writer* by Tom Dardis and *Equivocal Spirits: Alcoholism and Drinking in Twentieth-Century Literature*, by Thomas Gilmore, have approached the topic of alcohol in literature. Both of these works focus on the effect that excessive use of alcohol has on the writing of authors who have drinking problems. Both Dardis and Gilmore concentrate on authors of mainstream literature. Dardis, additionally, views the problem as generational, focusing on those authors who came of age when Prohibition made drinking seem rebellious and daring. While Hammett, Chandler and Block are known to have suffered from excessive drinking, others in this study have no known history of abuse. This is not, therefore, an examination only of detective stories by alcoholics. To have done so would have abrogated the premise that the relation between drink and the judgment of character in the hard-boiled novel is a cultural artifact, not the effect of a personal or psychological problem. Alcohol use is both endemic and problematic in American culture and this duality, not to say ambivalence, is reflected in popular culture in many ways, of which this is one.

The bibliography is divided between the primary works and works of criticism. It is the nature of genre fiction that books go out of print, that paperback editions may sometimes precede hard-cover and that full publication information may be missing. The editions of detective novels cited are those I found available, but there are no guarantees that the same editions will come to hand for those who wish to pursue further studies of these authors.

I would like to thank all the members of my dissertation committee at the University of Nevada, Reno: my advisor, Dr. Robert Merrill, Dr. Susan C. Baker and Dr. Susan Palwick of the English department; Dr. John C. Kelly of the Philosophy department; and Dr. Linda Curcio-Nagy of the History department. My thanks also go to my friend and colleague Dr. Linda J. Holland-Toll for her suggestions and sympathetic ear. My love and thanks go to my daughter, Senior Airman Rose Van Arsdall, United States Air Force, and my son-in-law, Sergeant Alexander Van Arsdall, United States Army, for providing me a home during the year in which I have brought this project to completion, and to my grandson, William Van Arsdall (b. January 2002), for keeping me from spending too much time at the computer.

Rita E. Rippetoe
Orangevale, California
May, 2004

Introduction

.

Dealing as it does with the darker passions and their criminal results, detective fiction, particularly of the category labeled "hard-boiled," has always featured characters who use, and sometimes abuse, alcohol. A part of Western culture from earliest times, alcohol has been depicted as a natural accompaniment of social meetings and an indispensable article of diet, and at the same time, it is depicted as a threat to good character and morality. From the ill-mannered suitors who plague Odysseus' household in his absence to the hard-drinking men and women of the Lost Generation and to the present day, authors have observed that characters can be defined, in part, by what, how much, how, and with whom they drink.

The encyclopedic work *The Oxford Companion to Crime and Mystery Writing*, edited by Rosemary Herbert, recognizes the role of alcohol in crime fiction by devoting an entry to the topic. It notes that alcohol can play a role in plots as a vehicle for poison or as a means to obtain information from an unwilling witness. It can also serve to facilitate the detective's thought processes or promote relaxation, as in the cases of Inspector Maigret and Inspector Morse. "Why, how and with whom one drinks," it notes, "becomes significant in a story because social drinking implies shared intimacy, often revealing questions of class and demonstrations of classiness." This work also cites James Crumley, James Lee Burke and Lawrence Block as writers who portray alcoholic detectives and calls Block's *When the Sacred Ginmill Closes* a penetrating study of a recovering alcoholic (Wedge, *Oxford Companion* 10–11).

A key factor for my interest in the ways in which authors of detective fiction depict alcohol use is my belief that detective fiction is a deeply moral art form. While there are exceptions, even among the classics, the basic premise of detective fiction is that crime, especially murder, should be punished. The malefactor, however clever, however self-justified, should be discovered. His or her methods are revealed as inadequate to escape discovery. His or her motives are revealed as self-serving and insufficient to exculpate the most serious of crimes, murder. Dennis Porter, in his essay "Detection and Ethics: The Case of P.D. James," comments on this aspect of detective fiction as a quality which sets it apart from other popular genres:

> Moreover, in a post-religious society like that of modern Britain, it [mass popular fiction] is frequently the only kind of widely read material that attempts to distinguish between right and wrong or set up models to be imitated. And among all forms of popular literature, nowhere is this more true than in detective fiction in the broad sense. Where else outside detective fiction does it still seem appropriate to raise questions about such theological categories as "good" and "evil" or such philosophical ones as "truth" and "justice"? [12].

One may disagree with the assertion that contemporary society is post-religious; certainly it is less so in the United States than in Britain. (According to *Britannica 2002 Book of the Year*, only 8.7 percent of U.S. inhabitants describe themselves as non-religious, compared to 30 percent in the United Kingdom [751–753].) But serious contemporary literature tends to mirror the cultural relativism and situational ethics of the postmodern academy rather than any belief in eternal verities of human behavior. This is not to say that popular culture does not respond to changes in mores; it certainly does. But although rules may change, there are still rules, and one of these is that only the most weighty of reasons will justify the taking of human life. The motivating force behind the action of most detective novels is the need to catch and punish the criminal.

The character of the detective is pitted against that of the murderer and against any others who would stand between him and the discovery of the truth. Any factor in the character of the detective that strongly affects his ability to do the job, or that may alter or mar his judgment, becomes important in the moral stance of the story. However, modern conventions in novel writing dictate that the author should show, not tell. It is no longer the fashion for an author to lecture the reader on the nobility of the protagonist. Instead, each character is to be revealed through action. In practice, action can be supplemented by physical description and details of style that may be assumed to elucidate character. The reader's own tendency to judge people by their clothing, habits, manners, speech and appearance gives the author a means to suggest information about characters without simply telling the reader what to think.

Drinking habits can be one such piece of information: Lord Peter Wimsey's knowledge of vintage wines, for example, encapsulates many of the differences of class and education that separate him from Kinsey Milhone, with her consumption of generic white wine. Certainly an author can use any item of diet as a convenient shorthand for character traits. In a column for *Gourmet*, author Elinor Lipman discusses her use of food choices as descriptive detail, observing that "Characters have to eat, don't they? ... I find that every interaction with the stove, refrigerator, plate, and fork provides an opportunity to mine the telling detail, to make abstract notions concrete in a way I hope is both subtle and economic" (106).

These abstract notions may be morally neutral, as in her example of a dull, unadventurous man who eats franks and beans rather than sweetbreads on a bed of polenta. But in popular fiction, choices involving alcohol can have a stronger role. One need only think of the famous scene in the film *Shane* in which a fight results after Shane orders soda rather than whiskey in the local saloon.

In the classic detective tale, the concern with morality shapes the plot toward a conclusion in which method, motive and murderer are all revealed. This usually occurs as a culmination of serious effort on the part of the detective in questioning suspects and gathering clues. The detective's genius lies in the ability to reach the truth despite apparently inadequate or contradictory clues. Indeed, so single-minded is this focus on the determination of guilt that the popular nickname for this type of story is "whodunit." Popular culture critic John G. Cawelti sees popular fiction as formulaic, embodying an ideal world rather than the disorder and ambiguity of mimetic fiction. In *Adventure, Mystery, and Romance: Formula Stories as Art and Popular Culture*, Cawelti makes the claim that each popular genre is shaped by a particular "moral fantasy" (39). For example, the moral fantasy of the romance genre is that true love is permanent and triumphant. Cawelti defines the literary formula of the classic detective story as embodying the "moral fantasy" that all problems have a desirable and rational solution (43). He terms this a moral fantasy because, despite the superficial realism of the form, the mystery reader knows that in actual life, crime may go unsolved and unpunished, just as the romance reader knows that there is no guarantee of finding true love.

In *Murder from an Academic Angle*, Hetta Pyrhönen questions Cawelti's distinctions, arguing that he falsely aligns all serious literature with the mimetic tradition. She also queries Cawelti's choice of the label "moral fantasy" for the escapist elements he analyzes in formulaic fiction (87). Cawelti is demonstrating that a fiction which does not tell the full truth about the nature of human character and society is as basically fantastic as one which constructs a fictional material world which differs from our known reality. Worlds in which true love always triumphs, in which criminals are inevitably found and punished while the falsely accused innocents are exonerated, in which dangers are courageously overcome and in which heroic individuals can endlessly struggle against crime and corruption without becoming corrupted or defeated, are as fantastic in their way as worlds in which unicorns roam the forests or Lovecraftian horrors lurk in suburban basements. However Pryhönen's theory that the equation of mimetic technique with serious intent in fiction leads to mislabeling of both serious and popular works that cross the proposed boundaries has merit.

Another way in which the classic detective novel departs from reality is that it tends to ignore the long-term consequences of crime; the story usually concludes with the explanation of the crime and the arrest or suicide of the murderer. The burden of unjust suspicion is lifted and the remaining characters are free to marry, enjoy inheritances, return to professions and otherwise resume normal lives. It is this aspect of the genre which leads George Grella to define what he refers to as the "formal detective novel" as a comedy of manners, in which the puzzle, confusion, hidden identities and other conventions of the comic genre are resolved in the final scene and all returns to normal in a "benevolent and knowable universe" ("Murder and Manners: The Formal Detective Novel" 55). The genre conventions do not encourage the reader to consider that if the characters were actual people so closely touched by murder, it is more likely that the trajectories of their lives would be permanently altered than that they would quietly return to an existence in which the village fete will be the most exciting news of the season. Grella, Cawelti and other critics agree in defining the type of mystery known variously as formal, classic, British or Golden Age as artificial and unrealistic, with little relation to the reality of either crime and its detection or the society in which murder takes place.

The hard-boiled genre, which usually features some type of professional, yet private, investigator, is regarded by some as more realistic than the classic form. As Raymond Chandler put it in "The Simple Art of Murder":

> The realist in murder writes of a world in which gangsters can rule nations and almost rule cities, ... in which a screen star can be the fingerman for a mob, and the nice man down the hall is a boss of the numbers racket; ... where the mayor of your town may have condoned murder as an instrument of moneymaking, where no man can walk down a dark street in safety because law and order are things we talk about but refrain from practicing; ... It is not a very fragrant world, but it is the world you live in, and certain writers with tough minds and a cold spirit of detachment can make very interesting and even amusing patterns out of it [990].

Plainly, Chandler believes he is describing a genre which is realistic, almost naturalistic, in its emphasis on the corruption and hypocrisy which underlie society. Most critics have agreed in seeing hard-boiled detection as more realistic than the classic mystery. However, Cawelti finds moral fantasy in the hard-boiled genre as well; it merely takes a different form than in the classic mystery. The benevolent universe of the classic mystery, in which all problems have a solution, is gone. Crimes may be solved, yet criminals go unpunished, as does Carmen in Chandler's *The Big Sleep*. Crime is no longer a diseased outbreak in an otherwise healthy body politic, but a symptom of a materialistic and morally corrupt society. Outright gangsters may commit most of the violence in the genre, although corrupt cops throw their share of punches, but the reader learns that powerful men with money seldom need to do their own dirty work. Furthermore, efforts to discover the truth may trigger violence and deaths that might otherwise not have occurred. The world of the hard-boiled detective is like a silty pond, which may seem clear and clean but becomes more fouled as the detective wades in after the truth.

For Cawelti, it is the detective himself who embodies the moral fantasy—not of solution and salvation, but of personal integrity, which is maintained despite assault or temptation. He is the one who instinctively protects the weak, defends the innocent, and avenges the wronged. He is "the one loyal, honest, truly moral man in a corrupt and ambiguous world" (151). Or, as Raymond Chandler puts it: "He must be, to use a rather weathered phrase, a man of honor, by instinct, by inevitability, without thought of it, and certainly without saying it. He must be the best man in his world and a good enough man for any world" ("Simple Art" 992).

Critics such as Cawelti have come to portray the hard-boiled detective as distinctively a man with a code: a code which leads him to protect the weak and innocent and which may bring him into conflict not only with criminals but also with the authorities. John Reilly, in the *Oxford Companion*, calls this code existentialist, a form of situational ethics. "Relentlessly honest and consistently devoted to the victims in society, the hard-boiled sleuth resists blandishment and bribery and sets his or her own high standards without regard for the conventions of a fictional world in which their style of morality seems unique" (Reilly 202).

The editors expand on this concept with cross references to an article on the code of chivalry, in which Marlowe is cited by Kate Charles and Lucy Walker as an example of the quintessential tough guy who is actually a modern knight (Charles and Walker 67). Even Sam Spade is counted as knightly in his quest to avenge his partner's death, although T. J. Binyon, in the entry on the private eye, contrasts the self-interested Spade with the altruistic and self-sacrificing Marlowe (354). The idea that the hard-boiled detective remains free of corruption while investigating the crimes of the rich is noted by Richard Bleiler as one of the features of the hard-boiled formula (166).

George Grella published one of the first detailed critical treatments of the hard-boiled genre in 1970: "Murder and the Mean Streets: The Hard-Boiled Detective Novel" (reprinted in *Detective Fiction: A Collection of Critical Essays* as "The Hard-Boiled Detective Novel"). This essay relates the detective hero to Natty Bumppo, James Fenimore Cooper's rugged frontier hero, who can only function on the boundaries of a civilization that is seen as inexorable in its westward progress, but as ultimately corrupting to the natural man. Unlike Bumppo, the detective is a creature of the cities but, like Bumppo, he must rely on his own moral sense rather than the corrupt institutions of his society. Grella finds Dashiell Hammett's protagonists notable largely for professionalism and loyalty. The Continental Op will do whatever it takes to complete a job; Spade will turn in the woman he loves because she killed his partner. To this stubborn professionalism Chandler adds compassion and wit in the character of Philip Marlowe. Ross Macdonald's Lew Archer possesses, according to Grella, "a limitless capacity for pity." Each of these heroes is also physically tough, able to stand up to beatings, druggings and other attacks while mocking their opponents with wise-cracking answers. Part of this toughness is the ability to hold their liquor; they can drink inordinate amounts and still function, shrugging off the effects of intoxication as easily as those of physical beatings. They continue investigations despite threats to their lives or their professions. "No matter what it may cost him, the detective follows his moral code," concludes Grella ("Hard-Boiled" 106–07). Although he categorizes hard-boiled detective novels as romance-thrillers, Grella denies that they are escapist in the sense of being wish-fulfilling, concentrating on the "hallucinated vision" they give of Western civilization and the failings of contemporary society (119).

Cawelti's major critical examination of formulaic fiction was published in 1976. As mentioned above, he sees the various genres in terms of the moral fantasy which underlies each genre's particular world view. In the classical detective story this moral fantasy is that of a rational and discoverable solution to the mystery, and the emphasis is on the intelligence and intuition of the detective which enable him to assemble clues into a meaningful story—the story of how and by whom the crime was committed. Cawelti sees the emphasis in the hard-boiled detective novel as shifting from the solution of the mystery to the adventures the hero must undergo to arrive at the solution. The hard-boiled detective becomes more emotionally involved in the mystery, either because he undertakes an emotional and moral commitment to another character or because his self-image is subjected to a crisis by some element of the crime. Cawelti finds the detective defining his own morality, defining justice, often in conflict with social authority, including the police. In the process, the detective may mete out justice himself, serving as judge and jury as well as detective (142–43). The hero's adventures may include violent confrontations with criminals, threats and offers of bribes, all intended to persuade him to give up the quest. The fact that he does not give up in the face of massive opposition may be attributed to toughness of character, but it is also attributable to the code. If the weak must be defended, the hero cannot quit until they are out of danger; if the injured must be avenged, the hero must do his best to avenge them. Cawelti sums up the character of the hard-boiled detective as

> a traditional man of virtue in an amoral and corrupt world. His toughness and cynicism form a protective coloration protecting the essence of his character, which is honorable and noble. In a world where the law is inefficient and susceptible to corruption, where the recognized social elite is too decadent and selfish to accomplish justice and protect the innocent, the private detective is forced to take over the basic moral functions of exposure, protection, judgment and execution [152].

Robert Parker analyzed the moral code of the detective hero in greater depth in the 1984 publication of *The Private Eye in Hammett and Chandler*, a non-academic presentation of material from his doctoral dissertation. He follows the critics cited above in seeing the detective as a development of the western hero, a solitary man who lives the virtues that society only preaches. A character based on this archetype has only three options, according to Parker: he can adjust to society, he can withdraw, or he can oppose society. Adjustment is not really an option if the character is to remain a romantic hero, for that would require him to compromise with the evil in society, to become part of it. Withdrawal is likewise impossible for a man of honor (2).

Parker traces the origin of this concept of individualistic moral idealism to the Protestant heritage of America. Once the Reformation caused men to stop regarding tradition and priests as the only reliable guides to moral action, Christians became individually responsible for their souls. Part of that responsibility entails practice of what Parker terms a warrantable calling. To qualify as warrantable, one's profession must serve the public good, use the individual gifts given by God, and be difficult. For Natty Bumppo, hunting is such a warrantable calling, whether he serves the community by providing meat or by using his skills to hunt men in times of war.

Parker sees the American character and the American literary hero as shaped by the hazards of colonization and the settlement of the west. Men like Daniel Boone set a pattern of individual initiative, willingness to fight and risk their lives for settlement of new areas, and a tendency to move on once that settlement was secure. This pattern was reflected in fictional creations such as Natty Bumppo and the many Western heroes who followed him (18–20). In the hard-boiled detective story, the hero is deprived of any option to move on. The frontier has been closed and the detective must cope with the result. For Parker, Hammett is the first significant writer of the hard-boiled genre (27). Hammett's heroes share certain moral tendencies, but display them in different ways. The Continental Op is job oriented. He likes detection and can't be bribed by his prey, whether offered money or sex. Yet despite his organizational affiliation he is not controlled by the agency. Based on some moral code of his own, he decides that Personville needs to be cleaned up and manipulates the putative client and the Continental Agency to that end. In the process, he commits acts that might be regarded as amoral or even immoral. Our only assurance that he has not actually "gone blood simple" is that he worries that he may have (35). The Op pays the price for his toughness in isolation. He is tough enough to save Gabrielle Leggett from drugs, but the price is that she sees him as a monster, nice and useful, but not a man to be loved.

Sam Spade is a more ambiguous character. As Parker notes, it is never clear whether he is honest or not. While other critics have singled out Spade's expressed desire to avenge his partner as the key to his code, Parker seems to find "I won't play the sap for you" a more central concept. Spade's code is a hard code, since he does feel love and feels its loss when he compels himself to turn Brigid over to the police.

In contrast to Hammett, Parker describes Chandler as more literary and comments that Marlowe is a man who sees the corruption in Los Angeles, but who is also capable of noticing that the jacaranda is in bloom. "[Marlowe's] triumph is not that he cleans up Los Angeles, but that he remains a man of honor." Part of being a man of honor is that he does not derive his values from the system, since the system itself, as exemplified by the bribe-taking vice cop Big Willie in *The Long Goodbye*, is pervaded by corruption (53).

Leroy Panek, in *An Introduction to the Detective Story*, published in 1987, sees the moral qualities of the hard-boiled detective as growing out of the genre's origins in the dime novel. "Dime fiction was boys' fiction and as such held as its main responsibility to inculcate morality in its reader.... Dime detectives therefore, are examples of determination, tenacity, pluck, chivalry and honesty" (147).

Obviously neither the Continental Op nor the more personable Philip Marlowe is a boy's fiction hero. They drink, smoke, and occasionally fornicate: adult characters for adult readers. Panek demonstrates the transition from the dime novel to the pulp magazine story by comparing the hard-boiled detective to a "whore with a heart of gold." Unlike the detectives of the classical detective story, the hard-boiled detective is a working man. He must take some "seedy jobs" to survive. And despite the code that leads him to protect the weak or to persist in seeking justice even when he is not paid, the hard-boiled detective has some traits which seem less than gentlemanly. He is tough when on the receiving end of violence, but he also may enjoy dishing it out. When necessary he may fight dirty, for he fights to survive against opponents who are not gentlemen (152). While recording the conviction of Chandler and other *Black Mask* writers that they were creating "realistic mystery fiction," Panek sees an "ultimate falseness" in details such as the detectives' ability to survive and function after being beaten, shot, and drugged, and a "basic sentimentality" that undermines these claims. In a later work, *Probable Cause: Crime Fiction in America* (1990), Panek summarizes the hard-boiled code of behavior as "an unspoken one predicated on fundamental values of which a boy scout could approve: friendship, courage, protection of the weak, truthfulness, perseverance and hard work." The detective is "a romantic who keeps the faith" (114).

In *Murder Most Fair* (2000), Michael Cohen analyzes the appeal of mystery fiction from its beginnings, which he traces to William Godwin's *Caleb Williams*. Among the traits of the fictional hard-boiled detective, he cites "philosophical individualism" and suggests that this type of protagonist appeals to the reader by validating "the integrity of the self as moral center."

Not all critics, however, find compelling the concept of the hard-boiled detective as bound by a code. In *Bloody Murder* (1985), Julian Symons, a mystery writer who is also a reviewer and critic of the genre, expresses the opinion that we can believe the crude code of ethics evinced by Sam Spade and the Continental Op, who were "rough people doing dirty work." However, for Symons, Philip Marlowe becomes, especially in the later works, a literary conception, "a piece of wish fulfillment," and "an idealized expression" of the author (131).

Robin W. Winks, a historian with an amateur's informed love of detective fiction, published *Modus Operandi: An Excursion into Detective Fiction* in 1982. He reiterates the idea of the private investigator as heir to the western hero, noting that "the land had run out." But he dismisses as "sentimental and impossible" Chandler's famous description of the hard-boiled detective as "neither tarnished nor afraid," adding that Chandler knew it was impossible when he wrote it. One cannot, maintains Winks, "go untarnished among mean streets." The best the detective can do is to remain unmoved by the things he must do to redeem society, because to be moved would make him part of society and unable to perform the redemption (87–89). He sums up the formula: "behind the facade of toughness is someone sentimental enough to care about both truth and people, though truth comes first." The detective embodies "quiet competence ... behind a shabby exterior." The client "buys the expertise but never the person" (99).

Lawrence Block, creator of alcoholic detective Matthew Scudder, finds the idea of "a man with a code" a "curious phrase." In a clear reference to Robert Parker's character, Spenser, Block remarks that he doesn't know anybody who sits and has conversations about his code. He explains, in an interview with Ernie Bulow, that he feels that making decisions about what to do is the main challenge in life and that Scudder, while he may have underlying precepts, must make up the rules as he goes (Block and Bulow 82).

Whether or not one accepts the concept of a detective code, the detective becomes the moral center of the hard-boiled novel and his character the touchstone against which others in the novel are tested. His role does not require perfection of character, but it does require a willingness to continue a sometimes hopeless job, to continue to oppose evil in a society which is all too willing to accommodate and compromise with that evil, particularly if the evil-doers cater to the hidden vices of the supposedly respectable.

This idea of the detective as a uniquely moral being is made more pertinent by the claims of both Cawelti and Thomas Roberts that the reader vicariously identifies with the detective protagonist. According to Cawelti, the formulaic hero confirms the reader's idealized self-image by being better or more fortunate, stronger, more courageous, more brilliant, more fortunate in love. The narrative flow carries the reader along, but does not manifest complex irony or subtlety (18–19). For Roberts, in *An Aesthetics of Junk Fiction*, the protagonist serves as a "model of deportment," a kind of person the reader would like to be, such as Adam Hall's coolly competent intelligence agent, Quiller (134). Yet Roberts undermines the simplistic view of reader identification which he labels "The Argument from Walter Mitty." He summarizes this argument thus: "life bruises some of us, and when it does we resort to the kinds of daydreams Walter Mitty created for himself. Alternatively ... we turn to popular fiction, whose stories, like so many daydreams, serve as psychic bandages. We especially seek out stories with strong heroes and heroines, for then we can slip inside their personalities and live, vicariously, the successful lives they are leading" (100–101). Roberts argues that this theory does not account for successful stories which do not have happy endings, or which do not feature a protagonist with whom the reader can identify. Nor, I would add, does it account for women reading and enjoying stories with male protagonists.

Theories of vicarious identification seem to assume that the reader wishes mainly to enjoy the good things that happen to the protagonist. The mystery or the battle or the treasure hunt is merely the means to the end. The real payoff is in scenes like the final scene of *Star Wars* with Luke Skywalker marching down the aisle of the Federation Senate and standing proudly as the medal is hung around his neck and he is kissed by the princess. More adult versions of the victory celebration may include champagne or a "vodka martini, shaken not stirred" and even the details of making love to the grateful princess, but the postulate remains the same, that readers enjoy these scenes because they would like to possess the medals, the champagne and the infinitely desirable sex partners, but are unlikely to obtain them in real life.

Whether it is read for simple vicarious satisfaction or for the more complex motives alleged by Roberts, hard-boiled detective fiction contains characters whose appearance and actions are described in vivid detail. Among these details are the habits of the protagonist, the upper-class clients, the gangsters and other denizens of the mean streets. As noted earlier, these details provide not just verisimilitude, but also a medium for delineation of character. This work focuses particularly on the role of descriptions of the consumption of alcoholic beverages in hard-boiled detective fiction, and the idea that portrayal of a character's relation with alcohol intersects in a meaningful context with the concept of the detective protagonist as a character defined by a moral code.

Before considering the role of alcohol in literature, one may consider its role in Western culture. For most of our recorded history, wine and beer were daily beverages. Before the introduction of coffee, tea, soft drinks, pasteurized fruit juices and safe tap water, fermented beverages were the expected accompaniment to every meal. These drinks supplied liquid and nutrition, both easily assimilated calories and vitamins and minerals. Yet alcoholic beverages are never merely thirst-quenching drinks or tasty additions to the menu. Because alcohol has certain specific effects on the mind and body, drinks which contain it have been seen as divine gifts, to be enjoyed by humans and returned as sacrifice to the gods. As the Bible puts it "wine, which cheereth God and man" (Judges 9: 13), is routinely listed among the blessings promised to the people of God: "thy corn, and thy wine and thine oil" (Deuteronomy 11: 14), the dietary triumvirate of the Mediterranean world. Other cultures that use alcohol have similar attitudes; for example *pulque*, the fermented juice of the agave, was regarded as the milk of the Aztec mother goddess.

Though wine is a blessing, drunkenness is a curse, and Proverbs 31: 4–5 warns princes not to "drink and forget the law and pervert the judgment." For commoners as well as princes, alcohol can lead to folly and even crime. Drunken quarrels may lead to assaults and homicide. Habitual drunkenness may contribute to poverty and hence to theft. A man whose senses are aroused and judgment dulled may commit infractions of his society's sexual code: seduction of virgins, adultery, consorting with prostitutes, or even rape. Whether seen as sinful or merely foolish, the drunken man is a threat to himself and the social order. Certain religious leaders have viewed the threat as greater than the blessing and forbidden their followers to use alcohol. Buddhism, Islam and some Protestant sects of Christianity are among the larger groups that forbid alcohol to their followers.

If the drunken man is a danger to society, even stronger disapproval awaits the drunken woman. In societies that place high value on female chastity, alcohol may be perceived as a major threat to a woman's virtue. According to Andrew Barr, in *Drink: A Social History of America*, in Republican Rome a husband could execute his wife for merely drinking wine, without any evidence that she had taken a lover (163). Centuries later, Ogden Nash made the succinct observation that in matters of seduction; "Candy is dandy, but liquor is quicker." Nor has the recent move toward sexual equality in Western societies removed concerns over women who imbibe. Earlier generations worried that overindulgence would remove the woman's will to refuse sexual relations or inflame her desire. Contemporary feminists worry that it will remove her ability to resist unwanted sex, a scenario for "date rape." Yet another area of concern is drinking during pregnancy. Chastity may be less valued as a female virtue, but motherhood is still sacred, and societal concern for the fetus may cause women who drink or take drugs during pregnancy to be regarded as disgustingly neglectful of their child's well-being. English social historian Andrew Barr seems to regard this as hysterical over-reaction to studies of fetal alcohol syndrome which failed to distinguish adequately between moderate and heavy drinking, noting that there have been instances of American women being refused service even of only one drink when visibly pregnant (Barr 154–158). Whether concerned about a woman's sexuality or her fertility, many people would probably still agree with the witness cited in *Drinking in America*. Accusing Goodwife Fisher of drunkenness in 1626, this witness testified that "It was a great shame to see a man drunk but more shame to see a woman in that case" (Lender and Martin 20). On the other hand, beer was traditionally recommended for lactating women and sometimes constituted part of the board or wages for wet nurses.

Whatever the problems with alcohol, most societies that used it regularly had developed social controls which maintained a balance between the risks of overindulgence and the real and perceived benefits of its inclusion in the diet. The introduction and increasing use of distilled liquor undid this balance. Brandy and whiskey were initially difficult to produce, probably discovered as a side effect of alchemical studies. This

concentrated essence of wine or beer, this "water of life" in many lan-
guages, was used as a medicine in its own right and as a vehicle for the
medicinal qualities of herbs and other substances in the early pharma-
copoeia. But when manufactured and consumed in quantity, distilled
alcohol was a mixed blessing. The hopeless urban poor of eighteenth-
century Europe welcomed the escape offered by gin made so cheap by
improved methods of distillation that one could be "drunk for ha'pence,
dead drunk for a penny." As a result, both health and work suffered. The
degree of alarm this situation caused middle-class Londoners is portrayed in William Hogarth's pair of cautionary prints, "Beer Lane" and
"Gin Alley"—the inhabitants of the former, virtuous, clean and hard-
working, those of the latter, destitute, neglectful and driven to vice.
Hogarth foregrounds concerns about the effect of hard spirits on women's
roles by displaying the appalling image of a nursing infant tumbling
headfirst toward the pavement from its drunken mother's arms while
prostitutes solicit clients in the background. The British government
responded to fears that the kingdom would be harmed by the moral and
physical damage this "gin epidemic" was causing to the laboring classes
by restricting the sale of spirits (Lender & Martin 7). Taxes and licens-
ing laws combined to restore the social equilibrium of alcohol use, with
beer remaining the affordable beverage of the working class while distilled drinks were reserved for emergencies, an occasional treat or for the
cocktails of the middle and upper classes.

Histories of alcohol use in America tend to focus on Prohibition. How
did it happen that America, alone of Western democracies, considered
alcohol a serious enough problem to warrant passing an amendment to
the Constitution to eliminate its consumption? And, if public sentiment
against alcohol was strong enough to establish Prohibition, why did it fail
after less than 14 years? In 1982, Mark E. Lender and James K. Martin
published a comprehensive history, *Drinking in America*. Their premise
is that drinking behavior both mirrors and shapes responses to social
issues and that the temperance movement was a more functional response
to the social problems caused by American patterns of alcohol use than
has been previously admitted. They see the republican ideology of the
American Revolution as critical in shaping attitudes about questions of
personal and public virtue: "from the very birth of the republic, drinking has been measured against an extremely exacting standard of personal and social conduct—a circumstance with profound implications
for the next two centuries of the American experience" (x).

The Atlantic colonies were settled primarily from England, a nation
of beer drinkers. In addition to traditional barley-based beer, cider, perry,
mead and beers made from corn or other fermentable grains were produced in the colonies. Wine was an expensive, imported product and

tended to be restricted to the upper classes. But, especially in frontier regions, distilled liquor had the advantage of greater portability and of not being subject, as was beer, to spoilage. Colonial America was a society that consumed large amounts of alcohol (an estimated six gallons of absolute alcohol per person over the age of 15, representing an estimated thirty-four gallons of beer and cider, five gallons of distilled liquors and less than a gallon of wine). Alcoholic beverages were a part of daily meals, including breakfast, and of every social occasion from baptisms to funerals, from harvest to militia practice. A tavern was central to every town, providing food and drink for travelers and a gathering place for locals. Yet, according to Lender and Martin, drink was not perceived as a major social problem. Pre-revolutionary America, like Europe, was a deferential society in which members were expected to accept their place in society and defer to the example and guidance of their "betters." Government was expected to compel good behavior, and habitual drunkards could be fined, imprisoned or whipped. Drunkenness was viewed as a sin and churches could cast out members who refused to reform (Lender and Martin 15–17). But, while individuals, such as Benjamin Franklin, might be moved to abstinence by philosophy or thrift, there was no movement to view alcohol use as a great social evil.

During this era, both lay and medical opinion on alcohol differed greatly from current beliefs. Beer was believed by most to be essential to the diet of those performing heavy labor. Witness the astonishment of Benjamin Franklin's co-workers in the print shop that he could work as well on water as they did on beer (*Autobiography* 50). Most manual workers consumed about six pints of strong beer daily.

Conversely, many believed that drinking cold water in hot weather or when heated by labor was injurious. Newcomers to the colonies especially were warned against yielding to the natural impulse to drink cold well water during the hot summers. Today we recognize that the agues and fevers which often resulted were probably the result of bacterial contamination. But at the time, physicians taught that sweating, by dispersing body heat, left the internal organs cold and that drinking distilled spirits was the proper remedy. So strongly was this believed that in Barbados even slaves were given drams of rum to preserve their health (Barr 39).

Conversely, by an odd sort of logic, liquor was also prescribed to warm and fortify in cold weather. There were a few medical men who protested that constant recourse to spirits was not healthful, but laborers accustomed to spirits were unlikely to heed Dr. Benjamin Rush's advice that fruit wine or water mixed with vinegar and molasses would be more healthful and refreshing (Barr 37). Lender and Martin note that farm and urban labor "was back-breaking, and timely jolts of beer, cider, or spirits helped deaden the pain" (10).

Barr agrees with Lender and Martin that rum became the favored drink in the colonies because it could be distilled from molasses, a by-product of sugar refineries. The liquor produced was so cheap that a man could stay drunk for a week on only a day's wages. Rum was also a very versatile spirit, being equally favored in the summer mixed with water, fruit juices and sugar, or in the winter in sweet, spicy hot drinks (Barr 44–45).

The Revolutionary War altered tastes by cutting off trade with the sugar islands of the West Indies. After the war, British embargoes continued to restrict trade. In the meantime, settlers in the newly opened trans–Appalachian areas distilled whiskey for their own needs and for trade. Rye whiskey and corn whiskey became the distinctly American beverages. The importance of frontier distilling is demonstrated by the Whiskey Rebellion, in which western Pennsylvania farmers rebelled against the imposition of a Federal excise tax on whiskey. The excise was eventually dropped, leaving whiskey distilled from domestically produced grain less expensive than rum made from imported and taxed molasses (Lender and Martin 51–52).

Whatever their source, distilled spirits continued to be a staple of the American diet. American eating and drinking habits were a great source of comment for foreign visitors. They observed that Americans ate extremely fast, sitting down to meals in hotels or boarding houses and clearing the table in less than fifteen minutes. Rather than drinking wine with a leisurely meal, American men wolfed down their food and retired to the bar to "liquor up." Barr gives a partial explanation, that the monotonous diet of the frontier, corn bread, salt meat and fried foods, needed whiskey to cut the grease and neutralize the salt (95).

In America, concern about the social role of alcohol took a particularly moralistic turn. Leaders of the Revolution believed that personal virtue was essential to enable America to fulfill its destiny. The break from a decadent Europe had created an opportunity to build a nation based on republican values of public duty and true liberty. Ironically, the Revolution also weakened the social fabric and made room for a more individualistic definition of liberty. This included a breakdown of social strictures on the use of alcohol, which, combined with the rise in the use of distilled liquor, alarmed leaders of the time. Dr. Benjamin Rush, the first Surgeon General, wrote *An Inquiry into the Effects of Ardent Spirits on the Human Mind and Body* in 1784. Rush worried that hard alcohol destroyed the health, and described chronic drunkenness as a disease whose progress led through distinct stages to illness and death. He also decried the social effects of intemperance, fearing that demagogues would be elected by voters corrupted by drink. Thus, in addition to suffering the crime, poverty and family destruction already known to be caused by intemperance, America would forfeit God's favor for having neglected the chance to build a new moral society. He suggested that asylums be established to confine confirmed drunkards and that the government restrict the number of taverns and raise alcohol taxes to reduce consumption (Lender and Martin 36–40). Despite these warnings, the U.S. consumption of alcohol continued to rise, reaching a high of about 7.1 gallons of absolute alcohol per person over the age of 14 in 1830 (46). Alcohol was part of nearly every social transaction and visitors to America reported that in some regions it was taken as an insult to refuse to drink with a man, an insult which might be answered with a challenge to fight (Lender and Martin 54). Yet by 1840 consumption had dropped by almost half, to less than four gallons per year.

Public attitudes had undergone a major change and 1851 saw passage of the first state Prohibition law in Maine (42). The slavery issue and the Civil War broke the momentum of the temperance movement, but by 1869 the cause was strong again as the National Prohibition Party was formed. Social reformers saw slavery to drink, not as a metaphor, but as a social evil analogous to chattel slavery and equally the responsibility of moral leaders to eliminate.

Industrialization packed the cities with urban poor, and social reformers concluded that alcohol aggravated or even caused the poverty, broken families, illness, insanity, prostitution, gambling and other sources of human misery against which the newly professionalized social workers struggled (88–98). Distrust of immigrant groups whose drinking patterns differed from those of older Americans also played a role. Anti–German feeling during World War I, for example, extended to beer drinking, with German brewers seen as un–American.

Many advocates of women's rights were also anti-drink because women dependent on male breadwinners were doomed to poverty, and sometimes violence, if that breadwinner spent his wages on drink instead of necessities (106–7). Progressive political groups saw urban saloons as sources of political corruption because city bosses used them as bases from which to oversee patronage in the neighborhoods (104). By 1917 Temperance forces had gathered sufficient political power to pass the 18th Amendment and its enforcement provision, the Volstead Act (130).

Lender and Martin claim that dry advocates realized that complete abstinence would not come overnight; a generation might be required to create a completely alcohol free society (148). But backers of Prohibition did grossly underestimate the costs of enforcement, both monetary and social, as criminal gangs took over manufacture and distribution of liquor, using bribery, corruption and violence to protect their illegal enterprise. Temperance leader Wayne B. Wheeler predicted that $5 million would suffice, but a Federal budget of $28 million proposed for enforcement of Prohibition in 1923 was completely inadequate. Many states refused to bear part of the cost, even failing to pass enforcement acts of their own (154). According to Lender and Martin, frustrated dry advocates responded by narrowing their efforts. The broader reform efforts, which had been supported by the Women's Christian Temperance Union and other temperance groups in earlier times, including outreach for world peace, education and research on treatments for alcoholism, were dropped. Temperance leaders were perceived as cold-hearted when they continued to support the denaturing of industrial alcohol even though it killed or blinded those who drank it.

In 1929, Women's Christian Temperance Union president Ella Boole dismissed the shooting of an unarmed bootlegger's wife by government agents with the comment, "she was evading the law, wasn't she?" (Lender and Martin 160–161).

Committed drys compared bootleggers and their customers to Bolsheviks and other traitors to the nation. By 1933, public opinion had been reversed and Prohibition was repealed. The Noble Experiment had failed.

Popular history and some literature has given the impression that drinking in America did not decrease during Prohibition, and may even have increased. Speakeasies and hip flasks are part of our mental picture of the "Roaring Twenties." In literary works of the time, such as Fitzgerald's *The Great Gatsby*, for example, none of the characters seems to question the availability of liquor. Yet Lender and Martin dispute this conclusion, citing research into hospital admissions and death rates from alcohol related disease, both of which declined during the Prohibition era, as evidence that drinking must have decreased as well.

The Salvation Army, which worked largely with the urban poor, reported less drinking and a decrease in broken homes and domestic violence. And despite the popular image of a flapper with a flask tucked into her garter, the authors believe there is little evidence to suggest that women began drinking in greater numbers than before (136–144). Since Prohibition raised the cost of liquor, drinking and serving alcohol became something of a status symbol for the upper and middle classes who could afford to do so. Consumption shifted from bulky beer and wine to distilled liquors, which were easier to smuggle and provided more profit for the bootlegger (146).

In 1934, the first full year after repeal, the annual consumption of alcohol was down to less than a gallon (absolute) per capita. Rates of consumption have risen since then, standing at 2.82 in 1978 (197). Writing in 1982, Lender and Martin felt that no national consensus on alcohol existed other than an admission that Prohibition did not work. They saw American attitudes as pluralistic, noting that laws can vary on a state-to-state or even county-by-county basis. Americans seemed to have accepted alcohol as a part of life while also feeling that society has a duty to deal with the problems it causes (195).

Andrew Barr, whose *Drink: A Social History of America,* appeared in 1999, differs from Lender and Martin on a number of points. He traces the historical and geographical circumstances which caused Americans to turn from beer to spirits, and which prevented wine from becoming a regular part of the cuisine. But he is far less charitable to the temperance movement than Lender and Martin, emphasizing its anti-immigrant and anti–Catholic aspects (330). He also accepts the conventional picture of Prohibition as having increased the attraction of liquor, especially for young people and women (237). He concludes by stating that Anglo-Saxon Protestant Americans should have learned from immigrants that alcohol could be enjoyed as a regular part of meals and social occasions without causing social problems. He berates Americans for seeing alcoholic drinks as a secret vice rather than as sociable conduct and for focusing on the problems of alcohol rather than its social values (398).

Lender and Martin do not agree with Barr about whether Prohibition was needed or about the effect it had on the nation, but all agree that the contemporary United States has no consistent attitude regarding alcohol. Consumption varies by race and ethnic group, by income and social class, by gender and by region. An author cannot assume that all readers share experiences with or attitudes toward alcohol. Some readers may never have taken a drink or entered a bar. The amount of possible variation in the audience may explain the attention often give to the drinking experience: descriptions of bars, names of drinks and the actual sensations of drinking—the taste, the harsh feel of alcohol in the mouth and throat, the often detailed description of its effects on body and mind. For some readers these details invoke the familiar, for other readers they may explicate the unfamiliar.

American hard-boiled detective fiction is not the only literature to describe the use of alcohol. Not surprisingly, given the ubiquity of alcohol in the life of Western society, it has appeared frequently in literature. Homeric heroes pour libations as prelude to every feast. Lyric poets celebrate the cheering cup while villains in a tragedy may conceal poison in a goblet. Yet in epic poetry and ballads, wine and beer or mead are only the expected accompaniments to feasting. The interest is more in who is honored by being offered the cup than in details of what is eaten and drunk. It is enough to know what the poetic epithets tell us, that the wine is blood red, that the goblet is brimming. While these beverages may bear symbolic weight the emphasis is on the provision of wine as evidence of wealth, abundance, and hospitality rather than consumption as evidence of personal worth or character.

Mimetic fiction, however, attempts to display the world as we know it, a world in which details matter and the observation that Sarah Gamp sips gin at the bedsides of her patients tells the reader much about both Sarah and her society. The answers to such questions as "why gin?" imply considerations about the habits and morality of the poor, the roles of women, especially poor women, and the role of alcohol in the society of Dickens' England. Although the main ingredient may be the same, there is a world of difference between Sarah Gamp's shilling's worth of gin and Mr. Pickwick's bowl of punch.

Although one may argue about how realistic it is in terms of plot, popular fiction is written within the mimetic tradition. And hard-boiled detective fiction is generally rich in mimetic detail, particularly details of the sordid side of society. The development of the hard-boiled detective story coincided with Prohibition and many critics relate this development to the concern about organized crime and government corruption caused by wide scale bootlegging. Panek denies this connection, pointing out that the hard-boiled story rarely deals with the type of gang crime actually generated by Prohibition (*Introduction* 160). Even the corruption of *Red Harvest* stems not from Prohibition but from the mine owners' willingness to use criminal gangs for strikebreakers. Certainly the Op, who drinks "when I can get it," has no intention of making Personville a temperance utopia. Marlowe's scorn for the fruits of Prohibition seems to be based on a disgust with social hypocrisy, which makes official corruption possible rather than a belief that Prohibition was a workable social policy that should have succeeded.

Since the hard-boiled detective story had its genesis during Prohibition, the depiction of alcohol could not be seen as morally neutral. Drinkers who bought from bootleggers became accessories in illegal activity and every favorably portrayed drinker could be seen as a negative comment on the law itself. (Drinking or possession of liquor was not illegal—for instance, members of the Yale Club in New York could drink from the club's supply purchased before Prohibition went into effect, as could private individuals wealthy enough to have stocked their cellars [Lender and Martin 140].) Richard A. Filloy, in "Of Drink and Detectives: The Genesis of a Literary Convention," claims that for Hammett, writing during Prohibition, drink became a useful marker of the moral ambiguity of his detective (253).

Given the contribution of alcohol to actual violent crime and of illegal drugs to continued corruption and violence in society, it is not unexpected that later detective novelists also give attention to the drinking habits of their detectives and other characters. Yet the hard-bitten private investigator with a bottle of whiskey in his desk drawer had already become a cliché by the time of Chandler, and some later writers appear to deliberately distance their protagonists from this hackneyed image.

Robert Parker's Spenser, for example, is more likely to worry about the effects of an extra beer on his waistline than to ponder the question of whether it is too early to pour a shot of rye from the office bottle.

Certain hard-boiled detective novelists reflect a uniquely American preoccupation with the effects of alcohol on the individual and society. While it would be excessive to claim that every beer or cocktail imbibed by a fictional character is an item of social commentary, neither are the drinking habits of major characters randomly chosen details intended only to flesh out depictions, what Lipman calls "the dialogue balloon next to a character's plate, an arrow pointing to his or her true self (106). Alcohol use has been a contested site within American society since Colonial times and remains so. The depiction of alcohol use by both the protagonist and by secondary characters has provided for authors a tool by which the moral character of the detective can be illuminated. As the protagonist chooses to drink or not to drink, or to approve or disapprove of the drinking of other characters, the reader is invited to concur in the standards on which these actions and judgments are based, and by extension, in the code that shapes them.

Given the many ways in which details of food and drink can contribute to the realism of a fiction, it is essential to demarcate the subject. The works dealt with are those which feature private detectives, what is commonly called "hard-boiled" detective fiction. Police procedurals are not considered because police officers work as part of a team under orders from above. They are agents of society, enforcing its codes, not freelance moral philosophers ready to put personal loyalties before the law. They are more like soldiers than like the knight errant figure of the private detective. As such, their individual characters are less in question, except where a possibility of corruption enters in. The police procedural is about the system, not about making and living by one's own moral code.

Most novels featuring the amateur detective fall into the classic or formal type, which critics view as being more concerned with the elaboration of a puzzle than with literary realism. The detective is usually an amateur. (Agatha Christie's Poirot is an exception, but even he is sometimes involved by happenstance rather than hired to solve a mystery.) This amateur detective becomes involved by accident. He or she is typically driven by curiosity or personal motives, such as freeing an innocent party from suspicion. Therefore the question of whether drinking will affect duty and performance, which is crucial to the professional detective, does not arise.

Thus, only detective tales of the hard-boiled school are considered in any depth. These are also the works that are most generally regarded as providing serious commentary on American society, if only because that commentary is often so bleak. In addition, only American works are considered. The mores regarding alcohol use differ greatly from one culture to another, making interpretation outside one's own culture difficult. For example, Colin Dexter's Inspector Morse may drink several beers in the course of a day's investigation without occasioning more than the exasperation of his Sergeant, whereas his American counterpart would be subject to discipline or referrals for counseling for the same habit.

Finally, only novel-length works will be treated at length. Short stories, while an important part of the hard-boiled genre, particularly in its early years, emphasize action over description and character development and are therefore less likely to give attention to nuances of what, and how much, characters drink.

Some critics have given attention to the subject of alcohol in relation to literary fiction. Certain critics have taken a primarily biographical approach, relating excessive drinking by authors to the quality of the literature they write. *The Thirsty Muse* by Tom Dardis is one such work. Dardis emphasizes the destructive effects of drink on the careers of four major American writers, William Faulkner, F. Scott Fitzgerald, Ernest Hemingway and Eugene O'Neill. According to Dardis, only O'Neill managed to quit drinking in time to salvage his life and career. The others, in Dardis' estimation, sacrificed their talent and cut short their lives through an inability or unwillingness to confront their alcoholism. Some critics include Dashiell Hammett in this category, an allegation which will be discussed later.

Other critics, such as Peter Wolfe writing on Chandler, take a psychological approach to analysis of an author's works, attempting to identify characters who may represent the author in whole or part, or situations that reflect incidents in the author's life. Thus, in *Something More Than Night*, Wolfe attributes Chandler's negative portrayals of physicians to the resentment he felt at their inability to save his wife. Both Wolfe and other biographers will be considered in greater detail in the chapter on Chandler.

Thomas Gilmore, in *Equivocal Spirits*, claims to be the first to treat the actual depiction of alcohol and drunkenness in American fiction. The author, a member of Alcoholics Anonymous, uses the AA theory about the nature of alcohol dependency to analyze both authors and their works. Although Gilmore does not discuss any of the writers dealt with here, his assertion that alcoholism in an author destroys the honesty of the work itself is certainly relevant to Hammett, Chandler, and other writers who are believed by their biographers to have been alcoholics.

Other critics, including Dardis, have explored the relationship of Prohibition to the generation of artists between the wars. Personal factors such as alcoholism undoubtedly affect any writer's work. And generations of writers are defined by the crucial social events that shape their lives and careers. But alcohol use and related issues appear in novels by writers with no reputation for personal problems with substance abuse and continue as a theme for writers after the Prohibition driven generation. Therefore, this work is not to be seen as a survey of detective story writers who write about alcohol because they are themselves problem drinkers.

Dashiell Hammett was the first of the pulp writers to acquire a literary reputation with his novels. He was a heavy drinker himself and lived and worked in San Francisco at a time when civic corruption was all encompassing, leaving vice laws virtually unenforced. Drink and drugs play a strong role in his novels, from the delirium soaked scene in which the Continental Op wakes from an evening of drinking gin and laudanum to find that he may have murdered Dinah Brand to the seemingly lighter hearted highballs for breakfast in *The Thin Man*. A chapter will be devoted to analysis of the role of alcohol consumption in defining the characters of the Continental Op, Sam Spade and Nick and Nora Charles.

Raymond Chandler continues the use of plots involving gangsters who came to power because of Prohibition and continue to profit from illegal drugs and gambling. However, the abuse of legitimate riches—oil money, film money, etc. takes an equal role in his works. Indeed, Chandler's gangsters sometimes seem soft compared to the ruthlessness of the rich. Chandler uses the drinking habits of his characters as something of a moral touchstone, to delineate characters' strengths and weaknesses. Philip Marlowe's inner dialogue about his own drinking and that of other characters provides a means for Chandler to obliquely expose aspects of Marlowe's character. Marlowe displays his own values through his comments on the behavior of others. Within Chandler's work, alcohol plays many roles. It can be a social lubricant, an emotional or physical comfort, or a symbol of a certain style of living. It can also be a symbol of corruption, personal or social. In respect to individual characters, the use of alcohol can indicate strength or weakness, respect for or disregard of moral and health standards. Because of the weight Chandler gives to this theme, his novels will be a central focus of this study.

A later generation of detective writers reflects a period distant from Prohibition-style gangsters and detectives. Mickey Spillane is unrivaled in popularity, if not in academic esteem, and therefore may be valuable to this study. Spillane's career has spanned five decades. Mike Hammer emerged in 1947 in *I, the Jury* and made a recent appearance in *Black Alley* (1996) in which Mike's life is saved by an alcoholic former surgeon. Do Mike's drinking habits change through the years? If so, does Spillane comment upon the change? If not, is the resistance to change a matter for comment? Mike Hammer is not presented as the type of character who just goes along with societal trends. If he has changed with the times this change may be seen as an admission that the times have changed for the better. If he has not, this refusal is equally a criticism of the present.

The 1970s saw the introduction of several new writers and new types of detectives. Robert Parker, an English professor, introduced Spenser in 1974. While definitely an heir to Philip Marlowe, Spenser breaks new ground by having a more fully developed life outside of his detective activities. Marcia Muller is credited by some with the first American woman PI, Sharon McCone, in 1977. In the 1980s several more female detectives were introduced, as well as women in police and other official investigative positions. In addition, changes in society occurred during this period, which are directly relevant to this topic.

An increasingly health-conscious generation no longer respected heroes or heroines who drank in quantities which had come to be regarded as excessive rather than sophisticated. The office bottle may still reside in the file drawer, but the detective who has too frequent recourse to it will probably be seen by readers as an alcoholic, and the author will be expected to have the character confront this problem in some fashion.

Several contemporary writers use detective characters who are admitted alcoholics. James Crumley's two series characters, Milo Milodragovitch and C. W. Sughrue, are both substance abusers (a nicely neutral term for characters who will get high by whatever means presents itself) who seem, at times, barely able to help themselves as they set out to solve the problems of their clients. Lawrence Block's Matt Scudder coasts through several volumes in a semi-controlled alcoholic haze, then sobers up and confronts society, including hard-drinking friends such as the Irish gangster, Mick Ballou, with the clarity of the reformed drunk.

Robert Parker's work is of interest for several reasons. His Spenser series features much discussion of food and drink. Spencer is more likely to whip up a tasty home cooked meal than to wash lunch counter food down with endless cups of coffee. In contrast, the Continental Op never cooked and ate nearly all his meals in restaurants, and Philip Marlowe's culinary talents seem confined to eggs and coffee. Spenser's girlfriend, Susan Silverman, on the other hand, has a near-anorexic relationship to food, which has been noted by several critics. The characters' relations to food and drink are obviously issues in the Spenser novels and are addressed explicitly in several scenes. Parker has also completed Chandler's last novel, *Poodle Springs*, and written a sequel to *The Big Sleep*, *Perchance to Dream*. While he has been successful in replicating Chandler's style, these works reflect the changed mores of the contemporary audience in respect to alcohol. More recently Parker has started a new series (*Night Passage*, 1997), which features a supposedly alcoholic police officer who has moved from Los Angeles to serve as police chief in a small New England town. The choice of an alcoholic character, in contrast to the usually moderate Spenser, suggests that Parker has an interest in the topic, or perhaps that he needed a plot device to put his character in place and to serve as an ongoing source of tension.

Analysis of the literary treatment of the use of alcohol reveals a number of binary oppositions. Sober/drunk, drinker/abstainer, alcoholic/heavy drinker, gentleman/bum, lady/drunken woman, man who drinks/woman who drinks, host/guest: in each of these pairs one term appears to be the privileged, preferred option. Yet, within the context of a given text the privileged terms may shift in ways which reveal a profound ambiguity about the subject. Sober is usually regarded as better than drunk, for example; yet, abstainer may not be correspondingly better than drinker. The abstainer may be seen as judgmental and narrow minded, or as para-doxically weak—not able to employ moderation. Nor are these simple opposites. Chandler, for instance, displays great interest in determining whether particular characters should be labeled as alcoholics, or merely as temporarily uncontrolled drinkers. Critics have displayed similar concerns about labeling the behavior of authors.

Certain attitudes about drinking have endured from the earlier years of the hard-boiled novel to the present. Tough men, including the hero, are expected to drink in an appropriate fashion. Yet American society has no unified standard of appropriate drinking. The social rules vary by gender, age, social class and ethnicity, while laws differ as well. So mixed are the cultural messages that it is actually illegal to sell Jack Daniel's Bourbon in the county in which it is produced. Authors, therefore, must give the reader clues as to what to consider appropriate and how the drinking behavior of any given character is to be judged. Since many hard-boiled novels are written in the first person these clues may take the form of an inner dialogue in which the character comments on whether it is or is not fitting to drink in a particular situation.

Female protagonists are more constrained in when and where they may drink and how they may behave without losing the approval of author and audience. This is especially true if an incident of drinking results in sexual activity, since such an incident plays into the belief that alcohol loosens sexual morality. First person inner dialogue on the subject and other authorial clues will be seen to reflect this difference.

A hard-boiled detective is unlikely to be able to compete with Lord Peter Wimsey in a wine tasting or share Nero Wolfe's obsessive gour-mandism. The hard-boiled detective will endure greasy spoon burgers or enjoy a well-cooked meal, but he does not obsess over either. He will sip fine brandy with a wealthy client or drink rotgut with an informant in a waterfront dive.

In later novels, attitudes change as a reflection of changes in American consumption patterns. For many people, white wine has replaced beer, and vodka has replaced scotch, or mineral water has replaced alcohol entirely, and authors portray these changes as part of the realistic detail expected of the genre.

Health concerns have also contributed to a more realistic attitude about the detective's ability to function physically. Modern detectives work out to maintain their prowess and may pass up a second beer out of concern for their health and mental alertness. Women detectives are particularly subject to such concerns since they are already at a disadvantage in strength-related fitness. Contemporary Americans are also more aware of alcoholism as a personal and social problem, and behavior which was normal for Philip Marlowe may be labeled alcoholic in a more recent text. On the other hand, alcohol and drug rehabilitation has emerged from the shadow world of questionable practice described by Chandler to become a recognized part of the social landscape. Close reading of the selected texts will reveal a depth of observation of American society which is little recognized by those who dismiss genre fiction as intended to be read only for escape or wish fulfillment.

Many of the texts have been singled out by critics as possessing more literary merit than the majority of works in the genre. Hammett's impersonal prose has been favorably compared with that of Hemingway, while many have commented favorably on Chandler's style, particularly his descriptive passages. To consider only works generally acknowledged to have literary merit outside the boundaries of genre would narrow this study unnecessarily and prevent the consideration of works too recent to have acquired a reputation. It is easy to fall into a pattern of studying certain texts because they have already been validated as worthy of study. Such concentration has another danger. Some academics who write on genre, quite simply, get it wrong. By concentrating on works which display "literary" qualities, they are led to generalizations based on an atypical and insufficient sample of works within the genre. Simply put, those who read only Chandler, Hammett, Macdonald, selected works by Christie, and Sayers don't really know the genre. For regular readers of a genre, expectations are based on reading a wide range of texts, not a select few classics. As Roberts explains, genre works enjoyed by the occasional reader, especially those works which break through to a general audience, are usually not typical of the genre. Critics celebrate them for the ways they differ from more typical works, rather than for the ways in which they are similar (80). Roberts estimates that it is necessary to read at least one hundred works in a given genre to acquire a basic understanding of its conventions. If detective fiction has important things to tell us about our culture's approach to social problems and concerns this information will not be found only in some author's works, but may be detected as a thread of information, description and commentary in many works, even those which may never be judged to have particular literary distinction.

In this respect, Roberts provides a useful critical vocabulary when he talks of "newspaper reality" in genre fiction. According to Roberts, among the pleasures found in reading genre fiction is the reflection of the readers' own era. This newspaper reality encompasses all the aspects of culture that are known by other than personal means. So, for a reader in the 1990s, newspaper reality would include crack houses and martini bars, even if he or she had never been in either. Even historical fiction and science fiction reflect the newspaper reality of the time in which they are produced and genre fiction gradually fades in interest to all but scholars as it becomes too dated to speak to readers of their own world (12–15).

In counterpart to newspaper reality is "literary reality" which reflects the literary heritage shared by author and readers. This includes serious and classic works as well as earlier examples of the genre concerned. Detective fiction is particularly apt to include direct references to literary reality, as characters may ask what Sherlock Holmes would do with the case, or assure one another that since this is a real murder, not a mystery story, the solution will be straightforward, not involving rare poisons or least likely suspects. Or, the reference may be oblique, as in the sentence that opens *The Big Sleep*.

Marlowe's deliberate description of himself as "sober" acknowledges the literary convention of the hard-drinking private investigator. The phrase "and I didn't care who knew it" is a wry commentary on these genre expectations. Normal, respectable people are expected to be sober and would have no reason to care who knew it. The Private Investigator is expected to be shady, so Marlowe engages in self-mockery of his "failure" to meet this lower standard of behavior. As Roberts sees it, genre authors engage in a conversation with readers and other authors about other books in the genre. Part of the pleasure of reading a genre is in following the changes that can be rung on the conventions, as entire works reply to other works. Roberts' examples are largely from science fiction, but the principle can be illustrated from fields more related to detection. For example, one can see the bleak world of John le Carré's *The Spy Who Came in from the Cold* as a reply to the glamour of Ian Fleming's James Bond series.

Each author and each book examined in this work will be viewed in the light of how the role of alcohol in the work contributes to the delineation of the limits of acceptable behavior. In broad terms we know that the detective has a moral and professional code because his major actions are shaped by it. That Marlowe will not betray Terry Lennox to the police is an example of such an action. But the fact that Marlowe will not share a last gimlet with Lennox is a telling detail about the end of their friendship. While some attention w;;ill be given to biographical details which may be relevant to an author's approach to the problems of alcohol or drug abuse, every effort will be made to avoid a biographical reductionism.

Dashiell Hammett is the writer credited by both his successor, Raymond Chandler, and by *Black Mask* editor, Joseph P. Shaw, as transforming the detective story into the hard-boiled genre. His works, therefore, are a natural starting point for this study.

Dashiell Hammett

"Behind in Our Drinking"

Dashiell Hammett's career has been examined by many critics and biographers. There is no need to discuss aspects, such as his screen writing career or his involvement in left-wing politics, that are not directly pertinent to the aim of this chapter, which is to examine the interaction between the ways in which Hammett portrays the drinking habits of his characters and the reality of alcohol's effects on the individual and on society in the world of Prohibitionist America. This seemingly narrow topic is in fact central to virtually everything Hammett wrote.

No thoughtful reader of the time could have been unaware of the rise in crime and the corruption of civic institutions that marred the prosperity of the 1920s. Yet Hammett and other hard-boiled writers portray their protagonists, who fight crime, as casually defying the law every time they take a drink, creating a tension between the concept of the detective protagonist as a basically good person in a corrupt world and the reality that working detectives are not likely to be temperance advocates.

Areas of Hammett's career that are relevant to this topic include his own heavy drinking, the brevity of his writing career and his employment by the Pinkerton Agency. His personal history with the effects of alcohol is clearly related to the manner in which he portrays drinking and drugs in his fiction. The brevity of his writing career may be related to his problems with alcohol, though this is not certain. However brief, Hammett's career as a detective writer is central to the definition of the hard-boiled genre, for he both provided enduring examples of the genre and inspired other writers to emulate his style and subject matter. His choice of subject matter was given credibility by his service in the Pinkertons, a credibility that extended to his critique of the conventions of the classic detective story, a critique that helped make the hard-boiled style the preferred form for American writers in later years.

Hammett joined the Pinkertons in 1915 and finally resigned in 1922. His service was interrupted from 1918–1921 by Army service and hospitalization for tuberculosis. Hugh Eames gives a brief history of the Pinkertons in *Sleuths, Inc.* Most earlier detective efforts had worked on the principle of "set a thief to catch a thief," relying heavily on informers and bounty seekers for information.

Allan Pinkerton served as sheriff of two Illinois counties and on the Chicago Police Force before resigning in 1850 to form the Pinkerton National Detective Agency, which specialized in crimes committed against railroads. Pinkerton maintained that an honest man can catch a thief and developed a repertoire of techniques—shadowing, disguise, role-playing—for the purpose. By 1896 the Agency had divisions for uniformed night patrol and detection, in addition to the railroad crime division. The agency manual defended its sometimes controversial practices: "it is held by the agency that the ends being for the accomplishment of justice, they justify the means used." Pinkerton originally refused to investigate legal union activity, but the poor state of the economy in 1872 led him to soften his stance and the Agency became famous for breaking the Molly McGuires, a coal miners' organization accused by owners of terrorism. The Pinkertons became notorious as hired strikebreakers in the violent labor strikes of the late 1870s (104–106).

Actual experience as a detective gave Hammett an advantage not shared by other writers in the genre of hard-boiled detective fiction. He knew what is was like to tail a suspect or to stake out a location. He had also experienced violence—bearing, among other scars, a dent in his skull from a brick wielded by the partner of a man he was tailing. His experiences also pertain to the issue of the detective code. The Pinkerton Agency, the largest and best known private investigation and security force in America, instructed its agents in proper procedures and ethics. William F. Nolan, in *Hammett: A Life at the Edge*, cites the instructions the young Hammett received from Jimmy Wright, his superior in the Baltimore office:

> Never cheat your client. Never break a law that violates your integrity. Stay anonymous. Never take physical risks unless absolutely necessary. And, above all, be objective; never become emotionally involved with the client or anyone else connected with a case [9].

The admonition to not cheat a client does not require much comment; common sense would suggest that any business that desires repeat business and referrals would follow this elementary ethic. "Never break a law that violates your integrity" is a more problematic instruction. This clearly implies that operatives will break laws in the course of their work and puts the decision as to which laws to break on the conscience of the individual. From this formulation, we see that the philosophical individualism of the private detective is not merely a fictional device employed by authors to justify plot turns that depend on the PI violating the law in pursuit of the solution to a case. The injunction to be objective is less observed in fiction. Readers might be little attracted to a protagonist who actually remained absolutely objective. However, the existence of the rule serves authors in certain ways. Normally, we are led to feel, the detective obeys this injunction and the fact that he becomes emotionally entangled in the tale we are reading provides assurance that the tale is worth reading, that it is exceptional in some way, not a dreary criminal casebook.

Some critics and biographers accept Hammett's explanation of having quit the Pinkertons because he missed out on a voyage to Australia by finding the hiding place of stolen gold before the ship left port. Others believe his health gave out as a result of TB contracted in the Army. As Sinda Gregory puts it in *Private Investigations*:

> He was thin, weak, and breathless and faint after any physical exertion.... Hammett was physically incapable of remaining a detective. He was unable to walk the distances often necessary when tailing a suspect, unable to work the long hours a case might require, and unable to defend himself in violent confrontations [4].

Both Gregory, and Dennis Dooley in *Dashiell Hammett*, express the opinion that a stronger motive existed than poor health, one Hammett himself never gave as a reason for giving up detection. These writers assert that Hammett had become disillusioned with the amoral nature of the job, the fact that anybody with enough money could hire their dirty work done (Gregory 5). Hammett's long-term lover, playwright Lillian Hellman, told biographers that Hammett repeated a specific incident to her, implying that it was a turning point for him as it led to the realization that he was living in a corrupt society. According to Hellman, Hammett claimed that an officer of the Anaconda Copper Company offered him $5000 to murder Frank Little, an Industrial Workers of the World organizer, who was urging miners to strike against unsafe working conditions in Everett, Montana. Little was later lynched by persons unknown. There is no clear assertion that Hammett knew or believed that other Pinkerton agents may have accepted the offer he rejected. However, Hellman claimed that when she spoke in defense of a relative who owned a fruit company in Central America, Hammett replied, "No, he just hired people to do it [murder] for him. I was in that racket for a lot of years and I don't like it" (Dooley 7). The Little incident, if true, may well have influenced Hammett's presentation of the ethical dilemmas faced by his protagonists.

Hammett's detective career, though short-lived, gave him an air of authority on matters of detection, which he drew on in his own fiction as well as in his reviews of other mystery novels. It also gave him experience with a greater variety of people than he would have met with in more conventional lines of work. A Pinkerton operative might mingle with the elite of society, guarding their possessions or obtaining facts in a case. He would also mingle with the criminal classes and have a working relationship with the police. Hammett's experience in actual detection lent his fiction an atmosphere of verisimilitude lacking in most mysteries written at the time.

The brevity of Hammett's writing career has puzzled many critics. The span from his first *Black Mask* stories in 1922 at the age of 28 to the publication of *The Thin Man* in 1934 is only twelve years. Although he wrote a number of screenplays in Hollywood and participated in comic book and radio projects as well, *The Thin Man* was his final major work of fiction.

Tom Dardis, in *The Thirsty Muse*, contends that many major American writers had careers marred by alcohol abuse. He argues that, because Prohibition made drinking seem a daring and subversive act, writers came to regard it as part of the creative lifestyle and underestimated its negative effects. He briefly mentions Hammett as a writer, like Faulkner and Hemingway, whose career might have been longer and more productive if not for alcohol.

Peter Wolfe, in *Beams Falling*, asserts that Hammett could not reveal his actual beliefs in his writing, and that his failure "to yoke detective fiction to Marxism ... finished him as a writer" (4, 8). It is not clear whether Wolfe believes such a link would be possible but that Hammett failed to make it, or whether he believes that the link is impossible and that the resulting incompatibility between Hammett's political views and his chosen literary form caused a creative impasse. This would explain, of course, only Hammett's failure to write more detective stories, not his failure to write other types of fiction.

Diane Johnson in *Dashiell Hammett: A Life*, describes Hammett's behavior during twenty years of writer's block as he tried in many ways to manipulate himself into producing another book. On some days he would drink before writing; on others he would force himself to wait until his day at the typewriter was ended before having a drink. He purchased new typewriters and eventually tried writing longhand. He tried warming up by writing letters to friends and family, but he never completed another novel (156). Yet Johnson reports that Hammett produced non-fiction for various left-wing publications and organizations, as well as helping to organize the Screen Writer's Guild and teaching writing. He also produced a newsletter for the Aleutian troops and wrote training materials while in the Army in WWII.

Nolan states that Hammett tried for years to complete another book and lists five titles of incomplete works, ending with *Tulip*, the autobiographical work usually cited as Hammett's unfinished last effort at a novel. Having exhausted the detective story, Hammett was unable to make a transition to other forms of fiction. Other critics believe that he put his creative energies into furthering Lillian Hellman's career as a playwright. Whatever the reasons for Hammett's long silence, his existing work remains a major milestone in the development of the hard-boiled genre.

Hammett's relation to alcohol is particularly relevant to this study. All evidence is that he was a heavy drinker from about the age of twenty until 1948, when a doctor convinced him that it would shorten his life. Nolan quotes Hammett as discovering "the joys of the bottle" in 1914 (6). Later, while hospitalized in San Diego in 1921 for the tuberculosis he contracted in the Army, he would get drunk on tonic remedies. "In those Prohibition days you drank whatever you could get" (19). His drinking continued through his years in San Francisco. Nolan claims that Hammett believed whiskey helped arrest TB. Whatever its medical virtues, it did ease the pain of the disease (38). According to Johnson, Hammett's wife, Jose, was already concerned about his drinking in 1927, when he was living in San Francisco and working on *Red Harvest* (61). Hammett's time in Hollywood in the 1930s was marked by continued heavy indulgence. "He drank, sometimes for days with [Ben] Hecht or others. At parties or alone. It was the drinking that counted, not the who or where of it" (Nolan 114). After citing the testimony of several of Hammett's friends and co-workers, who described him as drinking past midnight, with a blush on his cheeks and slurred speech, Nolan comments: "Alcohol loosened Hammett's tongue, allowing him to bypass his reserved, introverted nature and indulge in marathon conversations with a variety of drinking companions. Once he sobered up, he would reject such people, withdrawing abruptly" (149).

Julian Symons, in *Bloody Murder*, quotes an unnamed friend of Hammett as saying that the intensity of his drinking was explicable "only by an assumption that he had no expectation of being alive much beyond Thursday" (127). Johnson's biography reveals a Hammett who struggled with his dependence on alcohol, acknowledging as early as 1930 that it interfered with his writing. For instance, in a letter explaining his delay in completing *The Glass Key*, he blames "laziness, drunkenness and illness" (84–85). He periodically went on the wagon, once after a drunken assault on a woman friend, Elise De Viane, who later sued for damages and won (96). According to Johnson, his Hollywood friends, such as screenwriters Dudley Nichols and Sam Hoffman, were proud of his abstinence, seeing it as evidence that no one was really a slave of alcohol and that any of them could quit at any time (136).

However, an almost year-long period of abstinence in 1938–39 ended in a nervous breakdown. Hammett's friends in Hollywood managed to get him on an airplane to New York, where Lillian Hellman had him admitted to Lenox Hill Hospital. Underweight and in a state of physical collapse, he was diagnosed as suffering from neurosis, pituitary hypofunction and pyorrhea (infected gums)(152). His health was gradually restored and he returned to his political work and teaching.

In September of 1942 he re-enlisted in the U.S. Army and was assigned in July of 1943 to Fort Randell in the Aleutian Islands. He was able to stay sober while there, but would go on binges when on temporary assignments on the Alaskan mainland (178–200).

After the war, he returned to New York, where his drinking became wilder and more thoughtless. By 1948, Hellman would no longer see him and friends feared that he would injure his adult daughter, Mary, who was living with him at the time. Eventually this lifestyle took its toll and in June of 1948, he was hospitalized with delirium tremens (221–23). Told by a doctor that he would die within six months if he did not change, he declared: "I'll quit drinking. You've got my word on it.... I gave my word, and I keep my word when I give it" (Nolan 206). But with this resolution, which Nolan believes he kept, Hammett cut himself off from his means of socialization.

He skipped the drunken parties and spent much of his last twelve years alone (210). According to Johnson, he was consistently sober for his Thursday night class at the Jefferson School for Social Science, where he taught writing for ten years. Johnson, however, does not share Nolan's confidence that Hammett kept his promise not to drink. While no further binges are recorded, Johnson reports that in 1954 Hammett was allowing himself one drink a day to relax (274). It seems that he continued this pattern until his death, since Johnson cites Hellman as noting an evening in February 1960 on which he did not want his nightly martini (294). Hammett suffered a heart attack in August of 1955. He was later diagnosed with lung cancer and died January 10, 1961.

A crucial concept in the study and treatment of addiction is that of denial. The addict refuses to admit that there is a problem, that the use of alcohol or drugs is out of control, or that the habit is impairing everyday activities. Who has not heard a drunk proclaim that he can drive better while drunk than other men can sober, or a tobacco user claim that she can quit anytime, or the user of some harder drug protest, "it makes me more creative"?

The biographical evidence cited above suggests that Hammett, at least in his later years, was not actually in denial. The fact that he went on the wagon for periods of several months at a time illustrates both that he was worried about his drinking and that he retained some control over it. But however well Hammett dealt with his alcoholism in actuality, there is a strange progression of denial in his literary work.

Both Continental Op novels are fairly frank and realistic in depicting the effects of alcohol and opiates. In *The Maltese Falcon*, Hammett has Sam Spade drugged by the opposition, but does not indulge in the common pulp fantasy that sheer willpower on the part of the protagonist will overcome chemical effects. Yet in *The Thin Man* the major characters drink almost around the clock without displaying any ill effects. Hammett appears to have abandoned his objective style in respect to this particular aspect of life.

Thomas Gilmore, in *Equivocal Spirits*, describes a similar progression in the work of F. Scott Fitzgerald and concludes that Fitzgerald's inability to give "a full and honest portrait of a heavy or alcoholic drinker" reflected a compromise in his integrity as a writer, a compromise that essentially destroyed him as a major writer (101). A similar pattern of compromise is seen in Hammett.

In his short career as a novelist, Hammett produced three detective protagonists. The Continental Op is featured in many short stories and two novels, *Red Harvest* and *The Dain Curse*. Sam Spade makes a single novel-length appearance in *The Maltese Falcon*, as does Nick Charles in *The Thin Man*. Ned Beaumont of *The Glass Key* is not a professional detective. Whatever his characteristics, they do not bear on the question of the detective code, and are not pertinent to this study. All three of Hammett's professional detectives drink more than casually or socially in the course of the novels in which they are featured.

Although there is no evidence that Hammett intended *Red Harvest* and *The Dain Curse* to be read as a complementary pair, the novels do yield such a reading. The Op appears in earlier short stories as a man in control of himself. He cannot be bribed with money or sexual favors and seems to live only for the job. Yet, in *Red Harvest*, he surrenders his job ethic to the lure of revenge. He loses his temper when Chief Noonan tries to have him killed. He later loses physical and mental control to alcohol (and drugs), both in the course of trying to outdrink an informant and, later, in a deliberate attempt to hide from himself the extent to which he has violated his standards. He also loses control of the situation—having set the corrupt police and the local gangs into conflict, he is distracted and made less effective by his need to prove himself innocent of Dinah Brand's death. It is only when he is cleared of suspicion by Reno Starkey's dying confession that he can hand the mess over to the national guard. He even loses partial control of his own subordinates, sending Dick Foley back to San Francisco rather than confront Foley's unspoken questions about his role in Brand's death. Moreover, it is clear that the control over the city he has regained for Willsson is an illusion—Personville is ready to go back into chaos once external controls are withdrawn. The Op cannot even control his supervisor's perceptions; his carefully doctored report is scorned and the Old Man gives him a sharp reprimand. There is almost a sense of relief that this is so, that he has not gotten away with anything and will not be tempted again. Thus alcohol, and to a lesser degree laudanum, can be seen as crucial to major plot shifts and the effects of drinking on self-control and performance are relevant to almost every scene in the novel.

The Continental Op is an agent or operative of the Continental Detective Agency, assumed by most critics to be a fictionalized version of the Pinkerton Agency. As such, he is responsible to a superior—the Old Man—who is repeatedly described as having been rendered coldly unemotional by a lifetime as a detective. The Op also has the resources of the agency behind him. He can call on other operatives to help tail suspects or do stakeouts. The reputation of the agency is usually helpful in securing police cooperation, although there are exceptions. The Op's identification with his employer comes to the foreground in this statement to Elihu Willsson, who is hesitant over the Op's demand of $10,000 for the job of cleaning up Personville: "When I say *me*, I mean the Continental." (*Red Harvest* 44).

Given the history of the Pinkertons, there is an unspoken dimension to this dialogue. As an owner of copper mines, Willsson would certainly be familiar with the role of private detectives as strike breakers during the period before and during WWI. But Hammett hedges here by not making the direct connection. We cannot know his reasons, but might speculate that he, or his editors, knew that much of the pulp audience was composed of young, working-class men who might have been unreceptive to a protagonist who was painted too clearly as a tool of the bosses. As it is, the Op is allowed to sound fairly sympathetic to the unions as he recounts the information garnered from IWW (International Workers of the World) organizer Bill Quint about the strike that left Personville in the control of Elihu's hired thugs:

> Elihu hired gunmen, strike-breakers, national guardsmen and even parts
> of the regular army, to do his [bleeding]. When the last skull had been
> cracked, the last rib kicked in, organized labor in Personville was a used
> firecracker [9].

Later in the novel, when Elihu is trying to call off the cleanup, the Op invokes the agency once again in refusing to let Elihu's $10,000 buy him off, telling him that the agency has rules against its employees accepting bonuses or rewards from clients (63). But both his announcement to Elihu and subsequent actions make us believe that a desire for revenge has as much to do with his rejecting Willsson's offer as a dedication to company rules, since he bends and breaks those same rules in cleaning up the town.

Whatever its other rules, the Continental apparently has none about drinking on the job. Any such rule would have been impractical. As the Op's wallet full of fake identification demonstrates, its agents, like their real-life counterparts in the Pinkerton Agency, were expected to dissemble and role-play to obtain information. Blending into the underworld and befriending criminals and potential informants would have been a rather difficult task for someone forbidden to drink on the job.

In *Red Harvest*, the topic of alcohol is first raised by Mrs. Willsson, who is trying to discover what business the Op has with her absent husband. She asks whether the Op is a bootlegger, adding that her husband changes bootleggers often (5). The Op does not reply and only later does the reader consider the irony that Donald Willsson, who is leading a newspaper campaign against the corrupt politics of his hometown, apparently deals with the bootleggers who are part of the corruption.

After Donald Willsson's murder, the Op picks labor organizer Bill Quint out of the crowd gathered at the city hall. Over whiskey in a nearby restaurant, each spars for information from the other. The restaurant does not serve liquor openly—the bar is upstairs—but the casualness with which alcohol is mentioned makes it clear that neither man takes Prohibition seriously as either a reason not to drink or an impediment to obtaining alcohol. On the other hand, when the Op interviews Robert Albury over dinner in the hotel restaurant, the two men have a pre-dinner drink in semi-secrecy, going to the Op's hotel room and ordering ice water, then using the ice to chill improvised cocktails before going to the dining room (27).

Later, when the Op questions Dinah Brand in her home, she argues with him over payment for information on the case. Finally she wonders whether he will loosen up if he has a drink. Her friend, Dan Rolff, brings gin and soda, ice and lemons. Brand and the Op drink for several hours as he tries to persuade her to give him information and she tries to persuade him to pay for it. Finally the drink takes effect. "She made a face at me and put her glass where she thought the table was. She was eight inches wrong.... I do remember that I was encouraged by her missing the table" (36).

At last Dinah decides to tell the Op what he wants to know and a dialogue follows that makes it clear that both parties are feeling the effects of the gin.

> "Now listen to me. You're drunk, and I'm drunk, and I'm just exactly drunk enough to tell you anything you want to know. That's the kind of girl I am. If I like a person I'll tell them anything they want to know. Just ask me. Go ahead. ask me."
>
> • • •
>
> I laughed with her while I tried to keep my head above the gin I had guzzled [36–37].

The Op returns to his hotel at 2:30 A.M. only to find a message from Elihu Willsson. Before responding to the urgent summons, he goes to his room for a shot of scotch, commenting that he would rather have been sober but that if there was more work to be done that night he needed more alcohol to revive him (41). After discovering that Willsson has shot an intruder and has decided that he wants to hire the Op to clean up Personville, the Op listens to a harangue on the subject and comments, "I wished I was sober. His clowning puzzled me. I couldn't put my finger on the something behind it" (43).

Obviously, a detective who is not alert to the nuances of speech and behavior is at a disadvantage in his work, and the Op admits it. Despite his condition, he eventually intuits that Willsson's clownish bluster is a cover for the fright he feels because his former cronies in crime have tried to have him killed. There follows the scene in which the Op takes advantage of Willsson's fear by bargaining for a $10,000 fee and carte blanche for the investigation (foreseeing that Willsson will try to cancel the operation as soon as he feels that he is out of danger).

Later that day, Chief Noonan invites the Op along on the raid of Max Thaler's gambling establishment, and then sets him up to be killed in the crossfire. After escaping with Thaler and his men, the Op goes to a hotel in which he is not known and drinks some more scotch from his pocket flask before sleeping. Without any further drinking, the Op begins the morning by sending off the certified check from Willsson, then confronts the young cashier, Albury, as the killer of Donald Willsson. After Albury is delivered to the police, the Op eats a combined breakfast and lunch, shaves and changes, and visits Elihu Willsson. True to the Op's judgment of the previous night, Elihu tries to back out of the bargain. It is a sober and calm Op who explains that he intends to ruin Noonan and use Willsson's $10,000 to open "Poisonville up from Adam's apple to ankles" (64).

That evening the Op meets Max Thaler at Dinah Brand's house. Thaler tries to persuade him to leave town and he responds with a speech about finishing the job of cleaning up Personville and advises Thaler to clear out. It is evident neither will convince the other and Dinah calls for drinks—reported as a couple of drinks apiece with conversation about an upcoming evening of boxing. All part on apparently good terms. After a day spent spreading the information that the fight is fixed, using information given by Bob MacSwain to force Ike Bush to win instead, and seeing Bush killed by a thrown knife, the Op exits the arena to find Dinah Brand arguing with Max Thaler, who is upset with her for having cashed in on the Op's tip. When Brand and the Op return to Brand's house after dinner at a Chinese restaurant, they find Dan Rolff high on laudanum. Still angry about Thaler's confrontation with her, Brand has a couple of drinks and then announces that she will show Thaler that he doesn't own her (81).

Brand's earlier decision to give the Op information about Don Willsson's business with her the night of his murder was made under the influence of an evening of drinking. Clearly she is angry with Thaler before she drinks, but the drink loosens her inhibitions against acting on her anger. When Rolff reproaches her plan of selling out Thaler as "utterly filthy" she rounds on him and beats him, and then is ready to attack the Op with a seltzer bottle when he hits Rolff in self-defense after Rolff shoots at him. With the unconscious Rolff safely in bed, they have another couple of drinks as the Op explains his plan to clean up Poisonville by using whatever information he has to shake things up. They drink more as Brand tells the story which appears to implicate Thaler in the murder of Tim Noonan, Chief Noonan's younger brother (81–91). Brand and the Op eat breakfast and the Op returns to his hotel for a cold bath and a change of clothes, commenting on the need for its bracing effect and on the difficulty of substituting gin for sleep at the age of forty (91).

After engineering Thaler's arrest, the Op is resting with an after-dinner cigar when Thaler is broken out of the city jail by his gang. Finding MacSwain in an alley, the Op confronts him with the suspicion that he, not Thaler, actually killed Tim Noonan. MacSwain confesses, explaining that his confrontation with Noonan started with them drinking (113). Their altercation ended with a struggle over Noonan's gun, which left Noonan dead. The whole episode took place at a lakeside resort at which alcohol was sold openly, even with known police detectives such as MacSwain in attendance, thus confirming the virtual non-enforcement of Prohibition in the area.

When the other Continental operatives arrive the Op must explain events to that point. One co-worker comments, "'No wonder you're scared to send in any reports. The Old Man wouldn't do much if he knew what you've been up to, would he?'" The Op claims that "'It's right enough for the Agency to have rules and regulations, but when you're out on a job you've got to do it the best way you can. And anybody that brings any ethics to Poisonville is going to get them all rusty'" (117). As the Op explains matters to his colleagues, the depths of the city's corruption justifies any actions taken to clean it up; since the opposition owns the courts, merely producing evidence of crime will do no good. Both operatives appear to accept this logic and they depart for their assignments.

Next the Op is invited to join Chief Noonan in a raid on a roadhouse in which Thaler is supposedly holed up. The tip turns out to be false, but the police have riddled the building with machine gun fire, destroying crates of stored liquor and killing four men. Viewing the devastation, the Op pockets a bottle of counterfeit Dewars as they leave (123). Later he meets Dinah Brand, who wants to collect her payment for the information she has given him and bargain for the sale of more. Offered the choice between King George whiskey and the counterfeit Dewars, she chooses King George, and they share a few drinks while sparring over more information to trade. The Op agrees to meet Dinah later, and when he dresses to go out, includes the hip flask in his gear (128–30).

When Brand discovers that the Op has framed Thaler for a murder MacSwain has committed, she becomes convinced that Thaler will kill her for betraying him. She refuses to go out and instead cooks dinner. More gin cocktails precede and follow dinner and eventually, in a burst of Dutch courage, Dinah becomes as vehement about going out as she had earlier been about staying in. Once again the reader is given a description of alcohol-induced clumsiness as she struggles to untie her apron strings (134). The trip to another roadhouse turns into an impromptu rescue of Reno Starkey from an attack by another gang. After directing them to a cabin hideout, Starkey makes off with Brand's car. Frequent shots from the flask of scotch keep Brand's spirits up until morning when she and the Op are able to get a ride back to town.

Later that day, the Op meets with Chief Noonan, who has just learned of Lew Yard's murder. The Op urges the chief to set up a peace conference at Willsson's house. The meeting that follows is notable for its lack of any veneer of hospitality. Former allies sit around the table, but no food or drink, even coffee, is offered. It is at this meeting that the Op lets personal vengeance override any concept of merely cleaning up the town. He tells Thaler that Chief Noonan knew that Thaler had not killed Tim Noonan and that he set up the bank robbery in which Thaler's cohort Jerry was killed to provide false evidence of Thaler's involvement. The Op knows that as a result of this false information Noonan will be targeted by Thaler.

The Op returns to Brand's house where he receives news that Noonan has been killed. He fixes more gin and tonic and delivers the famous "blood simple" speech in which he both bemoans and justifies the tactics that have led to sixteen deaths in less than a week. The Op has killed one man directly—Big Nick, the detective who was shooting at him in the raid on Thaler's' headquarters. He is also responsible for setting up Noonan, as well as forcing Ike Bush to betray the gamblers who have paid him to throw a fight, with the result that he is killed by one of Thaler's gang. The Op's responsibility for the other deaths is less clear. Donald Willsson was killed for reasons that had nothing to do with his appeal to the Continental Agency, although the assumption that his death was ordered by Elihu to prevent the investigation or to give him an excuse to turn on Thaler leads to several deaths. And if the Op had allowed Elihu to call off the clean-up once Donald's murder was shown to be unconnected to the question of civic corruption, the remainder of the killings might not have occurred.

Critics disagree about the "blood simple" speech. Some argue that the Op has indeed become murderous in the pursuit of private vengeance. William Ruehlmann, in *Saint with a Gun*, states outright that the Op has gone blood simple and that readers are not meant to approve of the Op's personal vengeance (66–68). Gregory feels that the Op's normal professional methods, which include lying and the manipulation of others, are justified in pursuit of crime but become disastrous when he abandons professionalism in the pursuit of private vengeance (49–50). Wolfe agrees that the Op has sacrificed both personal and professional standards and notes that the Old Man is not fooled by the lies in the reports (87).

Other critics argue that the Op has retained moral sensitivity. According to Parker, the very fact that the Op worries about his actions is evidence that he is not really enjoying his role. Parker notes the ambiguity of a code of honor that is defined and defended by killing (*Private Eye in Hammett and Chandler* 35). David Geherin also supports the view of the Op as morally superior, not just to the citizens of Personville, but also to the Old Man, with his purported lack of feeling on any subject (*American Private Eye* 20). Geherin seems not to notice that this claim is inconsistent with both the Op's reluctance to reveal his methods and their results to his boss and with his final statement that the Old Man was not fooled and "gave me merry hell" (218). The Op's sensitivity to the moral ambiguity of his actions thus far is key to the remainder of the scene, for there would be no reason for the Op to use alcohol to blot out his consciousness of the results of his actions if he did not possess an awareness that these results are less than ideal and that the motivations for his actions are less than dispassionate.

In any case, the pragmatic Brand is unimpressed by the Op's moral quandary, remarking, that there is no point making a fuss over something he can't help (155). The Op drinks and then explains the events of the peace conference to Brand. He concludes that all partnerships are broken up and that each gangster will be gunning for the others in a bid for power and survival. This makes Brand uneasy, but she comforts him and offers more drink. The Op continues to explain, but his alternating self-blame and self-justifications make Brand uncomfortable. The conversation turns to who might want to kill Brand for her part. She continues to urge him to drink, and when the Op complains that there doesn't seem to be much body to the gin she offers him a drink spiked with Rolff's laudanum. After one drink of the mixture, the world becomes "rosy, cheerful, and full of fellowship and peace on earth." After more gin and another spiked drink the Op cannot see, even with eyes open, and passes out as he is helped onto the chesterfield (154–61).

As an example of how detective fiction is often carelessly misread by critics, one can take the comment by D. A. Labianca and W. J. Reeves that "the Op himself is doped by a gin and laudanum mixture and framed for a crime" (68), a remark which obscures the fact that the Op knowingly drinks the laudanum and gin mixture.

One can, of course, ask why he does this. His work up to this point has been marked by heavy drinking, but also a recognition of its negative effects on both his physical coordination and mental alertness. Moreover, much of the drinking has been, on the Op's part, a strategy to lure informants into giving him more information than they intended. As we have seen, this strategy worked with Brand, leading her to reveal the reason for the meeting with and payment from Donald Willsson. The Op has also imbibed for the physical stimulation, as when he drinks at 4 A.M. to counteract the fading effects of earlier drinking before answering Elihu Willsson's urgent summons. But in this chapter ("Laudanum"), the Op is drinking to smother his feelings, to escape from the ugly reality of his actions in Personville, in effect, to poison himself to escape the poisonous effect of Poisonville. Since he is already accustomed to alcohol and is in an excited state, the gin alone seems unable to accomplish the desired effect. The laudanum does, for a while, deliver a carefree world, but then it plunges him into a confused nightmare in which he chases first a mysterious woman and later a small brown man. He awakes to find himself in a genuinely nightmarish situation. Dinah Brand is dead, stabbed with an ice pick (which we are all too conscious the Op had described as a potential weapon earlier), and his hand grasps the handle.

Following this discovery, the Op drinks a long swallow of gin straight from the bottle, searches the house for evidence of intruders, then wipes away his own fingerprints and goes to Reno Starkey for a fake alibi. Gregory argues that the Op is "able to tidy up ... not because he is suppressing his pain, but because there is in fact so little pain" (54).

The tightly written narrative does suppress feelings—in striking contrast to the previous evening's venting of emotion. But what exactly is being suppressed? There does not seem to be any evidence that the Op feels any affection for Brand. He has been somewhat contemptuous of the range of men who have made fools of themselves over her, especially given her unconcealed mercenary motives. In addition, each time he describes a meeting with her he calls attention to some sign of slovenliness or crude habits. Her dresses are expensive, but do not fit properly and have ripped seams, and her stockings always seem to have runs in them. She spits on the floor and brutalizes Rolff in front of the Op. None of this information would lead one to believe that the Op is attracted to her.

However indifferent he may be to Brand's charms, the Op must be shaken by the possibility that he has murdered her in a drugged stupor or that someone has deliberately framed him to prevent him from playing any further part in the politics of Personville. We later learn that the frame was not deliberate and that the Op has evidence to suggest he had not committed the murder. But in the meantime, it is perfectly reasonable that the Op tries to protect himself by seeking the real killer and by continuing to destroy the power structure that could well railroad him for the murder.

Even after he learns that the police do not suspect him, his meditations on the situation are unpleasant. "I spread myself on the bed, smoked cigarettes end to end, and thought about last night—my frame of mind, my passing out, my dreams, and the situation into which I woke. The thinking was unpleasant enough to make me glad when it was interrupted" (174). These do not seem like the mediations of a man who feels nothing. That night, for the first time, the Op drinks alone and with no stated purpose or pleasure, "drinking unpleasant whisky, thinking unpleasant thoughts" (179). The reader can surmise that the thoughts are the cause rather than the result of the drinking.

However, as the pace of the case picks up, the Op does not drink again until offered a beer by Reno Starkey before being forced to join the assault on Pete the Finn's headquarters. Later he and Mickey Linehan go looking for the warehouse in which Thaler and Rolff have supposedly killed one another. The first building they try has a stash of counterfeit Canadian Club belonging to Pete the Finn. The Op lifts a bottle and leaves the old man who was guarding it plotting to profit from Pete's demise. Linehan and the Op each take a drink before continuing their search for Thaler's hideout. The detectives arrive in time to hear Starkey admit killing Brand to Thaler, who then shoots Starkey as they struggle. The dying Starkey explains how the killing occurred and how he left the doped up Op lying next to Brand's body. At this point, the Op leaves Linehan in charge and flees to Ogden to write his reports while waiting to find out whether he has been charged with any crime in Personville.

A notable part of this investigation is that the Op refuses to explain the events of the evening to either the laconic Dick Foley or Mickey Linehan. Foley's most explicit communication is to ask the Op how he knows details of the night of Brand's death which seem to include facts only the killer would know (181). The Op eventually tires of Foley's suspicion and sends him back to San Francisco. He explains to Linehan that Foley's suspicions were getting on his nerves. When Linehan responds with "Well?" the Op explains that he doesn't know whether he killed Brand or not. Linehan accepts the partial explanation as they run over the other events of the evening—for, as Linehan observes, the Op knows he did not loot Brand's house. But when they discuss other possible suspects Linehan asks, "Now where do you get the idea that you might be the boy who put it over [i.e., killed Brand]." The Op's responds, "Stop it," obviously reluctant to give a full account of the night even to a co-worker who has expressed confidence in his probity (205–207).

To tell Linehan all that the reader knows would entail revealing the laudanum-laced drinks. Since he could not plausibly pretend that he had consumed two heavily-laced drinks unknowingly, he would have to admit he had consented to the experiment. This would certainly lead to questions about his reasons and to the possibility that he would have to explain his state of mind and the reasons for it. A full explanation would involve admitting to a fellow professional that he had drunk and drugged himself in reaction to his guilty feelings over misuse of his professional position. Only by pretending to be serving Willsson's long-term interest in regaining control of Personville could the Op have forced the "peace conference." At that meeting he deliberately set up Noonan's death by announcing what only he and Noonan knew to be a lie—that Noonan knew MacSwain rather than Thaler had murdered his brother, Ted, with the implication that Noonan's pursuit of Thaler was political rather than personal. It is not the sheer number of murders that has gotten on the Op's nerves; it is the fact that he has violated his professional ethic in pursuit of private revenge. His desire to at least temporarily escape that knowledge also led indirectly to Brand's death. Ironically, it is laudanum, which was still legal at this time, rather than the illegal alcohol, which seems the more shameful transgression—perhaps because it identifies the Op with the weakling, Dan Rolff.

Once the full story is out, the Op leaves the wrap-up of the case to Linehan, ostensibly because he fears arrest by the still-corrupt Personville police department. But the flight to Ogden also spares him further contact with a colleague who has uncomfortable knowledge of his weakness—the fact that he was "coked to the edges" when Starkey stabbed

Brand, unable to defend either her or himself (215). The Op's account ends with the Old Man giving him "merry hell," but considering his admitted attempts to make his reports harmless, the reader may doubt that his superior's reprimand really went to the heart of the matter. How we judge the Op's performance in Personville will depend partially on how we define his task. In one sense, his job is over before he begins, when Donald Willsson is killed. But the Op both solves the murder and accomplishes the task for which he had been summoned by breaking the power of the gangs and the corrupt police force that have controlled Personville. And, although there is great deal of violence and a large number of deaths, no truly innocent person is harmed.

Ike Bush dies because he chose to betray his current criminal companions rather than face charges stemming from an earlier alliance with armed robbers. Dinah Brand may not deserve to die for her mercenary approach to life, but willingness to consort with criminals, to profit from other's weaknesses and to sell out her companions, make her a less a victim than a casualty of events. The Op's clearest culpability in the novel lies in setting up Chief Noonan's murder by Thaler. Significantly, it is this action that precipitates the Op's retreat into chemical oblivion, the retreat that is the crux of this analysis of the novel. But whatever the Op's internal struggles over his means and motivations, in the end he has completed the assignment.

If *Red Harvest* is a novel about loss of control, *The Dain Curse* is one of control regained. In the course of protecting Gabrielle Leggett from the cult of the Holy Grail, the Op struggles against the effects of a gaseous drug. Here his struggle is successful. He then leads Gabrielle in a successful fight against her morphine habit and helps restore the self-worth of which her strange heritage and the crimes against her have robbed her. By the end of the book the Op is confident that Gabrielle has fully recovered. The Op also controls any romantic feelings he may have for Gabrielle, feelings that would be inappropriate toward a young female client who is more than normally dependent on his integrity.

The Op's attitude toward the drug episode in *Red Harvest* is in marked contrast to his views in *The Dain Curse*. In the second work, he confronts an apparition projected on a column of steam in a darkened room. Partially drugged by a gas introduced into the room by the charlatans who run the Temple of the Holy Grail, he is convinced that there is a real entity against which he must struggle, until a broken window admits enough fresh air to clear his head. In *Red Harvest*, the Op refused to discuss his experience with laudanum with a co-worker, even to explain how he came to be on the scene of a murder, but he willingly discusses his even more bizarre experience in the Temple with a mere acquaintance, author Owen Fitzstephan. Although the episodes are superficially similar, there are important differences. In *Red Harvest* the Op deliberately seeks an intoxicated state as an escape from consciousness of his failure to adhere to company ethics. While drugged, he allows an innocent woman to be killed and himself to appear guilty of the crime, a situation which could jeopardize his ability to complete his assignment.

In *The Dain Curse*, he is drugged against his will or knowledge. The drugging is only partial because he has had the foresight to exercise vigilance by watching Gabrielle's room from a chair rather than the bed at the head of which the hidden gas pipes are deployed. He struggles against the influence of the drug and, although the delay in his response caused by the drugging allows Minnie to kill Dr. Reise, the Op recovers in time to save his client, Gabrielle, and clear her of her delusion that she committed the crime.

This is not to suggest that *The Dain Curse* reflects a more tolerant attitude toward drugs. The Op is not sympathetic to Gabrielle's morphine habit, even though we are still in an era when morphine was legal and alcohol was not. He refers to her condition in dismissive terms such as "coked up" or "skinful of hop," terminology which makes no distinction between cocaine and morphine although it is the latter to which Gabrielle is addicted. We never learn exactly how Gabrielle became an addict, although it is easy to assume that her aunt/step-mother engineered the process.

Although the Op clearly regards addiction to morphine as an undesirable condition, he is not an hysteric on the subject. When Gabrielle expresses the belief that it is too late to consider whether she enjoys morphine, he remarks, "You've been reading the Hearst papers" and assures her that breaking the habit is "not so tough" (170–71). Clearly yellow journalism's overstatement of the effects of drugs was already the order of the day in public discussion of drug problems. The Op appears to believe that the best way to help Gabrielle is to give her unadorned facts about the withdrawal process without the tabloid exaggeration that would, in effect, give her permission to over-dramatize her suffering. When she asks whether he will make allowances if she is not nice while going through the cure, he replies, "I don't know," musing, "I didn't want to encourage her to cut up on me." He adds, "I don't think so much of niceness that can be turned into nastiness by a little grief" (182). He also builds her self-confidence, assuring her that he does not believe she is cursed, that the strength of character she has inherited from her father will carry her through, and he finally lets her think that he has trusted her to be able to resist returning to the drug when the Mexican cook steals and gives Gabrielle packets they both believe to contain morphine, although the Op has earlier substituted powdered sugar.

Hammett as author seems as reluctant as the Op to magnify the effects of morphine. The account of Gabrielle's cure is not exaggerated for effect. The symptoms of addiction are described frankly, but unemotionally, when the Op tells Gabrielle that her disgust at her husband's sexual advances are probably owing to the fact that morphine would reduce her interest in sex to below normal (169). He later tells her that her lack of reaction to the deaths in her family was not the result of being callous but rather "going around coked up most of the time. That saved you from the sharp edge" (213). He does threaten that a return to morphine could "bring it back, clear and vivid." The symptoms of withdrawal are also dealt with straightforwardly: shaking, sneezing, yawning, sweating, cramps and extreme sensitivity to sound, light and odors are described but not lingered over.

In contrast to Hammett's clear, but unexaggerated, distaste for morphine addiction, the use of alcohol in *The Dain Curse* is given little attention. Prohibition is still in effect, but no one remarks on the fact except when discussing how to obtain alcohol when they are away from their normal haunts. When the Op meets with Fitzstephan to discuss the case, they drink together (19, 60–61), and when the Op tracks down Rhino Tingley, the boyfriend of Gabrielle's maid, he is described as having Italian wine on his breath (24). But these descriptions of drinking seem to be merely incidental details. While setting up the operatives who will be guarding Gabrielle during her cure in Quesada, a coastal town in which he has investigated the murder of her husband, the Op casually consults the local sheriff's deputy for a source of "gin, Scotch—whatever happens to be best" (175) and is directed to the elevator boy in the county courthouse. Clearly he assumes that the morale of his assistants will suffer if they are deprived of access to alcohol. The only negative commentary on alcohol use is found in the Op's account of Whidden's role in Fitzstephan's crimes. Whidden is described as having "fortified himself with whiskey" and later as possessing "enough drunken cunning" to disguise his handwriting (209–10).

Most critics have focused on the Op's relationship with Gabrielle rather than on the details of her addiction and cure. Is his interest in her that of a "hired man with only a hired man's interest" in her troubles? (167). Or has he fallen in love with the troubled young woman? Whatever his motivation, he endures the unpleasant process of helping her break her morphine habit and convinces her that she is not cursed by discovering who killed her father, her step-mother and her husband. As the novel ends, Gabrielle is cured and the Op concludes that "She seemed to have come back far enough," presumably far enough to be out of danger of renewing her addiction (213).

If we accept the conclusion of critics such as Geherin, who believe the Op acts out of affection for Gabrielle, the Op has once again violated

the detective code by losing his objectivity (*American Private Eye* 21).
However, in *The Dain Curse*, this break with the code leads to good results
as it motivates the Op to go beyond his original assignment as bodyguard
to help Gabrielle cure her addiction. Although many deaths occur in *The
Dain Curse*, none are engineered by the Op for his own purposes. The
control of self and situation sacrificed in *Red Harvest* has been regained
in *The Dain Curse*. Thus we see that though drink and drugs are central
to the action in both works, these actions move in rather different direc-
tions.

    Hammett's second protagonist, Sam Spade, also has problems with
control, although his problems are more with sex than with drugs or alcohol. The one time he does drink heavily is at least partially motivated by
woman problems, for after his partner is killed he anticipates (rightly) an
unpleasant scene with his mistress, the newly-widowed Mrs. Archer. Unlike
the Op, Spade is unable to fight off drugs administered by others, but he
does successfully maneuver all the forces contending for the falcon and
ruthlessly suppresses his sexual attraction for Brigid O'Shaughnessy for
the self-preserving necessity of turning her in for Archer's murder.

    In *The Maltese Falcon*, Hammett uses a new narrative technique. An
objective and unidentified narrative voice tells the story in the third person, giving no insight into Sam Spade's motives other than that provided
by his speech and actions. Accordingly, we know only what and how he
drinks, not why. When he returns to his apartment after viewing the scene
of his partner's death, he drinks three wine glasses of Bacardi rum. There
are clues as to why he is drinking. He has earlier called his secretary to
ask that she notify Miles' wife of his death. When the doorbell rings at
4:30 A.M. he mutters, "Damn her," apparently expecting Iva Archer, and
is relieved when two men appear instead. We later learn that Spade has
been having an affair with Iva Archer and fears that with Miles' death
the widow will assume that he wants to marry her.

    The two men who appear are police officers who suspect Spade has
avenged his partner by killing Floyd Thursby, the man Miles was supposed to be shadowing when he died. The scene between the three contains considerable information about the contemporary code of etiquette
surrounding alcohol. Spade invites the detectives, with one of whom he
is on a first name basis, to be seated and pours each a drink. Tom Polhaus
drinks his, but Lieutenant Dundy only sips his before he and Tom inter-
rogate Spade about the murder of Thursby. Although not completely
convinced by Spade's denial, Lieutenant Dundy finally finishes the glass
of rum before shaking hands and leaving. In the absence of enough evidence for an arrest, the policemen are constrained to treat Spade as their
host and a fellow professional. Spade makes this expectation explicit with
his comment, "But I'd feel better about it if you'd drink your drink" (28).

What dynamic is at work here? There is no "not while on duty" disclaimer such as readers of detective fiction have been trained to expect of a police officer offered a drink. Does Tom's willingness to drink indicate that he does not share Lieutenant Dundy's suspicion of Spade, or does it merely indicate a corrupt willingness to accept free booze, whatever its source? Is Dundy's initial sip intended to disguise the nature of their visit? And is his acceptance of Spade's insistence that he finish the drink a true concession of Spade's probable innocence or merely an attempt to put Spade off his guard by letting him think his claim not to have known Thursby has been accepted? The reader is left to guess, as the unadorned narrative gives clues but no firm information. As everywhere in Hammett, however, alcohol figures prominently in the behavior we are encouraged to concentrate on in "reading" the narrative situation.

The next occasion on which we see Spade drink is after his confrontation with Joel Cairo in his office. For thirty minutes he considers the information he has gained from Cairo, then drinks a moderate two-thirds of a cup from a bottle of Manhattan cocktail (63). Later that evening, he arranges a meeting between Cairo and O'Shaughnessy at his apartment. Significantly, he does not offer any refreshment until after Cairo has left following another visit by Polhaus and Dundy. Spade then fixes sandwiches and coffee for himself and O'Shaughnessy, adding brandy to the coffee, and then questions her as they eat. However, unlike the Op with Dinah Brand, he does not seem to expect the brandy to loosen her tongue, although he does take advantage of her spending the night to slip away to search her apartment.

Spade's first meeting with Gutman is a symphony of staged pseudo-hospitality. Gutman offers whiskey and soda, fine cigars and soothing talk of trust and openness, all in the service of deception and duplicity. At their second meeting, Gutman uses the whiskey to drug Spade. Spade fights the effect of the drug, but he collapses as Wilmer trips him and kicks him while he is down. The doping is apparently intended only to keep Spade out of the way while Gutman attempts to locate the Maltese falcon without his aid. Spade is cool and matter-of-fact about the incident, telling Perine that "he was fed knock-out drops, and came to twelve hours later" (164). Later, Spade is meant to believe that the same drug has been used on Rhea Gutman, who pretends to have struggled against its effects in order to pass a message from O'Shaughnessy to Spade. Rhea's disappearance from the suite before an ambulance arrives, as well as Spade's remark to Gutman that his daughter's belly is "too nice to be scratched up with pins," make it clear that he knows this was only a ruse to send him on a wild-goose chase to Burlingame. Had Rhea's story been true, she would have been found, drugged, in the hotel suite and Gutman would not have known about the scratches (218).

In the famous final confrontation, Hammett continues to use the details of drink and food very effectively to reinforce our sense of the relations between the antagonists. During this scene involving Gutman, Wilmer, Cairo, O'Shaughnessy and Spade, the latter offers O'Shaughnessy a drink, which she refuses, accompanied by the assurance that nothing very bad will happen. This offer may be intended both to reinforce her belief that he is still safely ensnared by her sexual relation to him and to keep her on his side as he matches wits with the apparently more dangerous combination of Gutman and Wilmer, with Cairo a more unpredictable quantity.

Later, Spade asks O'Shaughnessy to cook a late meal which she, Spade and Gutman eat while Wilmer refuses and Cairo takes only coffee. Since Spade, Gutman and O'Shaughnessy have reached an uneasy partnership, at this point it appears natural that they should eat together. However, the irony of the situation is that they are trapped in Spade's apartment by mutual distrust; no one will be allowed to leave and seek refreshment elsewhere until the falcon is delivered and paid for. It is natural that Spade does not offer drinks, since to do so would be an unwelcome reminder of Gutman's earlier violation of hospitality by using the host/guest relationship to drug him against his will. On a practical note, it is late at night and each party to the agreement has an interest in remaining as alert as possible, because their opponents will be likely to take advantage of any weakness.

Since Wilmer has been selected as the "fall guy" for the murders of Archer, Thursby and Jacobi, one can see his refusal to share the meal as recognition that he is now an outsider. Cairo's position is more equivocal—he is neither inside nor completely outside the plot, and his partaking only of coffee betokens a desire to stay vigilant in a situation in which his interests may change quickly. Spade makes another pot of coffee at daybreak before calling Effie Perine to bring the falcon to his apartment. After this, neither food nor drink figures in the novel again as the falcon is revealed as a fake, Wilmer escapes, and Spade has his final confrontation with Brigid.

Overall, alcohol plays a much smaller role in *The Maltese Falcon* than it does in *Red Harvest* or even *The Dain Curse*, and only the scene between Spade, Dundy and Polhaus serves to illustrate a principle involved, that a police officer should not accept hospitality from a suspect.

The fact that Spade drinks brand-name rum and bottled cocktails also suggests that he is willing to spend extra to get what he wants. Genuine Bacardi rum smuggled into the country would be more expensive than domestic bootleg liquor such as the counterfeit Canadian Club peddled in Personville by Pete the Finn. Nevertheless, if *The Maltese Falcon* had been Hammett's last work one might conclude that he had exhausted his interest in the topic of alcohol. But the publication of *The Thin Man* signifies a new turn in Hammett's treatment of drinking behavior.

The Op and Spade are portrayed in a fairly realistic manner, although Wolfe tells us that Hammett saw Spade as an example of what real detectives would like to be, "a hard shifty fellow," implying that such a self-image is something of a delusion (119). But Hammett's final protagonist, Nick Charles, is much more of a fantasy figure. No longer a working detective, at the beginning of *The Thin Man*, Nick is married to an heiress and lives a life of relative leisure. He rejects all notions of control over his drinking, yet seems never to lose control of mind or body as a result. What he cannot control is his wife, Nora, who pressures him into an investigation he does not want to conduct and to which he devotes minimal effort. Significantly, as a retired detective Charles has no official standing in the case. He cannot be strictly judged in terms of professional ethics since he is no longer a professional, and the novel in which he appears is much more a comedy of manners than a hard-boiled detective story.

The Thin Man begins in a speakeasy, as Nick Charles is approached by Dorothy Wynant, with whom he drinks a scotch and soda as they talk about her desire to contact her father, one of Nick's former clients. The next day, Clyde Wynant's lawyer calls to invite Nick to lunch. It is 11:30 A.M. and Nick is still in bed with a hangover. He has two drinks before Macaulay arrives and a third before they order lunch, commenting that he is feeling better than when Macaulay called. The next morning Nora wakes him with coffee and a news article about the murder of Wynant's secretary. He insists on a slug of whiskey "to cut the phlegm" and they drink together while discussing his earlier connection with Wynant (8).

As this pattern continues, it is possible to view the book as practically a non-stop drinking binge. When Nora suggests that Nick stay sober for one day he replies, "We didn't come to New York to stay sober" (134). And after finally unraveling the mystery, he declares that the excitement has "put us behind in our drinking" (180). Drinking is a constant in the story; Nick is even offered a drink in a policeman's office though Prohibition is still in force. Indeed, *The Thin Man* is Hammett's most elaborate depiction of the role of alcohol in contemporary America, or at least that portion of American society that centered its social life around the elegant speakeasy and the cocktail party. Dooley comments that the book contains so many references to drinking that it becomes almost a subtheme; everybody in the book drinks, and "Nick's preoccupation with alcohol and with getting drunk is so pronounced that it almost asks for comment. One continually expects Hammett to confront the issue in some way, but he never does" (125–26).

Here Hammett is remarkably inconsistent in portraying the results of drinking. While Nick does comment on hangovers and morning phlegm, he never seems to suffer from any lack of physical agility or mental acuity as a result of his alcohol consumption. Another drink or two, coffee, food, and a shower seem sufficient to restore his good spirits. Early in the case, Nora wakes Nick late at night to try to persuade him to investigate the Julia Wolf killing. He suggests that a drink might help her sleep and fixes himself one when she refuses. At one point Nora comments, "I wish you were sober enough to talk to," but it is not clear whether this is meant literally or whether she is using the comment to manipulate Nick into a promise to help Dorothy Wynant. Certainly the coherence of Nick's replies does not suggest that his judgment is impaired. Even after another drink, Nick is able to analyze details and cope intelligently with the arrival of a drunken and incoherent Dorothy. He realizes that her explanation of how she obtained a gun is false and that she is afraid her step-father will make sexual advances toward her if she returns home while drunk (13–18). While these may not be brilliant deductions, they do indicate rather more clarity of mind than one might expect of a sleepy man who has consumed two drinks on an empty stomach in less than an hour.

This ability to function effectively while under the influence of alcohol is not true of other characters. In the episode described above, Dorothy gives an incoherent account of how she obtained the gun she casually waves around and then passes out and is put to bed by Nick and Nora (17). Harrison Quinn, a married man who displays a drunken infatuation with Dorothy at a later party, has to be carried home semi-conscious, undressed and put to bed. From his wife's reaction, it is obviously not the first time this has happened. She tells Nick that she has given up undressing Quinn and wearily asks, "Where'd he pass out this time?" (99). On another occasion a drunken Mimi Jorgenson shouts to Nick to "tell your wife to stop pawing my husband," obviously an overreaction to Nora's hand on Chris Jorgenson's sleeve (42).

Critics have noted the lack of the usual effects of alcohol on the main characters. Gregory comments that Nick drinks often but his narrative is always lucid: "...drinking never makes him ugly, cruel or hostile, nor does it seem to affect his ability to function competently as a detective" (161). Wolfe asserts that Nick's "refusal of a drink in Chapter 27 [at Guild's office] proves that, though a hard drinker he is no alcoholic" (158). It is scarcely credible that anyone with a practical knowledge of alcoholism would make such an assertion, with its implication that only a completely out-of-control drinker can be defined as alcoholic. Gregory also comments on the dual role of alcohol in the novel. On one hand, there is a sense of fun and frivolity in the repeated party scenes; on the other, drink serves as a means of dulling an ugly and brutal world, as when Dorothy tells of being beaten by her mother (162).

The Thin Man displays a split between the honest portrayal of the effects of alcohol on characters other than the narrator and a refusal on the part of the narrator to admit the effect of alcohol on himself. Unlike the Op, Nick Charles never regrets a drink, never confesses to being less than alert or unable to cope with the physical effects of intoxication. Other characters get drunk and mean, or uncoordinated, or passionate, or even pass out. But Nick, even half awake and hung over, can banter with an armed gangster and attempt to disarm him with a pillow (25). This suggests that Hammett had difficulty being honest with himself about the effects of his own drinking.

As Gilmore says of Fitzgerald, "there are always signs of evasions, of a desire to mitigate the harsh ugliness of alcoholism" (101). It seems that Hammett was in a similar position. Nolan notes that the unfinished first version of *The Thin Man* featured a very different protagonist, John Guild, a "morose, job-holding detective" who "would have quickly rejected the spoiled heiress and her millions, and he would certainly never have had a drink before breakfast" (129). The characters of Nick and Nora Charles are not credible. Despite the passing references to hangovers and other ill effects, the reader is given the impression that constant drinking does no more damage to their spirits, minds, characters or bodies than would the same amount of plain soda water. As a result, the tale ceases to be hard-boiled, or even mimetic, and slips instead into a social fantasy.

In writing about the Op, Hammett is honest with the reader about his character's drinking, its effects on his behavior and his reasons for deliberate overindulgence. As narrator, Hammett gives less insight into Sam Spade. In the only scene in which Spade drinks heavily he is not explicitly described as acting in a drunken manner. However, one might surmise that his hostile and sarcastic attitude to the police is partially attributable to the effect of four glasses of straight rum. But for Nick and Nora Charles, for whom the day begins at noon with a whiskey and soda and ends at 4 A.M. with the same, drink seems to have no real consequences. Nick may claim to be hungover, but he never describes himself as less than alert or as unable to think clearly because of nausea or a headache. Nor does he become clumsy, rude or loud while actually drinking. Nora drinks almost as much as her husband, yet never becomes brash and loud, or jealous, or slovenly, or drunkenly seductive. When Nick takes Nora and Dorothy to a speakeasy run by Studsy Burke, a former safecracker whom Nick had once arrested, the speakeasy owner is not a ruthless gang leader like Pete the Finn in *Red Harvest*, but a charming "character" who declares, when he learns Nick has married, "A wife.... Think of that. By God, you'll drink champagne or you'll fight me" (69).

A reader who relied on such scenes for information on the effects of Prohibition would have no idea that bootleggers formed criminal gangs who warred over territories, corrupted public officials and undermined the entire justice system of the United States. Even a scene in which Studsy's employees beat and eject a customer who seems about to accost Nick is rendered almost as slapstick rather than as a vicious attack:

> An immensely fat blond man ... came over and said to me...: "So you're the party who put it to little Art Nunhie—"
> Morelli hit the fat man in his fat belly, as hard as he could without getting up. Studsy, suddenly on his feet, leaned over Morelli and smashed a big fist into the fat man's face. I noticed, foolishly, that he still led with his right. Hunchbacked Pete came up behind the fat man and banged his empty tray down with full force on the fat man's head.... With Morelli's help they got the fat man to his feet and hustled him out.
>
> • • •
>
> "You boys are impulsive," I said.
> Studsy repeated, "Impulsive," and laughed, "Ha-ha-ha" [111].

Hammett built his reputation as crime writer on his honesty in portraying crime and detection. If an unwillingness to tell the truth about the effects of alcohol forced him into dishonesty about the characters central to his work, that honesty about crime, criminals and detectives is necessarily lost. Although Nick and Nora became extremely popular characters, especially in the film version of the novel and the several sequels, Hammett himself came to dislike them. Johnson cites Dudley Nichols recalling Hammett's comment on the "charming fable of how Nick loved Nora and Nora loved Nick and everything was just one great big laugh in the midst of other people's trials and tribulations. Maybe there are better writers in the world, but nobody ever invented a more insufferably smug pair of characters" (145). This comment seems to be Hammett's recognition that his writing was no longer honest, no longer hard-boiled, but rather a pleasant fable in which charming, sophisticated people banter wittily over cocktails, encounter criminals who are "impulsive" rather than vicious, treat bullet wounds as minor inconveniences, and off-handedly solve murder cases between holiday shopping and a full social life.

In Hammett's best work, drink could be either an honestly portrayed major theme as in *Red Harvest* or a relatively minor element of character development as in *The Dain Curse* and *The Maltese Falcon*. When drinking behavior is handled honestly, as in these works, it contributes to a believable picture of Prohibition era America, in which the declared intent to eliminate drinking warred with a social reality of otherwise upright citizens supporting bootleggers. When this behavior is handled dishonestly, as in *The Thin Man*, it contributes to a fantasy of a society that can build its social life on relations with criminals without suffering from the results. For better or worse, alcohol is pervasive in Hammett's works. Hammett's emphasis on its presence and effects is coterminous with the emergence of hard-boiled detective fiction, which concerns itself with social realities as classical detective fiction did not.

Raymond Chandler was as familiar with the conflicted America of the Prohibition era as Hammett. Working as an oil executive in the Los Angeles of the twenties he was, like Hammett, a heavy drinker. Prohibition had been repealed by the time Chandler began to write detective fiction, but the America he portrayed was one which was still paying the price of civic corruption, in which former bootleggers like Eddie Mars turned to other forms of crime while continuing to corrupt the body politic. In Chandler's hands, the description of drinking and drinkers became even more entwined with the concept of a personal code of behavior to which the detective must adhere if he is to retain the self respect that is often his only reward in a corrupt world. In his attention to alcohol and its various effects then, Chandler is indeed Hammett's principal successor.

Raymond Chandler

"Alcohol Was No Cure for This"

Raymond Chandler is generally regarded as the heir to Dashiell Ham-mett's reconstruction of the hard-boiled genre from its forgettable pulp beginnings to what W. H. Auden termed "serious studies of a criminal milieu" (151). The careers of the two men resemble each other in several ways. Both started writing for pulp magazines when unable to support their families in any other way; both moved successfully from short stories to the novel; and both had major films made from one or more of their works. Each man spent some time in Hollywood as a screenwriter, and both men had lifelong problems with alcohol. Despite the overlap in their careers and Chandler's admiration for Hammett's work, these two writers apparently met only once, at a dinner for fellow *Black Mask* writers in 1936.

Unlike Hammett, Chandler never worked as a detective, nor did he have any other direct knowledge of crime or detection. However, his experience as an oil company executive gave him inside information about the ways fortunes are made in business and about the manners and lifestyles of the upper middle-class and the wealthy in Southern California. He also had an extensive knowledge of the Los Angeles area, due in part to his frequent changes of residence. The greatest of these changes, of course, had been his transformation from a midwestern American boy to British public school boy and his later return to the United States as a young man determined not to settle for a comfortable niche in the bureaucracy of the British empire. This streak of rebellion is reflected in the character of Philip Marlowe, who muses that if he had stayed in

Santa Rosa he might have become "small town rich ... with a brain like a sack of Portland cement" (*The Long Goodbye* 625).

Despite his rejection of the life he had been educated for, Chandler retained something of the attitudes of an English gentleman. As a result, he created a protagonist, Philip Marlowe, who acts by a code that is more than the merely professional ethic of the Continental Op, or the fierce determination of Sam Spade not to "play the sap" for anyone. Chandler demands a higher standard for Marlowe. Virtually every student of Chandler's work is familiar with his formulation of the private eye as hero: "The best man for his world, a good enough man for any world" ("The Simple Art of Murder" 992). Many critics appear to take Chandler at his word. Cawelti calls Marlowe "a chess-playing, Shakespeare quoting, supremely chivalrous tough guy, a complex character who guards his sensitivity and idealism behind a veneer of cynical remarks, wisecracks and overdrawn similes" (183). Robert Parker sees Marlowe as the American hero who has run out of frontier. For Parker, it is enough that Marlowe is able to stay an honorable man despite working in a Los Angeles which cannot be cleaned up (51).

One thing contemporary critics consistently noticed about Marlowe's world is the pervasivness of alcohol. In *The Critical Response to Raymond Chandler*, J. K. Van Dover cites reviews such as these (22–34): *The New Statesman and Nation* on *The Big Sleep*—"full strength blends of sadism, eroticism and alcoholism"; *The Manchester Guardian* on *Farewell, My Lovely*—"a world in which no one seems to have much idea of self-respect, where whiskey can be a man's sole sustenance"; *The Times Literary Supplement* on *The Little Sister*—"a half-world of whiskey and wisecracks"; Ralph Partridge in *The New Statesman and Nation* on *The Little Sister*—"a Hollywood saga of crime, drink and sex." Later, reviewing *The Long Goodbye*, Partridge comments that "all the reward Marlowe ever receives for his services is an occasional drink, an occasional woman, a succession of physical injuries and an addition to his embittered memories."

Chandler was aware of these reviews and commented on them in his letters to friends and publishers. Writing to a Mr. Inglis in October 1951, Chandler states that he is "a little tired of the numerous suggestions that have been made that he [Marlowe] is always full of whiskey. The only point that I can see in justification of that is that when he wants a drink he takes it openly and doesn't hesitate to remark on it ... compared with the country-club set in my part of the country he is as sober as a deacon" (MacShane, *Selected Letters* 294). This statement begs the question, however, of why Marlowe comments on his own drinking.

If one views Chandler's work through the lens of his personal life, the obvious answer would be that Marlowe is very conscious of what, when, and how much he drinks because his creator had problems controlling his own tendency to drink to excess. Many have taken this approach, especially in regard to *The Long Goodbye*. R. W. Lid, in "Philip Marlowe Speaking," sees the successful, but self-loathing and temporarily blocked writer, Roger Wade, as a character parallel in certain respects to the Chandler who had experienced difficulty finishing *The Little Sister*. He also detects a possible reflection of Chandler's war record in the character of Terry Lennox, stating that "Chandler is burying some ghost of his former self in *The Long Goodbye*" (58–61). Natasha Spender in "His Own Long Goodbye," describes Terry Lomax [*sic*] as representing Chandler's English upbringing and manners, but also his insecurity, "his anxious self," Roger Wade as representing Chandler's career as a writer of popular fiction, and Philip Marlowe as "Chandler's ideal self, the conscience, which punished the Roger Wade within him though not without commendation for achievement ... and befriended the Terry Lomax, within, not without censure" (134–35). More of this biography-based criticism could be cited. However, such biographical reductionism does not do justice to the complex role that alcohol plays in the novels.

Chandler combined ambivalence about the role of alcohol in his own life with an outsider's awareness of the national ambivalence about alcohol during the period in which his novels were conceived. When Chandler returned to the United States after World War I, the nation was trying to create a new society in which alcohol would have a greatly reduced role. There were high hopes for the "Great Experiment," hopes that were doomed to disappointment. Prohibition may have prevented some people from drinking, but it failed as a national policy, and its failure left a heritage of organized crime, disrespect for the law and continued uncertainty about the place of alcohol in American society. As a heavy drinker through the 1920s, Chandler had been part of the failure of Prohibition, as were so many in his generation. Inherent in Chandler's treatment of alcohol in his novels is an intersection between his personal problems with excessive drinking and the concerns of a post–Prohibition society that remains unable to come fully to terms with the role of alcohol in private or public life. This intersection allows the extensive discussion of alcohol in the novels to serve as a tool for probing personal morality and contributes to the enduring appeal of Chandler's work.

The frequent mention of alcohol in the Marlowe stories provides the author with a tool to display the moral code which underlies his literary creations. Chandler plainly expects the reader to recognize Marlowe, not just as a protagonist—that useful critical term made necessary by the fact that the main characters of many works are not particularly admirable—but as a hero. Readers are intended to see him as a decent man in a world in which being decent is difficult and unrewarding. He is a man with whom readers, who are assumed to share certain values with the author, can safely identify without fear that they will vicariously seduce virgins or brutalize unarmed suspects.

First-person narrative makes identification with the protagonist easy, as readers share the protagonist's thoughts and observations and are thereby led to share his judgments, particularly about other characters. First-person narrative can, however, handicap an author desirous of presenting a protagonist who attempts to live up to an explicit code. In a society which values at least a semblance of modesty the hero cannot be presented as frequently congratulating himself on his own high moral standards, physical prowess or cleverness. If he is to be a knight, he must in some respect resemble a Sir Gawain, who puts himself in line for a dangerous challenge because he is "the weakest, and in wit the most feeble; / My life would be least missed, if we let out the truth" (Gawain Poet 238). Centuries of Christian teachings about the value of humility lead us to expect a modest statement that, while the hero will do what he can, he does not arrogantly guarantee success. Marlowe, therefore, cannot praise himself without losing audience sympathy. For him to review his personal code in internal monologue would be to risk sounding prissy and sanctimonious.

The direct way around this stricture is in dialogue. Marlowe can be expected to speak about his professional ethics in two situations: when he is being interviewed by a potential client, or when someone is pressuring him to break a rule. For example, he tells Derace Kingsley, in *The Lady in the Lake*, that he does "Only the fairly honest kinds" of detective work (7). In *The Big Sleep*, he has to tell each of General Sternwood's daughters that, since he is working for their father, he does not feel that it would be ethical to make love to them (703, 707). In *The High Window*, he explains to Leslie Murdock that he cannot reveal why Murdock's mother has hired him: "If a man in my line of work is handed a job, does he go around answering questions about it to anyone that gets curious?" (1006). Marlowe can also express his ideals by speaking in an ironic, self-deprecating mode, as in his declaration to Bernie Ohls: "I hear voices crying in the night and I go see what's the matter. You don't make a dime that way" (*Long Goodbye* 651). He adds that he will never spend the $5000 bill given him by Terry Lennox because he is not satisfied with the way he earned it. Or he can perform ironic acts such as his "rescue" of the pink-headed bug from the office of Detective-Lieutenant Randall in *Farewell, My Lovely* (927–28). However too many such comments would risk seeming maudlin and too many such actions might brand Marlowe as eccentric rather than idealistic.

Discussion of alcohol gives Chandler another tool whereby Marlowe can reveal that he has a personal code, a code in which the proper use of alcohol plays an important role. Marlowe comments on who he drinks with, why he drinks and when he drinks. He is also given to remarks on the drinking behavior of other characters. These comments may be merely a matter of descriptive detail, as when a rich man serves brandy or champagne rather than beer. But they may also bear on character, as when Carmen Sternwood imbibes ether and laudanum before posing naked for Arthur Gwynn Geiger, suggesting that in her the Sternwood "blood," like the beverage, is indeed poisoned.

Chandler's biography gives some clues as to why the concept of a code of civilized behavior was so important to him and why he makes the use of alcohol by his characters a major descriptor for that code. Chandler's father was a heavy drinker who deserted the family when Chandler was only eight, forcing his mother to return to her family in England as a disgraced dependent. According to Frank MacShane, Chandler in later years referred to his father only as an "utter swine" (*The Life of Raymond Chandler* 4). Chandler spent his boyhood in the household run by his grandmother and his aunt Ethel and provided for by his Uncle Ernest, an Anglo-Irish solicitor in Waterford, Ireland. One of his childhood memories was that the wine served with dinner was not passed to his mother. MacShane sees this as a pointed reminder of her status as a dependent, who could not expect to enjoy luxuries at table, and as a possible reminder of her former husband (4). We do not learn when Chandler himself began drinking, although it is both possible and probable that he drank wine and beer while studying in France and Germany before applying to the British civil service. He may even have begun while at school, since attitudes about young men drinking were quite different in Edwardian England than they are in contemporary America. In any case, he had certainly been drinking for some time when he served in the Canadian Army in 1917. According to Tom Hiney, in *Raymond Chandler: A Biography*, by the age of twenty-nine Chandler was already a binge drinker who suffered from blackouts (61–62). This heavy drinking, and the womanizing that accompanied it, was a major factor in the loss of his job with the Dabney Oil Syndicate in 1932, according to MacShane. The unemployed Chandler stopped drinking, returned to his wife, and began writing short stories for the pulp market (69).

By 1943 Chandler had published three novels and attracted the attention of Hollywood. He was hired by Paramount Studios to work on the script for the film of *Double Indemnity*. As Hiney puts it, Chandler's "years as a nomadic recluse, and a teetoller [*sic*], were over" (132). He began to drink again, keeping a bottle in his desk drawer, and he yielded to the sexual temptation offered by a motion picture studio filled with secretaries and film extras. A major episode of Chandler's screen writing career is told by both MacShane and Hiney. Chandler was working on *The Blue Dahlia*, a script being rushed into production specifically for Alan Ladd, a rising star who was scheduled for induction into the Army. Although he had originated the plot, Chandler was having problems writing quickly enough to keep up with the filming, especially as changes insisted on by the Navy had forced a major revision of the plot. Studio executives became nervous, to the point of offering to pay Chandler a $5000 bonus if he finished the script. Chandler refused the bonus, which he regarded as an insult, and instead told producer John Houseman that although he had recently quit drinking for the sake of his health, he believed that if he began again he would be able to complete the script in time. He claimed to make this offer out of loyalty to Houseman as a fellow public school boy whose career would be seriously compromised if *The Blue Dahlia* were not completed for release in time to keep Ladd in the public eye during his Army service. Houseman was nervous but finally agreed, since he could see no other way to rescue the film and his own career. He later wrote about the incident in glowing terms, referring to it in "Lost Fortnight" as "when he [Chandler] risked his life for me" (54).

After agreeing to provide secretaries, chauffeured limousines, cars to deliver script pages and run household errands, and a direct phone line to the studio, Houseman took Chandler to lunch, preceded on Chandler's part by three double martinis and followed by three double stingers. The script was completed on time as Chandler spent a week or more living on bourbon and vitamin injections (glucose injections according to Hiney), writing, drinking, and napping: "never out of control: he was just in another realm" (MacShane 114). While MacShane appears to accept the story of self-sacrifice in service to the public schoolboy's code, Hiney presents another version in which, according to gossip by other writers, Chandler had already fallen off the wagon and set up the whole story in order to get permission to work at home rather than at his office. Hiney suggests that Chandler was given to self-delusion about his drinking and that his tale to Houseman may have been self-deceiving rather than devious (158).

Although MacShane seems to accept the possibility that alcohol helped Chandler complete *The Blue Dahlia* script, he does not generally credit drinking as a positive force in Chandler's career. He grants that some writers, such as Max Brand, Coleridge or Rossetti, need alcohol to spur their creativity, but he believes that Chandler is not among that number. "Chandler occasionally asserted that he also needed alcohol, but the results show that he never completed first-rate work while drinking." MacShane observes that Chandler's pulp stories, the first six novels and his best essays were written while living a reclusive life with little or no alcohol. The screenplays, unfinished work and his last novel were written while he socialized at the studios, had affairs and drank. Mac-Shane believes that when Chandler was alone he was thrown on his own resources and produced a vivid, convincing world of the imagination (117). MacShane describes Chandler's work habits after he left the studio and lived with Cissy in the quiet suburb of La Jolla. He worked 4–5 hours in the morning, ran errands after lunch and had tea with Cissy and his secretary, Juanita Messick, in the afternoon. Cissy and Juanita would have sherry, which he did not share as he was not drinking during this period. He began to drink again when he and Cissy visited England together in 1952. As Cissy's health continued to fail he drank champagne to numb himself and after her death in 1954 began to drink heavily and harbor a suicidal depression. But, according to MacShane, heavy drinking did not prevent Chandler from writing, as he completed *Playback* and began work on *Poodle Springs* before his death in 1959 (252–63).

Hiney's verdict on Chandler's drinking is somewhat different. "Two things stabilized him. Being drunk, which he often was, and Philip Marlowe" (vii). Hiney takes a psychological approach to the question of how Chandler's personal problem with alcohol relates to his writing, arguing that Chandler's drinking repeats the sins of his hated father and that "every self-loathing mention of alcohol by Marlowe in the later novels would have biographical resonance for Chandler" (66). Hiney also sees a connection between the frequent blackout scenes in the Marlowe novels and Chandler's personal history: "they beg at least two clear biographical correlations. First, the German bombardment that left Chandler unconscious during the First World War and ended his infantry career. Second, the blackouts that he experienced when he drank heavily" (63). In any case he cites Chandler's agent H. N. Swanson on the effect of drinking on Chandler's writing:

> Having served as agent to such infamous alcoholics as Fitzgerald and Faulkner, Swanson understood Chandler's own temperament well. "Some of the best writers I have known" said Swanson in 1989, "seemed to do their best work when they were drying out after a drinking bout. Perhaps the urgency of lost time and uncompleted work spurred them on." He included Chandler in this [153].

The episode of *The Blue Dahlia* script hinged on Chandler's expressed belief that he and John Houseman were the only gentlemen working at Paramount because they were the only men there who had been educated in the English public schools (Houseman 54). Chandler had been educated at Dulwich College Preparatory School, which, although not among the top public schools in England, was, according to MacShane, academically sound. The classics side prepared boys for university, the business side for careers in trade or the civil service of the pre-war empire.

Although he knew there was no money for a university education, Chandler did most of his studies in classics, which he later credited with helping him avoid literary pretension, and teaching him the difference between a vernacular style and an illiterate style he labeled the "faux naïf." But whatever path its students would take, Dulwich took seriously the task of instilling in them Christian, Greek, and Roman virtues. The headmaster, A. H. Gilkes, defined a man of honor as "one who is capable of understanding that which was good; capable of subordinating the poorer part of his nature to the higher part" (MacShane 6–10). Chandler had absorbed the values imparted by the school, even to the extent of enlisting in the Canadian Army to go to Britain's defense in a British uniform in 1917, though he had returned to America in 1912 and brought his mother to live in Los Angeles in 1916. After his infantry platoon was wiped out by German artillery, he transferred as a cadet to the Royal Air Force, but was still in training when the war ended. Settled into civilian life in the Los Angeles of the 1920s and 1930s, Chandler did not always live the values he had been taught, but when he came to create the character of Philip Marlowe, he combined the code of the public school boy with the cynical realism of the private eye.

One way that that code can be displayed is through references to alcohol. There are several reasons that commentary on the use of alcohol can serve as a convenient means to display a character's personal code of behavior. First, the use of alcohol is itself a coded behavior, with rituals such as offering drinks to guests, standing rounds at bars, waiting until certain times of day to drink, or drinking different beverages at different times and places. This codedness allows Chandler to use Marlowe's observations about others to shape reader response to those characters. For example, when Eddie Mars insists that Marlowe drink with him we learn both that Mars is a thug and that he dislikes being reminded that others see him as one.

Second, the codes are informal, not matters of law but of etiquette and personal morality. Thus lapses from the code are only as important as individuals or their associates believe them to be. The reader can be satisfied with Marlowe's level of self-criticism when he observes himself violating the code rather than feeling a need to judge him more harshly than he has already judged himself. Third, lapses from the code may be minor and excusable, or they may indicate an underlying weakness of character that will lead to accident, crime or moral decay. By itself, starting to drink too early in the day is more serious than not taking one's hat off to a lady, but less serious than cheating on one's wife. This is because one incident of starting to drink too early in the day usually has little effect except on the individual involved. However, even one such incident can conceivably lead to worse behavior, such as adultery or murder, which mere lapses of manners or violations of custom usually do not. Fourth, since alcohol is a potentially addicting substance, the desire and ability to control its use speak to the desire and ability to control one's behavior in general, a desire and ability that might reasonably seem advantageous to a hero who must seek to confront and defeat evil in others. As we saw earlier, the desire and ability to control one's relation to alcohol (and occasionally other drugs) was central for Hammett. However, for Chandler, self-control is only part of the dynamic involved in the discussion of alcohol use.

There are three major situations in which the use of alcohol is consistently mentioned by Marlowe: hospitality, manipulation, and self-medication. Discussion of any of these uses can, in turn, become a means of character evaluation. For example, when one character offers another a drink, it may be accepted or rejected, or one character may drink without inviting the other to join. Marlowe's descriptions of, and reactions to hospitality both illuminate and justify his judgments on the characters involved. Incidents that can be labeled "manipulation" occur when drink is offered in a context other than social, as when a witness is plied with drink to elicit information or an attempt is made to distract or deflect a character (usually the detective) from a goal by offering drink. "Self-medication" is the use of alcohol to deaden either physical or emotional pain. Such use may be morally neutral, as when the source of the pain is external and the remedy is used in moderation, or it may be a sign of moral weakness, as when the source of the pain is the character's own action or inaction and alcohol merely prevents or postpones behavior that could lead to an improvement in the situation or when the character continues to drink despite a recognition that alcohol will not help.

The general category of hospitality can be subdivided. The exemplar of hospitality is freely given, freely accepted, and of good quality. Chandler's first novel *The Big Sleep* provides an illustration. When Marlowe is summoned to General Sternwood's home the General offers brandy and soda, which Marlowe accepts and drinks as they talk. He also invites Marlowe to remove his jacket in the overheated greenhouse, to smoke if he wishes, and to help himself to another drink. The General confesses that he is, in part, enjoying the vices of alcohol and tobacco by proxy because his health no longer permits indulgence in "champagne as cold as Valley Forge and about a third of a glass of brandy beneath it" (593). The tone of the meeting is that of a gentleman conferring with a business associate. The relationship between Marlowe and General Sternwood continues as one of mutual respect, and in Marlowe's final conversation with Vivian Regan he gives his reason for the risks he has taken: "to protect what little pride a broken and sick old man has left in his blood, in the thought that his blood is not poison" (762). In contrast to the meeting between General Sternwood and Marlowe, some instances of hospitality lack one or more of the elements listed above.

In *The Lady in the Lake*, the initial meeting between detective and client also takes place on the client's premises. However, Derace Kingsley is less a gentleman than General Sternwood. First, he tries to inflate his own importance by making Marlowe wait, despite having been the one who summoned him. Then he tries to argue down Marlowe's fees and impress Marlowe with the necessity of confidentiality, thus impugning his professionalism. Only after he has launched into the story of his missing wife does Kingsley bring out a bottle of scotch and pour drinks for Marlowe and himself. As hospitality this seems an afterthought, and Marlowe seems to view it more as self-medication, (i.e. Kingsley is drinking "to help him in his worrying" [10–11]). At this point Kingsley appears not quite as sympathetic as General Sternwood, a little too self-important and worried more about his own concerns than about his wife's well-being. In fact, Kingsley never becomes a fully sympathetic character, as he is more concerned over the effect his wife's arrest for murder might have on his career than with whether it is right to help her escape if she has murdered Chris Laverty. Our last view of Kingsley is as he disappears into the bedroom of his cabin after a stiff drink, leaving Marlowe and Sheriff Patton with the problem of how to recapture Degarmo (109). Thus the unfavorable impression made by the initial interview is confirmed.

Farewell, My Lovely begins with a curious twist on the theme of hospitality. While seeking a missing person, Marlowe encounters Moose Malloy, who has just been released from prison. Malloy has returned to the bar at which his girlfriend Velma once sang and is confused to find that it is now a Negro establishment. For no clear reason he drags Marlowe upstairs with him, commenting, "I'm feeling good…. Let's you and me go nibble a couple." After Malloy floors the bouncer they order a drink, as Marlowe becomes the recipient of Malloy's memories of Velma. Malloy goes to the office for more information, kills the owner who tries to pull a gun on him and leaves with the gun. As he departs, Marlowe reminds him that he has failed to pay for the drinks. Malloy is obviously a violent and unpredictable man, the type who insists on treating a total stranger to drinks when he has something to celebrate and who would probably take violent offense if his hospitality were refused. But the concept of hospitality is mocked by the force used to impose the invitation, by the fact that the liquor is never paid for, and by Malloy's having made Marlowe an unwitting "participant" in his crime (*Farewell, My Lovely* 769–72).

In yet another work, *The Little Sister*, Marlowe visits Mavis Weld at her apartment. There, Dolores Gonzales offers him "The God damnest drink" after he flatters her acting. She pours scotch generously, but since she is not the actual hostess the drink is not really hers to give (*The Little*

Sister 259). It should not surprise us when Dolores turns out to be the most self-indulgent character in a novel filled with such figures.

Sometimes the quality of the hospitality is affected by the person who offers it. There are many scenes in which Marlowe drinks with people of whom he does not approve, usually to deflect their hostility or to gain information. Eddie Mars offers a drink when Marlowe visits his gambling club in *The Big Sleep*. Marlowe tries to decline, but there is a thinly veiled threat in Mar's response: "You'll have the drink and like it," a reminder of the frontier code which saw insult in refusal (687). But, although Mars goes through the forms of traditional hospitality to satisfy his own ego, he does not observe the substance. He will have Marlowe killed as readily after drinking with him as before, and they both know it.

In *Farewell, My Lovely*, Marlowe finds himself in a similar situation after he is smuggled aboard the gambling ship *Montecito* and is apprehended by the owner, Laird Brunette. Brunette treats Marlowe alternately as a prisoner and a guest, threatening him and then offering drinks. They part on terms of respect, if not friendship, and despite his disclaimers, Brunette does convey Marlowe's message to Moose Malloy. In *Playback*, however, Marlowe's attitude toward racketeers seems to have hardened. Clark Brandon is a major property owner in the resort town of Esmerelda. Marlowe suspects that he concealed the body of Larry Mitchell and hired a gunman to frighten off a Kansas City detective who might reveal his criminal past. But Marlowe wants only to have his guesses confirmed for his own satisfaction, since Betty Mayfield is not under suspicion and the police plan no action that might endanger her. Therefore, he is free to refuse a drink ("I'm not on that kind of terms with you, Brandon" [865]), and to tell Brandon as he leaves: "You hired a gun. That puts you out of the class of people I shake hands with" (868). In the meetings with Mars and Brunette, Marlowe had to compromise his standards to get information that might help his investigation. From Brandon, there is nothing he needs that would justify bending his personal code.

However, not every unpleasant character with whom Marlowe shares a drink is a gangster. In *Farewell, My Lovely*, he goes to the Chief of Police of Bay City. The chief treats him coldly when it seems that he has come to complain that Bay City officers illegally detained him outside city limits. But after Marlowe establishes that he is employed by the wealthy Grayle family, the chief offers drinks and complete cooperation. Given Marlowe's stated opinion of Bay City corruption, we may assume he would prefer not to accept hospitality from a crooked cop, but he does so in order to gain a chance to quiz the police officer about his arrest and the private clinic at which he was dumped. The chief's hypocrisy is underlined by the description of him locking the office door before bringing out the liquor, and his habit of chewing cardamom seeds to cover the smell of alcohol on his breath.

In yet another category is hospitality which is not offered at all. Marlowe's first meeting with Vivian Regan is in sharp contrast to the conference that has just taken place with her father. Vivian drinks without offering anything to Marlowe, even when she orders the maid to mix her another drink; she makes insulting remarks about private detectives as greasy little men; and she tries unsuccessfully to discover whether her father has hired Marlowe to find her missing husband. Even after Marlowe has repeatedly demonstrated his willingness to take risks for her family, Vivian continues to treat him inhospitably, even though she has on several occasions accepted drinks from him. Although we learn that Vivian's alliance with Eddie Mars was a bid to protect her father from the knowledge that his youngest daughter is a deranged killer, she remains an unsympathetic figure.

Mrs. Murdock, in *The High Window*, is a client whose first meeting with Marlowe establishes her as a less sympathetic character than even Derace Kingsley. She summons Marlowe, then attempts to intimidate him by questioning his fees and retainer. Unlike Sternwood or Kingsley, she does not offer any hospitality. Indeed, she drinks throughout the interview, sipping port from a glass that she replenishes frequently. Marlowe remarks to himself that he does not like to drink port in warm weather, but that "it's nice when they let you refuse it." Mrs. Murdock, perhaps sensing Marlowe's reaction, volunteers the information that she has not offered any wine because it is medicine for her asthma (*High Window* 992–93). The lack of hospitality, or even of courtesy, in this first meeting helps to establish Mrs. Murdock as a hard, selfish and manipulative woman who deserves to have the tables turned on her when Marlowe discovers that she killed her first husband, tricked Merle Davis into believing that she had done so then held this false information over Davis to make a virtual slave of her.

In yet another category is hospitality betrayed. When Marlowe visits the Grayle residence, he meets Mr. and Mrs. Grayle, and Mr. Grayle mixes him a drink. Marlowe continues to drink with Helen Grayle after her husband leaves the room. After several more drinks of what Marlowe describes as "the kind of liquor you think you can drink forever and all you do is get reckless," she sits next to him, falls across his lap, and demands a kiss. Marlowe is responding to her advances when Mr. Grayle re-enters the room and leaves again with an apology. Marlowe pushes Helen Grayle away and leaves, feeling "nasty, as if I had picked a poor man's pocket" (857–67). Marlowe has been guilty of a serious breach of the Western moral code by accepting a man's hospitality and then making love to his wife. The breach is made even worse by the fact that Mr. Grayle is elderly and in poor health.

Obviously, our judgment of characters cannot be based solely on whether they are charming and generous hosts. For Chandler, hospitality by itself is not enough to establish the moral worth of a character, for, as noted above, his gangsters are often generous and sophisticated, if not charming. Nor is lack of hospitality conclusive evidence of moral shortcomings. However, in describing social interactions in which alcohol is offered or withheld, accepted or rejected, Chandler typically provides a framework for evaluating certain aspects of character.

The uses of alcohol for "manipulation" can take either a strongly negative form in which the provision or promise of alcohol is used to prompt a witness to reveal information that he or she would prefer to conceal, or a milder form, which even verges on hospitality, in which alcohol is only an incentive for a witness to share information with the detective.

In *Farewell My Lovely*, Marlowe plies the befuddled Jessie Florian with gin until she is too drunk to realize that he is watching her conceal a photo of Velma so that she can attempt to palm off a substitute. She is also too drunk to object when he returns to the bedroom to take the photo for himself. Florian is so obviously dependent on alcohol and so disgusting in her greed for it that Marlowe feels soiled by the entire transaction: "A lovely old woman. I liked being with her. I liked getting her drunk for my own sordid purpose.... I was beginning to be a little sick at my stomach" (790). Johanna Smith rightly sees this statement as an attempt to "disinfect" Marlowe's behavior (189). The reader may be thinking that Marlowe's actions are disgusting, but his own self-disgust disarms the criticism by offering reassurance that he is capable of recognizing problematic behavior in himself.

Earlier Marlowe has shared alcohol with an informant without any such self-disgust. Marlowe approaches the clerk of the hotel opposite the club in which Malloy has run amok. After admitting that he is a private detective he offers the clerk a drink. "Brother, this don't buy you nothing at all," he said. "But I is pleased to take a light snifter in your company." In the ensuing conversation Marlowe establishes that the club had been owned by a Mike Florian, whose widow still lives in the area. Marlowe offers a third drink, but the clerk replies, "Two is all, brother—before sundown. I thank you. Your method of approach is soothin' to a man's dignity..." (781–83). In this interaction the witness remains in control of himself and of the situation. He gives Marlowe only as much information as he deems fit—although in this case it is apparently as much information as he has. Except for his initial approach of trying to pass himself off as an employee of a hotel protection agency, Marlowe treats the witness with respect and refers to him in terms that lead the reader to do the same. Neither party's self-respect is sacrificed in the transaction. Jesse Florian, however, is described in ways that emphasize her shabby surroundings, her lack of personal hygiene, her pathetic, drunken attempts at cunning and her hostility to Marlowe.

Similar incidents occur in other novels. The hotel clerk has a counterpart in the bellhop in *The Lady in the Lake*. Marlowe openly offers to pay for information, leaving the drinks he allows the informant to pour to serve as a hospitable accompaniment to the transaction rather than a bribe or a stratagem to obtain more information than the subject might have wished to share if sober. The bellhop takes offense when Marlowe suggests that he may be embroidering his story for a larger payoff, but harmony is re-established as the man goes over the details of Chris Laverty's meeting with the woman presumed to have been Crystal Kingsley. The bellhop finishes his drink and accepts payment for the information, and they part in mutual satisfaction.

Another witness like Jessie Florian appears in *The Little Sister*, as Marlowe finds the manager of the apartment building at which Orrin Quest had been living asleep in a room full of the fumes of gin and marijuana smoke. However, despite his obvious dependence on it, gin does not induce the man to give any useful information, except unintentionally when he dials Dr. Lagardie's phone number in front of Marlowe while making threats about having friends who "will take care of you" (221–22).

Marlowe is not the only character who uses alcohol to manipulate another. Geiger gives Carmen Sternwood drinks laced with ether to encourage her to pose for nude photographs. This disgusts even the gangster, Eddie Mars, who calls Geiger a "dirty pimp" after examining the evidence (*The Big Sleep* 640). In other cases the detective may be the victim. In *The Lady in the Lake*, Marlowe is stopped by Bay City cops who attempt to force him to drink whiskey so that their arresting him for drunk driving will be plausible. When he resists, they punch him in the stomach so that the whiskey is sprayed over his clothes (130). In an even more extreme version of alcohol as manipulation, drink can be used as a murder weapon, as when Mars' gunman Lash Canino poisons Harry Jones while pretending to seal an agreement with him with a drink (721). Marlowe, unarmed in the next room, is a helpless witness, but the information we gain about Canino's character is put to use later when Marlowe gets the drop on him and kills him without compunction. Chandler clearly wants there to be no question that Marlowe is justified in the one instance in the series in which he actually kills a person.

One might also note the reverse manipulation Marlowe tries on Terry Lennox, in *The Long Goodbye*, when he leaves this apparent alcoholic alone with a bottle of liquor to test whether he can resist (427). Whatever form manipulation takes, it is a slightly unsavory, but sometimes necessary, part of the hard-boiled detective's world. The private detective functions without the compulsion of the law to encourage truthful revelations from witnesses. He would not be employed at all if people did not have secrets and if truth were to be had merely for the asking.

As noted in the introduction, alcohol as medication has a long history in western culture. Distilled liquor, in particular, was used to counter both emotional shocks and physical injuries, to calm the nervous and to rouse the lethargic. Marlowe seeks comfort in alcohol on a number of occasions, and offers it to others as well.

In *The Big Sleep*, Marlowe arrives at Geiger's house to find Geiger shot and Carmen Sternwood drugged and naked. He drives Carmen home in her car, then walks back to his own car in the rain, where he drinks part of a bottle of rye whiskey before returning to the house. Geiger's body is gone, and after a brief search Marlowe returns home. Both the rye he drinks in his car and the hot toddy he mixes up at home may be intended to ward off the effects of walking for half an hour in a cold rain. But their effects in cushioning the emotional shock of encountering violent death must be considered as well.

Two days later, the Sternwood chauffeur has been found dead, Geiger's lover has shot Joe Brody, and there appear to be no leads in the disappearance of Rusty Regan. Sitting in his office, Marlowe muses that "life was pretty flat and that it would probably be just as flat if I took a drink and that taking a drink all alone at that time of day wouldn't be any fun anyway." After a brief call from Sternwood's butler Marlowe "took the drink and let my self-respect ride its own race" while he runs over the salient points of the case (684–85). In this instance and others throughout the series, Marlowe drinks to soothe his frustration over a case in which he sees to no constructive actions open to him. Two days later, Marlowe returns home after an evening in which he has helplessly witnessed Canino's murder of Henry Jones, been captured and knocked out by Canino, escaped with the help of Silver-Wig, and finally, killed Canino and reported the deaths to the police. It is relatively early in the morning and he is exhausted but cannot sleep. He takes a drink "although it was the wrong time of day" (745). Plainly there are times to drink and times to refrain, and a man should be aware of this code even if he occasionally allows himself to violate it.

This pattern is repeated in *The Little Sister*. After Marlowe has been threatened with a gun and offered a bribe, then fended off an invitation from Dolores Gonzoles, Orfamay Quest calls and suggests that she knows a murder has occurred. To brace himself for the coming interview he pours a drink of Old Forester (279). In *The High Window* the brand has changed to Old Taylor, but the action is the same as he sits in his office after discovering the body of George Phillips (1054). In none of these incidents does he drink to intoxication, although the amount consumed would have a stronger effect on a less-accustomed drinker. His goal is not to escape the reality of the violence and confusion that surround him so much as to cushion it temporarily.

Yet, on one notable occasion Marlowe does deliberately drink himself comatose. In *The Long Goodbye*, Marlowe is staying with the Wades when Eileen Wade tries to lure him into her bed. Marlowe is close to succumbing when the erotic spell is broken by an interruption from the Mexican houseboy. Marlowe flees downstairs and grabs a bottle of scotch and guzzles it until the bottle is empty and he passes out (594–95). The reason for Marlowe's urgency is not clear. If near discovery by Candy has really broken the erotic attraction, which his description of Eileen as merely a woman on a bed from whom weird noises issued certainly suggests, why the compulsion to put himself out of commission? The scene suggests that either he is afraid that he will be tempted again and will not be interrupted, or that he is ashamed of having become aroused by another man's wife, a man who is his host and whom he is supposed to protect. As earlier in his career, with Helen Grayle, Marlowe is deeply ashamed of having almost violated a major cultural taboo.

Marlowe is not the only character to use liquor to ease the pain of an unpleasant situation. When confronted about her sister's murderous nature, Vivian Regan admits that she knew and concealed the fact that Carmen had killed her husband, Rusty Regan. Knowing that he lies in the sump—"a horrible decayed thing"—explains her earlier behavior at times when, as she explains, "I had to get drunk quickly—whatever time of day it was. Awfully damn quickly" (*The Big Sleep* 762–63). Betty Mayfield has a similar reaction to finding the body of Larry Mitchell on her hotel verandah. Offered a drink by Marlowe, she first waves it away, then grabs the glass and empties it (*Playback* 776). Mavis Weld also needs a drink when Marlowe finds her at Steelgrave's mansion. Marlowe pours brandy and describes her reaction: "The second drink made her shudder. But the blue look had gone away from her mouth and her lips didn't glare like stop lights and the little etched lines at the corners of her eyes were not in relief any more" (*The Little Sister* 368).

Whatever its virtues in emergencies, alcohol does not always provide the expected solace. This is frequently made plain at the end of a case when the facts are in and Marlowe has completed his job. Seldom does he enjoy a sense of a job well done. Too many have died; the innocent have not been adequately protected, nor the guilty adequately punished. At the conclusion of *The Big Sleep*, Marlowe leaves the Sternwood mansion: "On the way downtown I stopped at a bar and had a couple of double scotches. They didn't do me any good. All they did was make me think of Silver-Wig, and I never saw her again" (764). *Farewell, My Lovely* has a double conclusion. First, Marlowe recaps the case for Anne Riordan as they drink at her house. She jokes that he should have played the role of the amateur detective, revealing his clever conclusions at a dinner party, like Philo Vance. Marlowe responds that it was not that kind of story. "It's not lithe and clever. It's just dark and full of blood" (978). Later he discusses Mrs. Grayle's capture and suicide with Lt. Randall, but they do not drink together. At the conclusion of *The High Window*, Marlowe drives Merle Davis home to the midwest. When he returns, the police have wrapped up the murder cases based on the false clues Marlowe had left and, after a brief visit with Lieutenant Breeze, Marlowe goes home, mixes a drink and plays over a Capablanca chess game. He seems to find some meaning or solace in the "silent implacability" of chess, and the novel concludes with Marlowe looking into the mirror and sipping ice water.

Neither *The Lady in the Lake* nor *The Little Sister* ends with Marlowe drinking; in both novels the final scene has him viewing the bodies of the murderers. *The Long Goodbye* concludes with Marlowe listening as the footsteps of Terry Lennox, now Señor Maioranos, recede down his office hall after Marlowe has refused a last drink with him. In *Playback* Chandler resumes the motif of Marlowe, alone at the conclusion of a case, pouring a drink. But his mood is more dispirited than ever.

> I opened a couple of windows and mixed a drink in the kitchen. I sat down on the couch and stared at the wall. Wherever I went, whatever I did, this was what I would come back to. A blank wall in a meaningless room in a meaningless house.
> I put the drink down on a side table without touching it. Alcohol was no cure for this. Nothing was any cure but the hard inner heart that asked for nothing from anyone [869–70].

His mood abruptly changes when Linda Loring calls from Paris to propose, overriding his objections about the differences in their circumstances. The call ends and he picks up his drink again, lost in visions of the night Linda spent with him a year and a half earlier. "I looked around the empty room—which was no longer empty…. The air was full of music" (871). Since Chandler did not live to complete another Marlowe story we will never know whether marriage would have provided a long-term escape from the feelings of meaninglessness that alcohol fails to suppress at the conclusion of each case.

The Long Goodbye is the work in which Chandler most fully explored his thoughts about the use of alcohol. J. O. Tate, writing in *The Armchair Detective*, feels that the novel is:

...at least superficially about drinking. It is what the characters do. Drinking is the basis of the relationship of Marlowe and Lennox. Drinking causes the acquaintance of Marlowe and Wade. Marlowe meets Linda Loring (his bride to be) at a bar. Marlowe meets Howard Spencer at a bar, and Mrs. Wade at that same bar. Chandler had mastered his desire for alcohol, at least temporarily; but alcohol was on his mind [394].

Yet, *The Long Goodbye* is not so much simply about drinking as it is about alcoholism. Chandler, through Marlowe, Wade and Lennox, obsesses over the difference, if any, between a heavy, even a temporarily out of control drinker, and an alcoholic. According to Marlowe:

> A man who drinks too much on occasion is still the same man as he was sober. An alcoholic, a real alcoholic, is not the same man at all ... he will be someone you never met before [569].

The events of the novel, however, give reason to doubt whether this distinction is valid.

Terry Lennox is the first character Marlowe meets who seems to have problems with alcohol. Lennox is drunk, falling out of the driver's seat of his wife's car in a nightclub parking lot (419). Although just short of passing out, Lennox retains his ability to articulate and his extremely good manners. The parking lot attendant, though, has a clear, unsympathetic philosophy that drunks may come in a number of varieties but that none of them are worth the extra trouble they cause. He does not share Marlowe's criticism of Sylvia Lennox for abandoning Terry, seeing no reason that she should stay around and waste her good looks on a lush (421). Marlowe disagrees to the extent of helping Lennox home, but he suppresses an urge to try to stop him from drinking, reflecting that alcoholics will always find liquor if they need it. Lennox, however, is no ordinary drunk. Although he seems doubtful about the possibility of quitting when Marlowe rescues him a second time, especially when Marlowe remarks that the process takes about three years, he is able to pass the test of being left alone with a bottle of whiskey. And, when he looks Marlowe up again after his remarriage to Sylvia Lennox, his drinking is still under control. Marlowe's offhand diagnosis is that perhaps Lennox was never really a drunk (432). The subsequent pattern of their friendship seems to confirm this. They develop a ritual of sharing a few quiet drinks about five o'clock in the evening in bars near Marlowe's Hollywood office. Lennox doesn't drink too much on these occasions and observes of his former drinking problem that, like a recurring fever, when it's not present it seems as if it never had been (433). We later learn that the extended binge that led to his initial encounter with Marlowe was sparked by the unexpected meeting with Eileen Sampsell, his secret wartime bride, who believed him dead and married Roger Wade.

Roger Wade is the second major character whose drinking is out of control. We learn of him first through his publisher, Howard Spencer, who tells Marlowe that Wade is drinking heavily, suffers from fits of temper, in one of which he has thrown his wife downstairs, and has disappeared for several days at a time. Eileen Wade has suggested to Spencer that her husband has a guilty secret which he drinks to forget. She suggests to Marlowe that Roger has fallen out of love with her. Marlowe counters with the idea that Wade is disappointed in the course of his writing career, in the type of writing he is doing (504). Later we learn that Wade's drinking is out of control because he either believes he killed Sylvia Lennox during an alcoholic blackout or suspects the truth, that his wife did. Wade's drinking patterns resemble those of Terry Lennox in some respects. While Lennox differs from the average drunk in maintaining a clear voice and precise articulation even when too drunk to walk, Wade differs in retaining the ability to type clearly, evenly and with no mistakes.

Lennox and Wade also share a contempt for the idle rich with whom their lifestyles have surrounded them. Lennox describes his life as lacking pleasure, filled with tennis, golf, swimming, riding, and watching his wife's friend suffer hangovers while trying to delay the first drink of the day (434).

Wade makes similar remarks about his dislike for his neighbors. He concedes to Marlowe that they are no different from anybody else and counters, "But they ought to be. If they're not, what use are they? They're the class of the county and they're no better than a bunch of truckdrivers full of cheap whiskey. Not as good" (654).

In addition to hating their neighbors, each man harbors a streak of self-contempt. Lennox is literally the kept man of a rich wife whom he has twice married for her money. Wade considers himself a literary prostitute because his best-selling historical romances are trash. Marlowe agrees with their self-evaluations, but brusquely discourages each man's self-pity, suggesting that they are capable of changing if they really wish to. He tells Lennox that he doesn't have to have it the way it is (434), and, when Wade suggests that he ought to portray history accurately in his novels, asks him why he doesn't (626). The answer in both cases is money; neither man is ready to surrender the luxuries which their prostitution has purchased. But Wade and Lennox are not completely alike in their drinking personae. Unlike Lennox, Wade is unpredictable when drunk. Although he maintains control when Dr. Loring assaults him at his own cocktail party, he later becomes suspicious and sarcastic with Marlowe (543).

Lennox and Wade are not the only drunks on stage in this novel. Several scenes are set in bars, giving Marlowe occasion to comment on the types to be observed there. For instance, in Victor's we see the type of habitual drinkers who have to try very hard to control their shaking hands as they begin an evening's drinking (433). In the bar of the Ritz-Beverly, Marlowe waits for Spencer and gives another commentary on habitual drinkers:

> ...a sad fellow ... you knew that he got up on the bottle and only let go of it when he fell asleep at night. He would be like that for the rest of his life and that was what his life was. You would never know how he got that way because even if he told you it would not be the truth. At the very best a distorted memory of the truth as he knew it. There is a sad man like that in every quiet bar in the world [489].

Nor are women exempt; one of the types of blondes enumerated in contrast to Eileen Wade is the type of blonde who is soft and willing and cares only about wearing mink and drinking dry champagne at the Starlight Roof (491). A sample female drunk appears at the Wades' cocktail party, engaging in pseudo-intellectual flirtation with Marlowe and staging hysterical scenes with her own husband (568).

Marlowe makes a clear distinction between a man who drinks too much on occasion, a category into which Marlowe himself would fall, and an alcoholic. As noted above, Marlowe believes that alcoholism alters character, that alcoholics are not the same people when drunk as when sober (569). Earlier, at his first meeting with Lennox, Marlowe had observed that interfering with a drunk, even one you know, may be a mistake and lead to a punch in the face (420). These observations on the nature of alcoholism are not mere window dressing. The emphasis on Lennox's politeness, both when sober and when drunk, helps the reader accept Marlowe's belief that Lennox could not have murdered his wife in the brutal fashion reported by the police. The syllogism would be: alcoholics are not the same sober as when drunk; Lennox is as polite when drunk as when sober; therefore Lennox is not an alcoholic. Lennox would not commit a brutal murder when sober, therefore Lennox did not murder his wife, whether he was drunk or sober at the time of her death.

Wade's bad temper when drunk and his record of alcoholic blackouts make him, on the other hand, a plausible suspect, to himself, to Marlowe, and to the reader. Yet this dichotomy is not in line with the way Chandler presents heavy drinkers in other novels. Can we imagine, for instance, that a sober Jessie Florian would be a pleasant, polite middle-aged woman, or that if Mrs. Murdock would lay off the medicinal port she would become a loving, kindly mother and generous employer? Nor does it agree with the line cited above which, since Marlowe has just met Lennox and has no way to know whether his condition is habitual, implies that any drunk, not only an alcoholic, may throw a punch.

There are two characters in *The Long Goodbye* who are not shown drinking. Dr. Loring does not drink at all and expresses contempt for alcoholics by refusing to treat them. However, the Demerol prescription he gives Eileen Wade, ostensibly for her asthma, may reveal a certain hypocrisy. The earlier discussion, while Marlowe was searching for Wade, of doctors who run sanitariums of doubtful repute has reminded the reader that a doctor's ability to prescribe narcotics is subject to abuse (512). Captain Hernandez's questions to Dr. Loring and Loring's defensive answers suggest that Loring is guilty of carelessness at best, of pandering to an addict at worst (685–87).

The second character who does not drink is Harlan Potter, although, when he summons Marlowe, he maintains a facade of hospitality in his daughter's home by ordering tea. He too reveals himself as a hypocrite; having grown rich on the revenues of newspapers, he expresses the utmost contempt for the salacious curiosity of the public and for the advertising that makes his riches possible. It should also be noted that neither Loring nor Potter respects the social bonds, which convention establishes between guest and host. Loring publicly insults and assaults Wade at a party in Wade's own home. As Marlowe observes, "If the rules mean anything at all any more," it is that one does not insult your host and your wife by accusing them of an affair in front of a roomful of guests (568). Loring compounds his rudeness with a lapse in professional ethics when he refuses to treat Wade after he injures himself falling while drunk. Potter, in contrast, does not create a scene with Marlowe. Indeed he deprecates the notion that he might threaten physical harm. He merely makes it clear that if Marlowe continues to suggest that Terry Lennox may have been innocent of Sylvia's murder, Potter will effectively deprive him of his livelihood by using his influence to have Marlowe's private investigator's license revoked. In this respect, Potter is morally equivalent to Eddie Mars, who similarly combines the facade of a host with threats of destruction. These portrayals of Loring and of Potter make it clear that in Chandler's view, sobriety is not necessarily a virtue.

Marlowe's drinking patterns in this work remain much as described in earlier novels. He drinks moderately in company, except when under emotional stress. When he returns to Victor's to drink Lennox's commemorative gimlet, he meets Linda Loring, and during the ensuing discussion of Sylvia Lennox's murder, the gimlet becomes three doubles. The drinks make him quarrelsome with Loring over whether Terry really killed her sister and over their father's role in squelching the investigation. On his way out of the bar, Marlowe accosts a gunman who works for Menendez and reflects to himself afterward that he may have been a little drunk (556–57). We see Marlowe drunk a second time a little later, in the scene described above in which he drinks himself into oblivion after

Eileen Wade nearly seduces him. The following morning he wakes with a hangover that persists even after he has returned home, showered and had breakfast. As once before, in *The Big Sleep*, he violates his rule against drinking in the morning. He explains that the Southern California climate is too soft, keeping the metabolism too low for drinking in the morning to be a safe habit. "But I mixed a tall cold one this time ... I was handling the drink carefully, a sip at a time, watching myself" (601). Just as in *The Big Sleep*, drinking in the morning is depicted as a risky behavior.

As in earlier novels, hospitality involving alcohol both symbolizes and cements social ties between people, especially between men. The relationship between Marlowe and Lennox is centered around the sharing of alcohol, but little else is shared. Marlowe never asks Lennox about his past; Lennox does not volunteer the information. When Lennox starts to open up about his current life and problems Marlowe walks out, telling Lennox that he talks too much about himself (437). This empty interaction hardly rates as friendship by most standards, yet a month later Marlowe is willing to aid Lennox's escape and shield him from the police. The shared drinks seem to symbolize a bond, which Marlowe cannot articulate or make sense of in any conventional way. This bond is only broken when Marlowe realizes that Lennox, while innocent of Sylvia's murder, is guilty of having sheltered Eileen Wade, thus leaving her free to kill her husband. Terry Lennox, returned in the guise of Señor Maioranos, is revealed as empty, either by nature or as a result of his experiences in the war. Twice Marlowe refuses to revive the relationship, even temporarily, by sharing their traditional gimlet. Like Silver-Wig, Mavis Weld, and many others through the years, Terry Lennox disappears from Marlowe's life.

Questions about Marlowe's relationships with drink and drinkers remain. Marlowe seems to represent a code of behavior concerning the use of alcohol: one drinks only at appropriate hours, not in excess except in exceptional circumstances, and preferably with people one likes or respects. This seems like a very moderate and reasonable set of standards for using a substance that is both a keystone of western cultural behavior and a dangerously addictive drug that can render users incapable of good judgment and endanger their physical well-being. Yet, despite the risks associated with its use, Chandler waxes oddly poetic over alcohol. At one point Lennox muses over the scene at Victor's:

> I like bars just after they open for the evening. When the air inside is still cool and clean and everything is shiny and the barkeep is giving himself that last look in the mirror to see if his tie is straight and his hair is smooth. I like the neat bottles on the bar back and the lovely shining glasses and the anticipation. I like to watch the man mix the first one of the evening

and put it down on a crisp mat and put the little folded napkin beside it.
I like to taste it slowly. The first quiet drink of the evening in a quiet bar—
that's wonderful [436].

In *The High Window*, there is a similarly lyrical passage as Marlowe
offers drinks to Spangler and Breeze, policemen investigating the murder
of George Philips. Breeze accepts and Marlowe describes his reaction to
an ordinary highball made with ginger ale and an inexpensive brand of
scotch: "…he picked the glass up and tasted it and sighed again and shook
his head sideways with a half smile; the way a man does when you give
him a drink and he needs it very badly and it is just right and the first
swallow is like a peek into a cleaner, sunnier, brighter world" (1068).
This description has echoes in *The Long Goodbye* when Marlowe relates
to Lennox that curing alcoholism entails several years and getting used
to different perceptions of the world, which will be quieter and paler than
the world of the drinker (426).

Oddly, Marlowe's description of the cured alcoholic resembles the
attitude of Dr. Largadie when he asserts that the treatment of drug addicts
is a complete waste of time involving more than merely depriving them
of their drug until they can do without it.

> That is not curing them, my friend. That is not removing the nervous or
> emotional flaw which made them become addicts. It is making them dull
> negative people who sit in the sun and twirl their thumbs and die of sheer
> boredom and inanition [*The Little Sister* 322].

Chandler presents a paradox. Alcohol can open a "cleaner, sunnier,
brighter world" and there is nothing wrong with liking that world or looking forward to the pleasures of a drink. Mutual recognition of and joint
entry into that world can be the foundation for a relationship either brief,
as with Spangler and Breeze, or prolonged, as with Lennox. Yet to be
too fond of the world offered by alcohol is a weakness, an addiction.
When supplied with their drug of choice, alcoholics are unpredictable,
not the same people drunk as they are sober. When deprived of their
drug they will be "dull and negative people" living in the less intense
world that Marlowe has described to Lennox as the world of the reformed
alcoholic. Balanced against the attractions of alcohol are the problems
that result from its abuse: Terry Lennox, drunk and abandoned in a
nightclub parking lot; Lennox again, filthy and about to be arrested;
Roger Wade, afraid that his alcoholic blackouts conceal a terrible crime.
These men are paying the price for overuse of alcohol to soften the
harshness of the world. These are the excesses that Marlowe strives to
avoid, the reason that taking a tall cold drink in the morning is cause to
watch oneself.

Part of the paradox of *The Long Goodbye* is that, while the nature of alcoholism works as a major theme, Chandler seems curiously unwilling to admit that any of the major characters are alcoholics. If one is intended to believe Marlowe's pronouncements on the subject, neither Lennox nor Wade need accept the label. Take for example, the dictum that alcoholics are not the same drunk as sober. Marlowe sums up Lennox's character when he returns as Señor Maioranos by saying that he was a nice guy because he had a nice nature (733). This is true whether Lennox is drunk or sober. In the parking lot of The Dancers, Marlowe comments that Lennox was the politest drunk he had ever met (421). Marlowe also claims that curing an alcoholic takes about three years. Yet in much less time Lennox is not just clean and sober, which could indicate the desperate clinging to sobriety that Alcoholics Anonymous doctrine calls the "dry drunk," but is actually able to drink sociably and in moderation, a goal that most substance abuse experts regard as impossible for the real alcoholic.

If the essence of Wade is his writing ability, that also endures. He can write and type clearly while drunk. His drunken self-disgust may seem like an alcoholic character trait, but it is only a less-inhibited version of his contempt when sober for the quality of his literary production. Even Wade's supposed violence becomes less certain under closer examination. Spencer tells Marlowe that Wade threw his wife down stairs while drunk, but there is never direct evidence that this occurred. If, as it seems reasonable to assume, Eileen Wade plotted to bring Marlowe into her household in order to discover whether he had any suspicions about the Lennox murder that might lead to her, it is perfectly possible that she either deliberately provoked Wade into pushing her downstairs, or that she faked the entire incident to give credence to the necessity for Marlowe's presence. Spencer is not the sort of person who would demand proof of such an allegation from the wife of a valued author.

If alcoholism is the theme of *The Long Goodbye*, why is Chandler at such pains to deny that his characters are alcoholics? For this one book at least, a biographical explanation seems to fit. Chandler had struggled with alcohol most of his adult life. Its abuse had cost him jobs, had threatened his health and probably strained his relationship with Cissy, especially when associated with his repeated unfaithfulness. As Chandler was writing *The Long Goodbye*, Cissy's health, which had been poor for a long period, was declining even more. In a letter written after Cissy's death, Chandler speaks of all his work as having been an offering, "a fire for Cissy to warm her hands at" (Houseman 66). Given the circumstances of its composition *The Long Goodbye* may be seen as a more specific offering to Cissy. Chandler creates a prolonged explanation for the problems his drinking had caused by creating characters who exhibit out of control drinking while they embody aspects of his own personality. Wade is not living up to his potential, writing trashy romance, as Chandler wrote mysteries, instead of serious literature. Lennox is an American with English manners and war record, as Chandler was himself. The presentation of the idea that an alcoholic is not the same drunk as when sober seems to ask the reader (and Cissy) to accept the sober aspects of each man and forgive any alcohol-induced aberrations as being out of character. Yet this "apology" is marred by the simultaneous claim, as outlined above, that the characters who stand in for Chandler may not really be alcoholics at all. Later readers know that Chandler's drinking slipped out of control after Cissy's death, letting us see the "denial" at the heart of the novel—the alcoholic's deluded assertion that he is in control, that he can quit any time, a claim that is given credence during periods of abstinence but revealed as empty by the next drinking binge. The extent of Chandler's denial of his problem is displayed in a letter to Jessica Tyndale written in September, 1955. "I start off with a drink of white wine and end up drinking two bottles of scotch a day. Then I stop eating ... the withdrawal symptoms are simply awful. I shake so that I can't hold a glass of water."

Yet after describing in himself the clear clinical symptoms of alcohol dependence he muses that his father was an alcoholic and that he had feared becoming one, as though that fear were groundless. In a later letter (October 1955), Chandler delivers the pronouncement that he had put in Marlowe's mouth, that a heavy drinker need not be considered an alcoholic if "he is the same guy even with a load on" (MacShane, *Selected Letters* 392–93). Clearly Chandler wishes to believe that so long as he does not undergo some Jekyll/Hyde transformation when drunk, he can avoid the label that he hangs on his despised father. Perhaps because of the degree to which he had put himself into the novel, Chandler felt that *The Long Goodbye* was his best work. In any case, its writing seemed to purge him of his preoccupation with alcoholism. In *Playback*, alcohol retreats to its earlier supportive function in reporting the moods and characters of Marlowe and the people he encounters.

Mentions of alcohol in Chandler's works serve as much more than mere descriptive detail. Repeatedly Chandler allows Marlowe to make evaluations of other characters based, at least in part, on their use of alcohol. Hospitality, of which drink has been a central item in western culture, is a test of character applied to those whom Marlowe meets in a context in which it would appropriately be offered. Some, such as General Sternwood and Terry Lennox, display behavior that earns from Marlowe more than the normal loyalty of the detective/client relationship. Others, such as Mrs. Murdock, who provokes scorn for her self-centered hypocrisy, condemn themselves in part by failing to treat Marlowe hospitably. Conversely, Marlowe subjects himself to severe censure for his violation of guest morality by almost yielding to the sexual advances of Helen Grayle and Eileen Wade. Marlowe also shames himself when he uses alcohol to manipulate others, even when such manipulation is necessary to his investigations. While alcohol can be used to exploit others, it can also be used to help, as when it is offered to someone who has suffered a physical or emotional shock. Marlowe also uses alcohol to help himself through physical strain, as when he escapes from the sanitarium room in Bay City. However, the dangers of alcohol are most commonly brought home to Marlowe when he uses or is tempted to use it as self-medication for the sense of despair that threatens him when a case is not going well, or when the case has concluded in the usual manner of a hard-boiled detective story with too many people dead and too little justice dealt. It is then that he must remember that alcohol is no cure for these feelings. Throughout the series, Chandler uses Marlowe's actions and attitudes toward the use of alcohol to reinforce his presentation of Marlowe as ultimately a superior man, a man who is, despite a humble profession, "good enough for any world." That this strategy is successful bespeaks the importance of alcohol to western culture, and the degree to which American culture in particular had become obsessed with its cultural role, as well as Chandler's skill in presenting his personal obsessions in terms that the reader can find palatable.

Chandler is secure in his place as the creator of the knightly private detective who has earned the approval even of critics and academics. There have been many contenders for Chandler's place in the canon. However, one who is not usually nominated for this position is Mickey Spillane. Spillane and his creation, Mike Hammer, tend to dismay critics who believe the works display a sadistic pleasure in descriptions of physical violence. But as a worldwide best seller whose career spans five decades from the publication of *I, the Jury* in 1947 to *Black Alley* in 1997, Spillane can hardly be ignored, especially since he himself became part of the culture surrounding alcohol use in America by participating in a series of beer commercials that played on his tough-guy persona.

Mickey Spillane

"Can't Spell Cognac"

Mickey Spillane is one of the most controversial of contemporary detective story writers. The works featuring his major creation, Mike Hammer, exemplify all that literary critics and academics disdain in pulp fiction: excessive violence, preoccupation with sex, and conservative (some would say reactionary) politics. Yet these works undeniably found an audience, as there are an estimated 200 million copies of Spillane's works in print. Nor can his popularity be considered purely an artifact of American culture, for in 1995 he was the fifth most translated author in the world, according to an interview with Julie Baumgold published in *Esquire* (132). Mike Hammer is known to non-readers as well, an additional audience reached by six feature films, a radio show, two made-for-television movies, two television series, and a syndicated comic strip (Collins and Traylor 184–85). Obviously, Mike Hammer is a character whose appeal transcends the boundaries between readers and mass media audiences, between nations and between generations, for his career has spanned five decades.

Mike Hammer would seem to be the likeliest of any literary character to fit the clichéd image of the trench-coated, trigger-happy and hard-drinking private eye. Indeed, even Max A. Collins and James L. Traylor, who defend Spillane's literary achievements in *One Lonely Knight, Mickey Spillane's Mike Hammer*, refer to Hammer as drinking "a prodigious amount of beer, wine and hard liquor (usually rye or Four Roses and soda) in a day's time" (33). Spillane himself traded on the image his creation had acquired when he was one of the celebrities hired to advertise

Miller Lite beer in the 1980s. Yet the image of Hammer as a consistently excessive drinker is based on little in the actual texts. Indeed, except in his first appearance in *I, the Jury* and later in *The Girl Hunters*, Hammer is portrayed as a rather moderate drinker, especially when one considers that the post-war years were the era of the three-martini lunch, a time when comedy sketches about drunks were a staple of family-oriented television shows and the role of alcohol in domestic violence, automobile accidents and other social ills aroused far less concern than it does today. This examination of several Hammer novels will demonstrate that the image of the detective as an extraordinarily hard-drinking man appears to have been imposed on the texts by Spillane's critics. The stereotype of the fictional private investigator has overtaken the facts.

Although Mickey Spillane has patterned his protagonist on himself in many ways, to the point of saying, "He only drinks, dresses, or does what I do," it is important not to confuse the author with his character (Baumgold 132). Frank Michael Morrison Spillane was born in Brooklyn, New York in 1918. He was a friendly and athletic young man who grew up in the rough neighborhood of Elizabeth, New Jersey, where his father was a bartender (Geherin, *The American Private Eye* 127). He began to write while in high school and contributed stories to various slick and pulp magazines under a number of pen names. After a short time at Kansas State Teachers College, he returned to New York and eventually began writing comic books. Among the titles he worked on were *Captain Marvel, Captain America, Plastic Man,* and *Prince Namor* (Van Dover, *Murder* 93).

When World War II began, he enlisted in the U.S. Army Air Force and became a combat pilot and later, when his skill at conveying information was recognized, he was made a fighter pilot instructor. After the war, he planned to return to writing comics but found that the comic industry was in a slump. He converted his planned comic character "Mike Danger" into Mike Hammer and in 1947 *I, the Jury* appeared. Although it sold slowly in the hard cover edition, the paperback editions have sold over eight million copies (Collins and Traylor 5). There have been thirteen Mike Hammer novels published to date, the most recent *Black Alley* in 1996 (Penzler).

In the sixties, Spillane created another series character, a freelance spy, Tiger Mann, called "an imitation James Bond" in *The Oxford Companion to Crime and Mystery Writing* (Traylor & Collins 423), who is featured in four novels from 1964 to 1966, a time span illustrative of Spillane's notorious speed in composition, especially considering that two Hammer novels were published during the same period. According to Otto Penzler, Spillane claimed to have completed *The Day of the Guns,* the first Mann novel, in three days (24). Spillane has also written short stories and novellas for magazine publication featuring other characters, several non–Hammer novels, and two books for juveniles. Yet despite being able to write a private eye story in a matter of weeks, Spillane does not display the steady production for which some series authors are noted— "a Christie for Christmas." There was a ten-year gap between the publication of *Kiss Me, Deadly* in 1952 and the next Mike Hammer novel, *The Girl Hunters,* in 1962, an even longer 18 years between *Survival, Zero* in 1970 and *The Killing Man* in 1989, and again seven years before the publication of *Black Alley* in 1996. Some critics attributed the disappearance of Mike Hammer after 1952 to Spillane's conversion to the Jehovah's Witness faith, since that denomination frowns on excessive drinking, smoking, gambling, and extramarital sex, and teaches that violence is only justified in the direct service of God. The official Jehovah's Witness Website contains the statement, "It is wrong to take revenge or to return evil for the bad things that others might do to us." The site also counsels moderate use of wine and other alcohol, adding that "heavy drinking and drunkenness are wrong in God's eyes" (Watchtower). However, Spillane himself has never confirmed that the articles of his faith have affected his writing career, attributing his non-productive time instead to prosperity. According to Geherin, Spillane told *Life* writer Richard W. Johnston; "Why write if you don't need the money?" to explain the hiatus in his career (129). The religious explanation seems weakened by the fact that Spillane returned to writing Hammer novels without changing his character's habits. In the later novels, Hammer continues to drink, smoke, engage in casual sex, and resort to violence on a regular basis when dealing with criminals or their associates. Meanwhile, Spillane is noted in a recent interview with John Meroney in *The Washington Post* as being a regular and active member of his church in Murrells Inlet, South Carolina (C1). According to Collins, Spillane refuses to discuss his religion in connection with his work (x). On the other hand, Collins reports a rumor that Spillane has manuscripts of Hammer stories that he will not publish because he is uncomfortable with the level of sex and explicit violence they contain (viii). In the absence of a persuasive statement by Spillane, the question of whether his faith influences the content of his fiction cannot be determined with any confidence, but the supposition does not seem likely in view of Spillane's writing history.

No full biography of Spillane has been published, but a few more details of his life are available. He has been married three times: in 1945 to Mary Ann Pearce, in 1965 to actress Sherri (Selma) Malinon, and in 1983 to Jane Johnson, a fitness instructor who grew up near his home in Murrells Inlet. In addition to writing, Spillane has worked as a circus performer for Ringling Brothers, Barnum and Bailey circus, doing a trampoline act and being shot from a cannon. He has aided the FBI in a drug investigation, and acted in films, including a portrayal of Mike Hammer in *The Girl Hunters* (1963) and a part as a circus performer in *Ring of Fear*, produced by John Wayne. He has also appeared in television commercials, notably the series of advertisements for Miller Lite beer, which featured sports stars and other minor celebrities. He has also kept his image before the public by appearing on television game shows with his second wife and by putting in appearances at events such as the mystery readers' convention, Bouchercon. The public tendency to identify Spillane with his fictional creation may be related to his having posed for cover photos for some editions of some of his works, usually with his second wife. His hobbies have included stock car racing, fencing, diving, flying and sports fishing. In addition to being a regular churchgoer, he is a grandfather and family man, married almost 20 years to his third wife. (Biographical material not otherwise credited from Collins and Traylor.)

Spillane's drinking habits appear to have changed through the years. At the 1981 Bouchercon, he informed Max Collins that he never drank while working, including the conference in the category of work. Collins juxtaposes this observation with the image projected in the Miller Lite commercials of the writer "at his typewriter with a gun, a blonde and a bottle of Lite nearby" (x). A still shot of this commercial was used as a cover photo on a reprint edition (undated) of *Kiss Me, Deadly*.

In 1995, Spillane told interviewer Julie Baumgold, "All I drink now you can put in one eye. It's good to be seventy-seven. I can get a nice glow from two beers" (132). In 1999, writing for *The Guardian*, Peter Lennon reports that Spillane doesn't drink (S2). As Collins observes, Spillane "likes to play into his image as the beer-drinking, blue-collar mystery writer" (vii). An example of this tactic is his repeated pronouncement that there is no symbolic significance to Hammer's drinking habits.

Edwin McDowell cites Spillane's declaration to the Mystery Writers of America that "Mike Hammer drinks beer instead of cognac because I can't spell cognac" (16). Coming from a man of Spillane's obvious intelligence, one doubts that this pronouncement is intended to be taken seriously, but is rather a humorous way of reminding fellow writers to know their audience, for it is the members of that audience who drink beer and may not be sure how to spell cognac.

It is perhaps also a continuation of Raymond Chandler's sniping at the unlikely upper-class heroes of classical detective fiction, such as Philo Vance and Lord Peter Wimsey, who do drink cognac and other expensive beverages, a continuation of the argument that it is utterly unlikely that men of such backgrounds and tastes would be involved in tracking criminals and a way of agreeing with Chandler's assertion that the American detective novel, as started by Hammett and practiced by Chandler

himself, located fictional crime in more likely settings with more likely
protagonists. Clearly this remark tells us that Spillane regards the drinking habits of his characters as among the telling details that contribute
to the success of his fiction in attracting a loyal audience.

Despite his commercial success in a genre which has been accorded
some degree of critical respect, Mickey Spillane has possibly received
the least favorable critical attention of any major detective writer and is
rather pointedly excluded from the Hammett, Chandler, Macdonald triumvirate of hard-boiled writers who merit literary study. George Grella,
in his 1974 essay on the hard-boiled detective novel, refers to Spillane as
representing "the perversion of the American detective novel" (116):

> The detective's solipsistic belief in himself, his unerring rightness, his
> intensely lonely virtue, all become a vivid argument for a totalitarian moral
> policeman whose code, no matter how vicious, must be forced upon every
> man. Mike Hammer is convinced he is the hammer of God, free to tor-
> ture, maim, or kill all who get in his way. The whodunit's implicit endorse-
> ment of a system of justice and the hard-boiled novel's explicit sense of
> morality are transformed in Spillane into dictatorial apologetics, advance
> propaganda for the police state. A thug and a brute, Hammer would have
> been the villain of most mysteries, but in Spillane he is the new superman,
> a plainclothes Nazi [117].

Grella also detects a brutal homosexual fear of women in the final
killing of the naked seductive woman, Charlotte Manning, in *I, the Jury*,
though his generalization on the subject may leave the reader with the
impression that such a killing occurs in each of the Hammer novels, which
is not the case. He also claims that, while more knightly detectives are torn
between the perfect blonde and the seductive brunette but end possessing neither, Hammer has both and kills the guilty. In the case of Charlotte
Manning, this is definitely untrue, since Hammer never makes love to
Manning, having fallen in love and proposed to her. Hammer is a devoted
practitioner of the double standard, by which women worthy of marriage
are to be left untouched until after the ceremony. Such careless readings
threaten the critical structure built upon them and seriously undermine
Grella's credibility. Grella's final judgment on Hammer is that he is "in
no way a man of honor" (118). This conclusion is extremely debatable.

Another noted critic of the genre, John G. Cawelti, judges Spillane
as atrocious by literary standards. He rather bluntly adds that Spillane's
"popularity is often attributed to the unregenerate depravity and stupid-
ity of the mass reading public." Curiously, Cawelti does not make clear
who is responsible for such an attribution, using the passive voice to distance himself from the expression of such a negative opinion. Having
raised the specter of "mindless millions of cretins slobbering idiotically
as Mike Hammer pistolwhips another naked female," he then admits that

this sort of generalization only relieves the feelings of critics who are upset at the large market reached by works of which they disapprove (183).

Cawelti deplores Hammer's "pathological blood-lust" (152), discusses Spillane's use of violent and quasi-pornographic images to heighten the pattern of the formula through intensification of the emotional response (184) and explores the psycho-sexual implications of the female villains in the Hammer novels, especially in cases in which a woman who has attempted to seduce the hero is revealed as the villainess and is killed by him (186–87). Cawelti claims that the tension built up by the voyeuristic seduction scenes is released by the violence of other scenes. He claims to find an "alternating pattern of sexual provocation and orgies of shooting or beating that seem to function psychologically as a partial release of the emotional tension built up by the unconsummated sexual teasing" (186). But this seems a feeble argument given that Hammer yields to as many seductive women as he rejects. If Spillane's protagonist were celibate it might make sense to imply that he is substituting violence for sex, but since Hammer has sexual relations with a number of women in the series, the hypothesis simply does not work. It is also unclear who is doing the sexual teasing in the above quote. Female characters typically do not tease Hammer; they offer themselves aggressively. It is Hammer who picks and chooses, accepting the advances of some women while rejecting others. He seems to take pride in the fact that they cannot arouse him against his will, or that, even if aroused, he is capable of walking away from the opportunity for sex with an attractive, naked and willing woman. Yet he does not always walk away. Cawelti may mean that Spillane, as author, is teasing his audience with unconsummated sexual scenes, then compensating them by satisfying their blood lust with a scene of violence. In short, Cawelti's argument here seems to lack coherence, although it is clear that he has an extreme distaste for Hammer as a character and Spillane as a writer.

More pertinent to this study is Cawelti's claim that Spillane's work resembles the didactic temperance novels of the nineteenth century in which the hero:

> encounters the disturbing temptations of the sophisticated city: the corruptions of wealth, the destructive habits of tobacco and alcohol (and the dangerous seductiveness of the Scarlet Woman). Spillane … transmutes the animus against liquor into a fear of drugs…. The temperance novel even tends to manifest the same pattern of social hostility as Spillane: the corrupters represent sophisticated wealth on one side and non-white or non–Protestant groups on the other. For the nineteenth-century didactic novelists, popery plays the role assumed by communism in Spillane: a foreign conspiracy associated with threats to the sexual purity and moral asceticism of the American way of life. Finally, the temperance novels characteristically end with a terrible providential vengeance against the corrupters, just as Spillane's novels end with the violent death of the Scarlet Woman [189].

In other words, Spillane represents a strand of primitive morality found in other versions of popular fiction that predate the hard-boiled detective novel.

Other critics respond to Spillane in a similar vein. Comparing Spillane to other million-selling authors, Erle Stanley Gardner and Ian Fleming, J. Kenneth Van Dover finds "a radical failure to establish positive values," which makes Spillane's achievement of high sales figures "certainly the most disturbing" of these three examples of popular success. According to Van Dover, "the moral myth which provides a context for the actions of Spillane's heroes is neither as decent as that which guides Perry Mason nor as definite as that which governs James Bond" (*Murder in the Millions* 150–51). Geherin calls Spillane the "black sheep of the private-eye brotherhood" and notes that Hammer is the "most violent and sadistic of all private eyes" (*American Private Eye* 127).

Spillane's supporters are not much kinder. Although they deplore the critical neglect of Spillane's works, Collins and Traylor describe Mike Hammer as crazed or psychotic. Collins' major claim for the importance of Spillane as a writer is that his "dark, surreal vision of the post-war urban jungle" is a "wilder, more daring vision than Hammett or Chandler would ever have risked" (viii). In *One Lonely Knight*, these critics suggest that the violence in the Hammer novels does not come out of nowhere, as other critics seem to assume, but out of World War II. Spillane's audience was composed largely of ex-servicemen who had returned from a hard-fought war to a society in which victory over evil was no longer clear cut (7).

Collins and Traylor accuse other critics of failing to understand the series as a cathartic fantasy (39). One could describe this as a fantasy of a world in which evil is embodied in individuals who can be beaten or shot to death as opposed to the reality of faceless urban crime and Cold War dangers that cannot be conquered by the ordinary or even the extraordinary citizen.

Given this overwhelmingly negative critical reception, which seems to add up to the conclusion that Hammer is a mindless, amoral thug, one might legitimately wonder whether a consideration of Spillane's books is necessary in a work dealing with the importance of the moral code for the fictional private investigator. However, Hammer cannot accurately be accused of acting amorally or aimlessly. As Collins and Traylor express it in their comparison of Hammer and Sam Spade:

> Both Spade and Hammer follow personal codes, the laws of society meaning little to either. Spade, however, sees the world (perhaps the universe) as devoid of meaning, and society itself as arbitrary and absurd. Hammer, on the other hand, sees society as unresponsive to the demands of a higher morality. Spade's code requires that he dispassionately "send

his lover over" to an executioner; Hammer's code demands that he himself carry out the execution. Spade is an amoral man who chooses a conveniently moral route; Hammer is a moral man who chooses (as he sees it) a necessary amoral route [13–14].

Later Collins and Traylor cite the basics of Hammer's code as duty and friendship; compassion for suffering; distrust of society's ability to deal justice; acceptance of violence as a permissible tool; and a sexual double standard (41). Certainly, Hammer's loyalty to friends is unexampled. In *I, the Jury*, he makes clear that his pledge to avenge Jack Williams, the man who had lost an arm while saving Hammer's life by coming between Hammer and a Japanese bayonet in the Pacific, is nonnegotiable. He will not wait for the police to solve the case and arrest the killer, but will race them to the culprit in order to serve as judge, jury and executioner. Even when the murderer is revealed to be the woman he has fallen in love with and proposed to, he refuses, as Collins and Traylor emphasize, to step aside for the process of the law. He had promised Jack retribution in kind rather than a delayed and humane execution or the possibility that the murderer may escape on legal technicalities. Retribution in kind, in other words, a bullet in the gut like the one that killed Jack, is what Charlotte Manning receives. In a later novel, *Survival ... Zero*, Hammer continues to pursue the killer of school chum and army buddy, Lippy Sullivan, even though he is privy to the information that Soviet-planted germ warfare canisters may soon destroy the entire human race. Neither logic nor despair will deter him from his course. One may disapprove of Hammer's individualistic interpretation of law and order, but one cannot deny its moral foundation, the firm belief that murderers should die for their crimes and that a man has a duty to avenge a friend.

What Collins and Traylor label as Hammer's compassion for suffering is displayed in his almost instant sympathy for those who appear to be frightened or threatened. For instance, *Kiss Me, Deadly* (1952) begins with Hammer picking up a female hitchhiker who throws herself in front of his car. Her obvious fear when another car passes them makes him aware that she is in trouble, although he initially assumes that she has been dumped by a boyfriend. Without asking for details he negotiates a police roadblock by pretending they are married, even when the officer on duty reveals that the search is for an escapee from a sanitarium.

Further down the road they are held up, and she is tortured and killed and her body put in the car with Hammer before it is pushed over a cliff. He manages to escape and regains consciousness in the hospital. He vows to hunt down the men responsible for the attack, even though he knew little about the woman he almost rescued. There are many other instances in the novels in which Hammer immediately moves to protect or avenge those who seem to be victims.

Collins and Traylor are also accurate in reporting that Hammer distrusts society's ability to serve justice. His position is made clear in the rant he delivers at the beginning of *I, the Jury*:

> I'm not letting the killer go through the tedious process of the law. You know what happens, damn it. They get the best lawyer there is and screw up the whole thing and wind up a hero! ... A jury is cold and impartial like they're supposed to be, while some snotty lawyer makes them pour tears as he tells how his client was insane at the moment or had to shoot in self defense. Swell. The law is fine. But this time I'm the law and I'm not going to be cold and impartial [4].

Hammer's acceptance of violence is a given in every novel. He will kill in self defense, in defense of others and for vengeance. He will slap or punch or shake needed information out of any potential source foolish enough to be reticent, and all seems to be justified in his mind so long as he believes the information gained by such methods will contribute to the solution of the case and the apprehension or death of a criminal. This is not to say that Hammer is completely unreflective about his activities. *One Lonely Night* begins with Hammer walking around Manhattan, stung by a an incident earlier in the day. Apparently he has been charged in a death; the judge has ruled it self-defense, but followed up with a stinging indictment of Hammer and his methods. The judge accuses Hammer of having learned to like killing in the war and of being unfit to live in normal civilization. Hammer walks the streets considering this accusation: "Maybe he was dead right and I'd never be satisfied until I knew the answer myself. If there was an answer" (9). Needless to say, the ensuing plot contains enough problems that only Hammer can solve to justify fully his violent methods. Collins, in his introduction to *Tomorrow I Die*, describes *One Lonely Night* as having been written to respond to the critics who attacked Spillane's works for containing too much violence (ix).

Obviously it is possible to agree that Hammer possesses the code attributed to him by Collins and Traylor without feeling that the code makes him an exemplary or even an admirable character. Nonetheless, it is a code. Hammer is not amoral, focused only on his own pleasure or survival. He is willing to take risks to fight those he perceives as enemies of his society, whether mobsters, drug dealers or communists.

Spillane has written thirteen full-length Hammer novels including: *I, the Jury* (1947), *Kiss Me, Deadly* (1952), *The Girl Hunters* (1962), *The Twisted Thing* (1966), *Survival ... Zero!* (1970), *The Killing Man* (1989), and *Black Alley* (1996). This selection represents the entire span of Hammer's career to date.

Most critics are more interested in the sex and violence in the Hammer novels than in the detective's drinking habits. However, the latter do figure in general discussions, as when Elizabeth Bullock remarks that Hammer "punches, drinks, shoots, seduces, and beats his way to victory" (cited in Collins and Traylor 24). Another critic, Kay Weibel, refers to drink in passing in her evaluation of the attraction of Hammer for the ex-serviceman. She states that Hammer continues the social code of the war, in which lonely servicemen overseas found relief from tension and boredom in smoking, drinking and enjoying sex with local women.

The ex–GI still has a bottle and cigarettes, whereas he had to leave his "Tiger Lily," Weibel's term for those sexually available foreign women. Mike, however, still has eager, aggressive women available to him (116). Thus Hammer is seen as continuing to live the life of a bachelor warrior, using violence to solve cases while solacing himself with sex and booze. The problem with these critical evaluations of Hammer's drinking habits, however, is that they are not accurate. It is as if the critics automatically assume that all excess is the same. If Hammer is excessively violent and indulges in too much casual sex, he must also be intemperate in the use of alcohol. A close examination of several novels will show that this is not uniformly the case.

I, the Jury appeared in 1947. Mike Hammer and Pat Chambers, his homicide detective friend, are in Chambers' office after viewing the murdered body of their mutual friend, Jack Williams. Chambers pulls a bottle of bourbon from a lunch box in his desk drawer and pours "a man-sized slug" each for Hammer and himself. Hammer gulps the drink but refuses a second (31). Later they lunch together and each has a bottle of beer (48). That afternoon, after an encounter with the sexually provocative Mary Bellamy, Hammer is described as having "a few quick ones" (rye and soda) at a bar near his office while he reviews his notes on the case. This evidently is a regular habit as the bartender expresses surprise that he leaves "after so few" (67–69). He then goes to the Hi-Lo Club for information on George Kalecki's numbers running racket and has a beer while questioning the proprietor, Big Sam (69). That evening he has dinner, which is not described as including alcohol in any form, with the seductive Charlotte Manning. He leaves completely besotted with her and stops on the way home for a drink to clear his head, noting that it didn't work (89).

The next evening Hammer follows a lead from Williams' notebook to a brothel where he is offered a drink by the woman he has come to question. He turns it down and the woman is killed before he can discover her connection to Williams' death (108). The next day he meets Manning in Central Park and she suggests drinks later at her office. But when they are shot at by Kalecki they return to her apartment instead, where she asks Hammer to fix drinks while she showers. Hammer has two or three highballs before leaving (137–39). He has a meeting with Chambers, then consumes a quart of beer with dinner in his office (161). After nine that evening, he meets with Mary Bellamy, who is posing as her sister Esther. They drink scotch together and Hammer allows himself to be seduced (163–66).

After returning to his apartment Hammer spends the evening with a case of beer, smoking and going over the case. We are not told how many beers he consumes before he suddenly realizes that Hal Kines' college room may contain clues and he drives to upstate New York to check his hunch, only to end up in a shoot-out with Kalecki. He returns to New York and goes to Manning's apartment to question her about the Bellamy twins, then falls asleep. He awakens in the late afternoon and has a scotch and soda with her (181) before leaving to run errands and ending up following Pat to the scene of Bobo Hopper's death.

That evening he meets Manning again. They go to a movie and then to a bar where they both order beer, despite Hammer's protest that Manning can have anything she wants. She replies that she likes beer (197). The next day at the Bellamys' tennis party Hammer has an unspecified number of drinks at the bar while Manning mingles, then returns to his room and falls asleep. He comments that the "drinks did more to me than I thought. I didn't pass out. I simply fell asleep" (207).

He rouses himself for the tennis match and is recalled to duty when Williams' former fiancée is killed. A shocked Mary Bellamy starts drinking whiskey and by the time Hammer takes the bottle from her to "salvage a drink," she is dead drunk (218–21). The next day is Sunday and Hammer is completely frustrated by the lack of progress on the case. Five more people are dead and there seem to be no leads. He spends the day pacing the floor, drinking beer and eating, then falls in bed exhausted. It is unclear how much beer he has consumed during the day (228). Monday he seems equally frustrated and follows lunch with a visit to a bar in which he sits drinking highballs from one in the afternoon to six in the evening (230). When he reaches for a pack of cigarettes he pulls out the envelope he found on Myrna's body and takes it to a chemist for analysis of the traces of white powder. The revelation that it contained heroin is the clue he needed and he goes to Manning's apartment for the final confrontation.

This novel establishes a few basics about Hammer's drinking patterns. He seems to drink, if only beer, on most days. However, he is capable of turning down drinks. Of hard liquor he drinks either highballs or rye and ginger ale, although in later books he switches to Canadian Club. He assumes that beer is a man's drink, that women prefer cocktails if their date's budget will allow it. Hammer drinks alone when thinking over the case, either highballs in a bar or beer at home. At no point does Hammer, as narrator, voice any concerns about the effect of his drinking on his performance, physical or mental. There is, for instance, no apology for driving across New York state at night after an evening spent drinking beer. Nor does he ever report a hangover. The only narrative concessions to the effects of alcohol occur at the Bellamy estate when Hammer reports that his afternoon of drinking made him sleepy (but, we are assured, not passed out) and when he takes the whiskey bottle from Mary Bellamy in time to ease her "dead drunk" into a chair. In this respect he is utterly unlike the Continental Op, who reports rather dispassionately the effects of booze on himself and other characters, and Philip Marlowe, who comments both on the effects and on the appropriateness of his drinking.

The categories of drinking that can be perceived in Chandler are also present, in part, in Spillane's work. Hospitality appears to be taken for granted, as characters offer and accept drinks without much narrative comment. The quality of the drinks is occasionally mentioned, either in respect to the mix or the quality of the liquor. For instance, at a party given by mobster Carl Evello, Hammer picks a drink from a tray and remarks, "It was a lousy drink but I threw it down anyway" (*Kiss Me, Deadly* 104). But he does not reveal whether the drink was lousy because it was too weak or too strong or because the liquor was of poor quality. In *The Twisted Thing*, he takes a drink from Alice Nichols and comments, "Old stuff isn't it?" Alice confirms that the liquor is twenty years old, given to her by her wealthy uncle. The fact that she is receiving expensive gifts from her uncle is perhaps what Hammer wished to discover by making the remark (85).

Manipulation by means of booze does not seem to figure in the Hammer methodology as it does for Hammett's Continental Op or for Chandler's Marlowe. As critics have noted, Hammer simply beats the answers out of people, not hesitating to threaten or assault even uncooperative hotel clerks or other relatively innocent people who may have information he wants. The third category, that of self-medication, is, however, present, as when Mary Bellamy responds to the murder in her household by almost emptying a bottle of scotch and collapsing dead drunk. Hammer himself is careful, however, not to overindulge in drinking for emotional comfort. He and Pat have one drink after the death of Jack Williams, and Hammer turns down a second. When Velda is a hostage in *Kiss Me, Deadly*, Hammer thinks about recourse to the liquor cabinet, but is sickened by the smell when he tries to drink. He can only pace the floor, waiting for the police (111). The major exception to this self control occurs in *The Girl Hunters*. At the opening of the novel we learn that Hammer has been on a seven-year drunk because he believes Velda is dead, killed while on an assignment he had given her. This novel will warrant more lengthy analysis. In general, however, the excessive use of alcohol for self-medication, especially for emotional hurts, is treated as a danger, a weakness to be avoided, an obstacle to the job of solving the case and bringing the criminal to justice.

By 1952, with *Kiss Me, Deadly*, Hammer seems to have moderated his drinking from the level found in *I, the Jury*. He has a couple of beers with Velda as she explains the state of the police investigation after he was found unconscious near his burned-out automobile in which a woman's corpse was discovered (30). Later he meets Velda at a bar, where he has a beer and she has lunch (59). He has another beer at a different bar, "while the facts settled down in my mind" (64). When he learns that the dead woman had been the mistress of Mafia boss Carl Evello, Hammer goes to Evello's house to question him, is offered a drink and turns it down without comment (83). We are not told whether the refusal is based on moral qualms about accepting hospitality from gangsters or a prudent wish to keep his wits about him as he beards the enemy unarmed (his gun permits have been canceled by the police because federal investigators want to keep him out of the case). He kills two hit men who try to take him into the countryside to be murdered and then tours underworld hang-outs to make himself available for another attempt. At one of the bars he turns down beer and orders a Coke, once again a sensible precaution for someone trying to outwit armed men sent to kill him (96).

When Evello's sister, Michael Friday, takes him to her brother's cock-tail party Hammer drinks two drinks from the trays being circulated through the room (104). Later there is a moment of crisis when Hammer discovers that Velda has been captured by the Mafia after the man she sedated with choral hydrate in his drink recovered consciousness in time to discover her searching his apartment. In the empty apartment Ham-mer paces furiously, waiting for the police: "There was a full cabinet of liquor I was going to try, but the smell of it sickened me when I got the bottle near my mouth" (111).

Interestingly, the alcohol that has the greatest role in the novel is not the beverage but rubbing alcohol, which the woman who has passed her-self off as Lily Carver, a friend of the woman Hammer tried to rescue, uses for alcohol baths. Her bathrobe is soaked with it when she leans down to kiss Hammer after shooting him, and he sets her afire with a cigarette lighter (175). The novel ends with Hammer lying wounded in the burn-ing building. Other than the observation that Hammer is portrayed as drinking less in *Kiss Me, Deadly* than in *I, the Jury*, it is difficult to discover any significant patterns concerning alcohol usage in the novel. One can only surmise the reasons for Hammer's decreased consumption in this novel. It may be that Spillane realized that the level of drinking portrayed in *I, the Jury* was simply unrealistic for a protagonist expected to display both intellectual and physical performance at above average levels.

Ten years passed before publication of the next Hammer novel. *The Girl Hunters* (1962) opens with Hammer drunk in the gutter. He is picked up by police who take him to Pat Chambers. The next scenes reveal that seven years earlier Hammer had sent Velda on a routine case to body-guard a wealthy couple and protect the woman's jewels. The couple disappeared, together with Velda, and although the woman's body was discovered, the husband and Velda have never been found. Hammer assumes Velda is dead and blames himself. He has been drinking for most of the time since. He has lost his PI license and his gun permits. But most of all he has lost the friendship and respect of Pat Chambers, who declares, "We stopped being buddies a long time ago ... nobody's friends with a drunken bum. He's nothing but a lousy lush" (12–14). How does a man who is strong enough to reject a second drink after seeing the bloody body of his best friend (*I, the Jury*) change into a man who meets personal tragedy by crawling into a bottle? Spillane has the doctor explain it to Hammer as "Guilt complex. Something you couldn't handle. It happens to the hardest nuts I've seen. They can take care of anything until the irrevocable happens and then they blow. Completely." Hammer acquiesces in the description: "Like me?" (28). But there is another implied factor at work. In *I, the Jury* Spillane gave Hammer a goal—to beat the police to Jack Williams' killer and perform the execution himself. There is simply no time to waste in drunken mourning.

In addition, Hammer has no responsibility in the death itself; Williams was conducting an investigation among people Hammer did not even know. Similarly, in *Kiss Me, Deadly*, Hammer is waiting only for the police to reach the scene of Velda's abduction so that he can explain the circumstances before continuing the hunt himself. He has a momentary impulse to take a drink, but recoils from it. Now, in *The Girl Hunters*, he has been confronted with a situation in which there is nothing more for him to do. The investigation is dead-ended; there are no clues to Velda's whereabouts. The longer she is missing the more likely it seems that she is dead. Her body has not been discovered, but that fact offers scant hope to a New Yorker who is aware that many victims consigned to the river are never found. Hammer is eaten up by his loss and by his guilt, since he feels that he unwittingly sent Velda to her death. Further, he was working another case that evening, so it could appear that greed led him to give Velda a field assignment. He describes his feelings as Chambers tells the story to the doctor in attendance: "That great big place in my chest started to open up again, a huge hole that could grow until there was nothing left of me, only that huge hole" (16). This is the hole he has attempted to fill or obliterate with alcohol.

Spillane leaves no question that Hammer is as thoroughly damaged by alcohol, if not more so than Terry Lennox had been the second time Marlowe rescues him. The doctor Chambers calls to sober Hammer up describes him as in a "Typical alcoholic condition.... From all external signs I'd say he isn't too far from total" (14). Later we learn that Hammer has lost thirty-seven pounds from his normal weight and is dehydrated. He is too weak to fight back when Chambers hits him and is even delirious to the point that he tries to shoot Chambers with a gun he no longer carries, squeezing an imaginary trigger as Chambers tells the doctor about his part in Velda's presumed death (16–17).

Sobered up, Hammer is taken to see Richie Cole, who is dying of a gunshot wound from a gun used earlier in a political assassination. The FBI wants the information he may have, but he refuses to talk to anyone other than Hammer. Cole tells Hammer that Velda is alive but in danger, then dies as Hammer tries to assimilate this information: "my thoughts groping for a hold in a brain still soggy from too many bouts in too many bars. I couldn't think..." (23). Nevertheless, he is clear enough about what this revelation means to him to dissemble when questioned by Chambers about Cole's statement.

Up to this point Spillane's description of a man ravaged by alcohol abuse seems fairly realistic. But the revelation that Velda may be alive acts as an almost miraculous cure. Even the doctor can see, in some unspecified way, that Hammer has pulled back from the brink of self-destruction and that he will not relapse. As the recovering Hammer puts it, "Medics don't talk seriously to D and D's" (28). Hammer, who a few hours earlier had demanded a drink before meeting with Cole, now refuses one even when the doctor advises it (31). Later, after he has been nursed back to health, he will have "Maybe a couple of Blue Ribbons [beer], but nothing else" with a meal (49).

Spillane does not go into detail about the process of rehabilitating Hammer. Three days of rest, soup and an unspecified series of shots (perhaps vitamins) seem to be the only treatment he receives, yet at the end of this period he is weak, but cured (40). As he begins his investigation he reproaches himself as "what was left over from being a damn drunken bum, and if there were anything left at all it was sheer reflex and nothing else" (43). Yet he proceeds to solve the case, and at one point the FBI man, Rickerby, comments, "for someone who was an alcoholic such a short time ago, your mind is awfully lucid" (50). In short, Hammer's supposed alcoholism has no very lasting effects and is shrugged off as easily as a bout with the flu when it is no longer needed as a plot device. In this respect Spillane's treatment of alcoholism resembles Chandler's. Terry Lennox does not need the three years predicted by Marlowe to achieve a cure, and neither does Hammer.

The creators of these characters display little awareness of alcoholism as a disease with long-term physical effects. It is treated solely as a mental and emotional escape hatch to be used when one is faced with a situation one can neither endure nor cure. Hence Lennox goes on his first bender when he learns that his war bride is alive and remarried, and Hammer descends into drunkenness when he believes that Velda is dead and that he is to blame. We will see this pattern of treating alcoholism as a temporary disability, or in essence as a plot gimmick, again in *Black Alley*, as well as in books by other authors.

The Twisted Thing (1966) finds Hammer back at work at more conventional detection. He has intervened to rescue a friend accused of kidnapping a rich scientist's son, a prodigy. After rescuing the family chauffeur, an ex-con named Billy Parks, whom Hammer knows from an earlier case, from a brutal local policeman, Hammer is hired by Rudolph York to find his missing child. He rescues the child, but other crimes follow and Hammer eventually discovers that the prodigy himself, resentful of having been denied a normal life, has engineered them.

When Hammer initially meets York and his relatives he remarks on the "nightclub pallor and squeegy skin" of York's nephews, and when they attack him for speaking disrespectfully to their uncle, he easily subdues one, "I smacked him on each side of that whisky-sodden face until my hand hurt. When I dropped him he lay on the floor crying, trying to cover his face with his hands.... 'In case anyone else has ideas like that, he'd better have more in his hands than a whisky glass'" (13). This episode functions to demonstrate the self-indulgent weakness of the nephews, who, like York's other relatives, are basically parasites hoping for an inheritance that they are "earning" only by being toadies. It also demonstrates that while Hammer is able to drink without becoming a weakling, others are not. With the exception of the scene mentioned above, in which York's niece serves Hammer the expensive liquor her uncle has given her, *The Twisted Thing* contains few other scenes describing or commenting on alcohol use. Ruston York does tell a story of having been able to escape from his kidnappers when they became drunk, but since the kidnapping itself was faked under his direction the supposed drinking merely provides a false clue as to the course of events.

In *Survival ... Zero* (1970) Hammer is tracking down the man who killed a former school chum and army buddy, Lippy Sullivan. In the course of the investigation he stumbles across a top-secret case being handled by the federal government—a Soviet agent has planted canisters of bacteria engineered for germ warfare in locations across the nation. No one in the current Soviet government knows the locations, and unless they are found the human race may be destroyed, as the Soviets have discovered that the vaccine they planned to use to protect themselves is ineffective. Against this background Hammer continues the search for Sullivan's killer, even as others in on the secret express despair.

Television newsman Eddie Dandy speculates that if the canisters are not found in time he will cry and "get drunk as hell and not have to fight a hangover" (220). As it turns out, Hammer finds the key to the germ warfare plot in the course of finding Sullivan's killer. Hammer himself has not materially altered his drinking habits in response to the threat of destruction; he continues to drink beer at bars and in his office and highballs with women he is interviewing. As in earlier works, a vengeance-driven sense of purpose seems to shield Hammer from despair and self-destruction.

This sobriety-preserving sense of purpose also appears in *The Killing Man* (1989). Hammer comes to his office for a Saturday appointment only to find Velda badly beaten in the anteroom and a dead man at his desk. After the ambulance crew removes Velda he "walked over to the miniature bar by the window and picked up a glass. Hell, this was no time to take a drink. I put the glass back and went into my office" (13). Later he drinks a beer in a bar with a journalist friend. On another occasion he meets a mobster in another bar and orders a Canadian Club and ginger ale. He is well into the conversation before he tastes the drink, "Charlie had given me a double charge and barely taste it was all I did" (75). There is no further explanation, so we do not know whether he does not like the flavor of a double strength drink or, more likely, wishes to keep his wits about him in a conversation with a potentially dangerous man. On this and other occasions Hammer seems to be working on the assumption that to refuse to drink in a man's company will be perceived as an insult, a concept rooted in American frontier culture. When his journalist friend, Pete Benson, meets him at the Plaza Hotel with inside information about the ambitious woman assistant district attorney who has threatened his license, Hammer acquiesces in ordering a drink, but thinks to himself that he would rather read the notes (47).

Drink is involved, though not heavily, in a quasi-seduction scene with the woman DA. She and Hammer have dinner together and a highball at her apartment afterwards. He bets her that he knows her life ambition, which he has learned from Benson. If she loses she will undress. Since the bet is fixed Hammer wins, but he stops her when she begins to unzip her dress. The moderate consumption of alcohol seems crucial to the psychology of the final scene in which she voluntarily drops her dress and stands naked as he exits (83–94). Throughout the series we are reminded that women do not need to be drunk to lust after Hammer; he is irresistible to intelligent, aware, extremely attractive women, even though he is never described as physically attractive himself. It is apparently his air of self-confidence and his self-control that arouse the passions of these women. This impression, and the male fantasy behind it, would be materially weakened if the females in question were intoxicated when they displayed this strong attraction.

In the remainder of *The Killing Man* alcohol is treated matter-of-factly. General Ruddy Skubal of the CIA describes his secure compound to Hammer, remarking that "if you're a drinking man, those needs are supplied too" (215). Later, as Hammer and Velda are being hidden from the killer in a mountain cabin, the supplies are listed as "groceries, beer and plenty of toilet paper" (279). In neither case is alcohol seen as possibly detrimental to discipline or safety.

The most recent Hammer novel is *Black Alley* (1996). In it Spillane revisits the return from supposed death and recovery from alcoholism themes of *The Girl Hunters*. This time it is Hammer himself who is presumed dead when he is caught in a shoot-out between rival Mafia factions at the docks. Badly wounded, he had been ignored by medics who assumed he was dead. A man leaving a nearby bar recognizes that there is a spark of life in Hammer's eyes and tries to attract attention, but he is ignored by police and medical personnel because he is a drunk. This drunk is a former doctor who takes Hammer home and operates on him, saving his life. Dr. Ralph Morgan explains that he became disillusioned with his life and walked away from a thriving surgical practice. Since then he has been a drunk, declared dead by a family who never even searched for him when he disappeared. But the challenge of using his rusty skills to pull Hammer from the brink of death has given him a new lease on life:

> "A month ago I wouldn't have given a hoot. Hell, I would have welcomed the *big out.* Then you go and show up all blown to pieces and I take the challenge and make it real again, suddenly turning into a doctor who pulled off some kind of a modern miracle...."
>
> "Now you're ... sober?"
>
> "Permanently" [14–15].

Readers will note the similarity to Hammer's immediate return to sobriety in *The Girl Hunters* once he learns that Velda is alive. Also like Hammer, Dr. Morgan is able to resume drinking in moderation. He drinks one or two light beers at a sitting and shows no tendency to return to out-of-control drinking. Not coincidentally, these beers are Miller Lite, the brand for which Spillane made commercials.

Hammer, in the meantime, is unable to drink at all since his digestive tract has been severely damaged by the bullet wounds. Morgan makes it clear that Hammer's recovery is anything but complete, that physical or emotional strain can still kill him. At the beginning of his recovery even a full cup of coffee is too much to stomach. Needless to say, given the conventions of the action hero, Hammer pushes the limits of his endurance as he tries to find out who was behind the double-cross that led to the Mafia shoot-out. But he does obey the doctor's order to avoid alcohol, at least until his meeting with Don Ponti. He is offered and accepts a Canadian Club and ginger ale, which he sips as they talk. Like the mobsters in Chandler's works, Don Ponti freely violates the laws of hospitality as, despite the shared drink, he orders Hammer killed after he leaves the house. However, we are not particularly struck by this betrayal since Hammer's history tells us that he is equally ruthless in killing those who have become a threat, regardless of previous social interaction.

Spillane's treatment of alcohol consumption in the Mike Hammer series is not as extensive or sophisticated as that of Chandler, nor as honest as the early Hammett. As noted above, the extent of Hammer's drinking in *I, the Jury* stretches the reader's credulity yet is never admitted to be excessive by the narrator-protagonist. We are simply expected to accept that an afternoon spent downing highballs can culminate in brilliant detective work as soon as the vital clue is rediscovered while groping for a cigarette. We are apparently not expected to suspect that the detective's beer and highball consumption may have caused him to forget the evidence in the first place. Hammer's alcohol consumption declines in later novels, although the critics fail to recognize this decline, treating Hammer as a relatively unchanging character who can be discussed as though each volume in the series follows exactly the same pattern. By contemporary standards Hammer's drinking remains excessive, at least on occasion, yet Spillane's only concessions to the changes in national drinking habits during his and his protagonist's career is the introduction of light beer. This denial of the negative consequences of heavy alcohol use is as telling as the aggressively seductive women characters in branding the Hammer novels as adult male fantasies, in which the protagonist rarely suffers the logical consequences of his actions. Hammer drinks excessively without suffering from loss of performance or hangovers; becomes an alcoholic, yet cures himself with little effort; assaults and kills without ever being convicted of a crime or suffering long-term punishment. He is a superhero who wears a trench coat rather than tights and enforces his one-man version of justice with fists and a .45 rather than an esoteric superhuman power.

Nevertheless, Spillane's descriptions of Hammer's use of and attitudes about alcohol can be related to the code of behavior Hammer follows in his work. In Hammer's world a man is supposed to take on a job and get it done. Drinking is acceptable as a form of relaxation when not actively working on a case, or when socializing with colleagues or friends. It is even permissible to drink with enemies if necessary to further an investigation. But alcohol should not be used as a means of escape when there is action to be taken. Hence Hammer's revulsion from liquor when Velma is in danger. Alcoholism is regarded, not as a disease with biochemical causes, or a mental disease, or a symptom of social ills, but as a simple failure of will, a loss of desire to work or live a normal, productive life. Hammer, when he believes Velma is dead, has no reason to carry on, so he becomes a drunk. When he learns she is alive, he is cured and needs only to recoup his physical and mental strength before returning to his normal state as a man able to use alcohol appropriately and at what earlier novels have established as his level of moderation. And he does not seem to expect sympathy for his decision to drink excessively.

In later novels he shows no resentment of Chambers for having disdained his friendship during his time as a "lush." The case of Dr. Morgan is treated in a similar fashion. When the challenge of keeping Hammer alive revives Morgan's desire to function he is able to abandon his alcoholism as quickly as he started it, with no tendency to backslide. Just as other aspects of Spillane's work may be seen as fulfilling male fantasies about sex and violence, these incidents can be seen as an alcoholic's fantasy: "I can quit anytime." Unlike the cases of Hammett and Chandler, however, this less than realistic approach to alcohol abuse in fiction does not seem to be tied to any aspect of Spillane's biography. No source consulted suggests that Spillane has had any history of excessive drinking. One may surmise that Spillane has not turned away from realism on the subject from internal pressures, but is rather responding to his market, readers who expect fiction to provide an escape from life's complexities rather than an examination of them.

Despite its popularity with the public, Mickey Spillane's work is as generally despised by academics as Chandler's and Hammett's are admired. It contrasts strongly with that of former academic Robert B. Parker, whose Spenser blends the physical toughness of Mike Hammer with an ability to recognize and confront his feelings and a penchant for literary quotation and who has attracted both a wide popular audience and a sympathetic academic audience as a result. Spillane may be seen as having reverted to the pulp origins of the hardboiled genre with a protagonist given to black and white judgments and a violent response to any threat to his values. Parker is credited with creating a detective who reflects more contemporary values, a tough guy who has dropped the sexism and racism typical of earlier times while maintaining the traditional detective code.

Robert B. Parker

"This Was No Job for a Poet"

Robert B. Parker entered the academic world as author of a dissertation dealing with the works of Dashiell Hammett, Raymond Chandler and Ross Macdonald. In this work he emphasizes the role of the Protestant ethic and the ethos of frontier America in shaping the hero of the hard-boiled detective novel. Finding the academic life uncongenial, Parker set out to create his own version of the hard-boiled hero in Spenser, a PI who works out of Boston. With the creation of Spenser, a literate yet irreverent detective, Parker was hailed by some critics as the heir to Chandler. This became literally the case when he was chosen to complete *Poodle Springs*, the novel left unfinished at Raymond Chandler's death. He later wrote a sequel to *The Big Sleep, Perchance to Dream* (1991). As of 2002 Parker is the author of thirty novels in the Spenser series. He has also created two other series characters, Jesse Stone and Sunny Randall. The Stone series will not be considered here because Stone is a police officer rather than a private investigator. The Sunny Randall series is too new to have received much critical examination.

Parker is an appropriate subject for this study for several reasons. As in the case of Spillane, his popularity over several decades indicates that he provides a pattern of heroism that the public finds acceptable. His work has also attracted considerable academic attention, possibly in part because he is a former college professor, a fellow academic. Another reason for this critical attention, however, is that Spenser early acquired a reputation as an exception to the usual hard-guy, loner PI. From the third volume on, Spenser has an ongoing relationship with Susan Silver-

106

man, who is a professional who refuses to sacrifice her career to further their relationship. Spenser also deals on what appear to be terms of equality with feminist activists, male homosexuals and persons of diverse races. He is presented as having left behind the sexism, racism and homophobia found in many early hard-boiled works. But he has not left behind the idea of a masculine code by which the detective shapes his behavior. In fact, he is far more explicit about the code than earlier PIs. Nor has he left behind the office bottle or a tendency to find revelations about other characters in their drinking habits. Parker has also contributed to the Chandler oeuvre by completing *Poodle Springs*, an action that must be of interest to students of Chandler. Both the common view that the works featuring Spenser have broken new ground in the genre and Parker's close ties to Chandler, an acknowledged classic, make Parker an obvious choice for this study.

Robert Brown Parker was born in 1932 in Springfield, Massachusetts, where his father was a telephone company executive. He attended Colby College in Waterville, Maine, graduating with a B.A. in English in 1954. Two years later, he married Joan Hall, who became the prototype for the character of Spenser's lover, Susan Silverman. Parker served with the U.S. Army infantry in Korea, then worked a variety of jobs before returning to college to earn a M.A. at Boston University in 1962. From 1964–68 he taught at various colleges before attaining a position as an assistant professor at Northeastern University, which he held from 1968 through 1978. In 1971 he was awarded his Ph.D. in English by Boston University for his dissertation on the hard-boiled detective tradition. Rather than continue to teach while writing and publishing in the academic world, Parker turned his energy to fiction and in 1974 published *The Godwulf Manuscript*, which introduced the character of Spenser (Corrigan 716–717 and Geherin, *Sons of Sam Spade* 5).

In *The Godwulf Manuscript*, Spenser is described as being thirty-seven years old, 6' 1" tall and weighing 195 pounds. He is a former heavyweight boxer, a veteran of the Korean Conflict, and worked with the Suffolk County District Attorney before being fired for insubordination. He works out regularly, running and lifting weights, and is experimenting with wood carving as a hobby. He also cooks and appreciates good food, a trait that will be richly developed in the series. Parker establishes his ties to the hard-boiled tradition by emulating Chandler's use of simile in the novel's first sentence, as Spenser compares a university president's office to the front room of a Victorian whorehouse (5) and later describes campus football players as having "necks like pilot whales" (13).

Spenser's statement to Dr. Forbes that he "went to college once" (6) echoes Philip Marlowe's first meeting with General Sternwood in *The Big Sleep*. Spenser's office also resembles Marlowe's: "second floor front, half a block down from Tremont. One room with a desk, a file cabinet, and two chairs in case Mrs. Onassis came with her husband. The old iron radiator had no real control and the room, closed for three days, reeked with heat" (72). Yet Spenser is not a Marlowe reinvented for the last quarter of the twentieth century. Nor, despite his penchant for cases involving troubled adolescents and dysfunctional families, is he a rewrite of Macdonald's Lew Archer. Most noticeably, Spenser is far more physical and violent than either Marlowe or Archer. Marlowe kills only one man in his entire chronicled career, the gunman Canino in *The Big Sleep*. And while Marlowe does engage in physical combats, he is more likely to be beaten than to triumph in a fight. As for Archer, Geoffrey Hartman rightly remarks in "Literature High and Low: the Case of the Mystery Story": "… in Ross Macdonald's novels generally, violence is as offstage as in *Oedipus Rex*" (212). In Parker's work, on the other hand, violence is brought to the foreground, with vivid descriptions of dead bodies and physical confrontations between Spenser and various villains.

In *The Godwulf Manuscript*, for example, Spenser discovers two corpses on separate occasions, beats up a mob enforcer, forcibly extracts information from a member of the radical organization suspected of the theft of the manuscript, kills two gunmen while rescuing the man they are about to execute, and chokes a third mobster to death. In the course of these struggles he sustains a black eye, some bruises and a bullet wound in the side.

Violence is not the only form that physicality takes in Parker's works. As mentioned earlier, Spenser works out, running and lifting weights, to maintain his fitness. He also keeps up his fighting skills with drills on the punching bags and, in later novels, sparring at Harry Canoli's gym. One can hardly imagine the Continental Op, Sam Spade or Philip Marlowe jogging or doing bench presses. Physicality is also manifest in appetites. Spenser can exist on junk food or diner coffee when necessary, but he thrives on meals he has prepared for himself, whether learning French recipes from a book or improvising sausage and fried apple slices. Indeed, V. Louise Saylor charges that Spenser "eats and exercises at a near excessive level" and that "these recurring and explicit episodes propel the story, rather than functioning as incidental trimming … frequently running the risk of stopping the plot cold" (115–16). Physical indulgence also extends to the sexual realm. When introduced to readers Spenser is apparently between relationships. He mentions a cookbook given him by a former girlfriend and a package of cigarettes left behind by the same or a different woman. But in the course of the investigation he makes love to both the mother of the murder suspect and to the suspect herself. He also flirts with secretaries and comments on the physical charms of other women he encounters during the investigation. After he establishes the mostly monogamous relationship with Susan Silverman their dialogue is still laced with flirtatious remarks and references to past and future episodes of lovemaking. This is a typical passage from *Hush Money* (1999), as Spenser and Silverman discuss his current case:

> "Then I'll try to establish whether there was or was not a relationship between Nevins and Lamont, and if there was why people didn't know and if there wasn't why people said there was."
> "And if that doesn't work?"
> "I'll ask you," I said.
> "For some psychoanalytic theory?"
> "Can't hurt," I said.
> "What I think we should do is go take a shower and brush our teeth and lie on my bed and see what kind of theory we can develop."
> "I'm pretty sure I know what will develop," I said.
> "Should we shower together?" Susan said.
> "If we do, things may develop too soon."
> "Good point." Susan said. "I'll go first" [72].

Critics tend to make a great issue of the fact that Parker breaks with the "loner" tradition of the hard-boiled genre by giving Spenser a long-term relationship with a woman who is described as being independent and intelligent. Susan Silverman is introduced in *God Save the Child*, the second novel in the series. In the early Spenser novels she is a high school guidance counselor in an area outside Boston. Because neither she nor Spenser is willing to relocate, they maintain separate residences despite developing a relationship both describe as committed. Later in the series, Silverman begins to study for a doctorate in psychology, leaves the Boston area for an internship in Washington, D.C., and then relocates to the San Francisco Bay area. Her separation from Spenser is complicated by a relationship with another man who pressures her for commitment and from whom Spenser and Hawk "rescue" her in *A Catskill Eagle* (1985). Spenser and Silverman restore their relationship, but continue to dwell separately, even though Silverman has established her psychotherapy practice in Boston. As Maureen Corrigan notes in *Mystery and Suspense Writers*, the writing of the novels in which the relationship between Spenser and Susan is conflicted coincides with the period during which Parker was separated from his wife (716).

According to Geoffrey Norman's interview with Parker, the separation lasted from May 15, 1982 to August 2, 1984 (108). Both sources agree that Parker and his wife have since maintained separate quarters within a shared house. Parker tells Geoffrey Norman that he and his wife "date" each other, travel together and spend weekends together at a country place (108). Parker has stated in a number of interviews that his marriage to Joan was the most important act of his life and asserts in the interview with Anne Ponder in Robin Winks' *Colloquium on Crime* that she influences all his women characters (Parker and Ponder 201).

The ongoing presence of Silverman in Spenser's life is one reason that critics have proclaimed him a model of the new detective. Norman notes that most book buyers in America are women and comments that they "don't want to read about Mike Hammer with a babe in one hand, a 1911 .45 Colt in another, and a glass of whiskey in his third hand, if he had one" (55). Corrigan sees the Spenser series as a sign that "Hard-boiled America is no longer the domain of socially conservative, wealthy, white, straight men; instead, it has been turned over to enlightened guys like Spenser and his rag-tag band of feminists, African-Americans, gays. and ethnics" (725). Donald Greiner, in an article in *Critique*, comments that Silverman is a pro, like Spenser, and that because of this professionalism she able to talk with Spenser about hard things, the hard things that his profession requires of him, including killing (40). Greiner's insight is partly confirmed by a Spenser novel published after his article, *Valediction* (1984).

In this novel Silverman leaves for California, and in her absence Spenser dates Linda Thomas, a woman who works in an office in the building opposite his. Although Linda is a woman with a profession (She is an art director.), she is not a "pro" in Greiner's sense. After Spenser kills four of five men who have attempted to ambush him outside a mall in which he and Linda attended a movie, she is unable to deal with the fact that Spenser is a man who can kill without apparent compunction, and she terminates the relationship.

However, not all critics agree with the idea that Parker's creation of Silverman enhances Spenser's liberal credentials. Corrigan notes that some feminist critics object to the need for Spenser to rescue Silverman (729). A more sustained critique of Spenser's relation to other major characters is made by Christina Root, in an article for *Clues*. Root observes that "Spenser's enlightened views are achieved with no loss of power or moral authority ... Spenser remains the central moral arbiter" (27). Spenser never changes his views in response to critiques from Silverman or any other woman. Indeed, as Root points out, the women are often left humbled and awed by Spenser's statements of his philosophy.

For instance, Root analyzes a scene in *A Savage Place* in which Spenser and the journalist he is guarding have just made love. They discuss his apparent double standard in making love to Candy while asserting that it would be different if Silverman were to be unfaithful. Root comments:

> Candy ... gives up too easily and seems to have no experience of her own to match his expression of a principled rather than expedient position....

Spenser is able to maintain his status as a being completely sui generis. Candy and Spenser don't conflict over issues of sexual politics and decorum—she seems to have no position despite her feminism; everything he says has for her the force of revelation. She's pictured as fragmented and empty, Spenser as mysterious, full, whole ... [30].

Root asserts that other characters, and Silverman in particular, seem to be set up by Parker only to be cut down to size. She sees a ruse to put Silverman in her place in the plots of *Valediction* (in which Silverman leaves for California) and *A Catskill Eagle*. It is, she asserts, hard to credit that an intelligent, educated woman would fall for a man who is a lobbyist for his anti–Semitic, right-wing father and let herself be lured into a relationship from which she cannot extricate herself without involving Spenser and Hawk (35). Having established that Silverman is less than insightful in her private love life, Parker proceeds in *Crimson Joy* to portray her as an idiot in her professional capacity as well, unable to detect that one of her patients in therapy is a serial killer, unwilling to believe the truth once Spenser has detected it and, once again, needing to be protected and rescued. Root calls this novel an "assassination of Susan's character" (36).

Gregory Eisman, in "A Catskill Eagle Crashed," is more concerned with the effect of Silverman on Spenser, blaming her for the demise of Spenser as a moral character. He asserts that Silverman is never in any real danger in *A Catskill Eagle*, but her supposed peril is used as a justification for uncontrolled violence on the part of Spenser and Hawk. A Spenser who, in a previous novel, *Early Autumn*, could not bring himself to execute a criminal who had made direct threats against his and Silverman's lives is now able to kidnap two whores, rob and kill their pimp and his bodyguard, kill private security guards whose only crime is carrying out the work they were hired for, among other acts of violence. As Eisman puts it, "By the time Spenser gets to *A Catskill Eagle*, any voicing or acting out of these rules [about when and how it is appropriate to take a life] becomes nothing more than a lead slug tossed into a blind man's cup. And throwing up after performing a reprehensible act [killing the pimp] does not make that act any less reprehensible" (112–13). Eisman's analysis brings us to the question of Spenser's code and its relation, if any, to the portrayal of alcohol use in the series.

That Spenser lives by a code is one thing the critics agree on. In "Spenserian Ethics" Steven Carter writes of Spenser:

He eschews abstraction and preconception in favor of a judgment grounded in a through understanding of the specifics of a situation, his primary aim being always to help and protect those who, through pardonable folly or circumstances beyond their control, are unable to help themselves.

In doing so, he demonstrates that the traditional American hero, redefined with an awareness of feminist, gay and pacifist challenges, remains a figure to be admired and emulated [117–18].

Herbert Fackler, writing in the library journal of Parker's alma mater, Colby College, relates Spenser's conscience to his New England background. In the words of Cotton Mather's "Essay Upon the Good," Spenser is a "stranger to the gain of oppression; the common refuge of the oppressed, and the distressed" and "stoops to do good" (254). Fackler also finds the influence of Emerson in Spenser's seeking of original solutions to problems and his nonconformity in such acts as sending April Kyle to be schooled by an experienced madam, in *Ceremony* (1982) when she refuses to be rescued from a life of prostitution. Spenser's reasoning is that the madam, Patricia Utley, who has helped him in an earlier case, will educate April and protect her from the dangers of street-walking, whereas left on her own the girl will run away from home again and fall into the hands of pimps (256). While not a solution one would expect from Emerson himself, it is Emersonian in its refusal to take easy recourse in conventional morality.

A final New England influence, according to Fackler, is Thoreau, as Spenser takes Paul Giacomni back to nature in *Early Autumn* to teach him autonomy away from the influence of his toxically self-centered parents (267). They work together to build a cabin, using hand tools in preference to power tools or hired help, in a rather obvious allusion to Thoreau's efforts at Walden Pond. David Geherin, who has written extensively on the hard-boiled genre in *Sons of Sam Spade*, summarizes what he sees as Parker's message in the Spenser novels: "One must develop a code for responding to the situations of life, and it is the quality of one's response that is the ultimate measure of character" (9).

Greiner's examination of the code by which Spenser lives is more detailed. He finds several elements to this code and also conflict between the elements. Spenser works independently rather than for the police or district attorney because his sense of honor requires that he not do things he does not want to do or thinks he should not do. He seeks his own version of justice, rather than merely enforcing the law as even good cops such as Lieutenant Quirk must do. Spenser's code requires that he strive to protect the weak and to refrain from killing unless it is necessary for self-defense or to defend others. Greiner also discovers elements of what he terms the "jock ethic," which requires that one play by the rules, even if to do so means losing. But this code is in opposition to that of the professional, who must put expediency ahead of rules and win at any cost. In other words, one does not give criminals a sporting chance (37). Greiner elaborates that a professional must do what he can, not what he ought to, and that Spenser finds he cannot obey both the imperatives of the playground with its jock ethic and the gutter, where his profession takes him (43).

Doug Robinson, in *No Less a Man: Masculist Art in a Feminist Age*, dwells on the ways in which he sees Spenser as fulfilling or changing not so much the detective code as the general cultural expectations of masculinity. He claims that Parker's importance lies in his exploration of masculinity, in asking questions such as "What is a man?" and "Why do men have to be so hard-boiled?" and "What is this masculine obsession with violence?" and "Why is the macho man so obsessed with protecting others, being the knight in shining armor?" (40). Robinson feels that readers use Spenser to test themselves by projecting "our tough, would-be autonomous self-images" onto the character to examine how such a self would function in the imaginary actions that Parker provides (44).

Robinson also examines the role of violence in the masculine self-image in Parker's work, noting that to fight effectively one must have self-control and that emotionally this reverses to the idea that to have self-control one must be able to fight effectively. Spenser, says Robinson, justifies his violence as part of his autonomy, but though he uses it to help people he also enjoys the violence for its own sake (82). Ultimately, though, the code fails because it cannot be adjusted if it fails; if the code changes, it is no longer the code.

James W. Zalewski and Lawrence B. Rosenfield agree that an important feature of the code is that it cannot be adjusted. Further, when there is a conflict between Spenser, with his code, and other characters, the majority of the other characters convert, and many of those who fail to convert are killed ("Rules for the Game" 75–76). In addition to obsessively exploring the subject of Spenser's code in the novels themselves, Parker has had much to say on the subject in interviews. In *Colloquium on Crime*, Parker states that: "In each book.... The stakes are mortal and a person can prevail insofar as he or she is not finally overwhelmed by a corrupt world." (Parker and Ponder 198)

Parker adds that he is interested in an "image of a hero who is self-disciplined, reasonably autonomous, and able to control his fear of death and his desire for sex and money" (198).

Norman is the only critic to make direct comments on the role of alcohol in Spenser's code. He says, "Drinking is also important in Spenser's universe, and there is a right way to do it. Drinking must be approached with a sense of measure." He relates this to Parker's habits as they meet for lunch. Parker orders cranberry juice and soda and remarks, "'Don't do as much [drinking] as I used to.... And I still haven't done any work today.' Strong drink has strong appeal, but it comes after work. Part of the code" (59).

A close reading of the novels themselves will clarify both the statement and workings of Spenser's code of behavior and the relation of
alcohol use to this code. Given the number of novels in the series it is
impractical to attempt a comprehensive survey. *The Godwulf Manuscript*,
as first in the series, introduces the detective himself and begins to give
a sense of his attitudes. *Mortal Stakes* (1975), the third in the series, contains discussions of the code and its application to a case in which there
is no solution which will spare the innocent. *Valediction*, in which Silverman leaves, and *A Catskill Eagle*, in which she is recovered, are important
in demonstrating what Eisman sees as a breakdown of the code. *Pastime*
(1991) is a good example of Parker's more recent treatment of Spenser,
containing extended discussions of alcohol and manhood. *Potshot* (2001)
is the second to most recent novel in the series and contains significant
discussion of the code.

The Godwulf Manuscript (1973) seems clearly derivative of Chandler. Spenser is hired to investigate the theft of an illustrated manuscript
from an university library. He interviews Terry Orchard, secretary of a
radical organization suspected of the theft and ransom request. That evening she calls him for help when she is framed for the murder of her lover,
Dennis Powell, the organization's leader. Terry's father hires Spenser to
clear her of the murder charge and, when his investigation focuses on
faculty members, the university fires him. Spenser persists and eventually discovers that a member of the English department is allied with a
local mobster in selling heroin on campus, an act the professor believes
will finance and further "the revolution." Spenser is wounded rescuing
the professor from the hitmen sent to kill him. Finally, the professor's wife
is killed by another hitman and Spenser turns the professor and the results
of his investigation over to the Boston police. In the course of this work,
Parker uses references to liquor in the modes that were defined in the
examination of Chandler's works. Spenser offers or is offered drinks in
social or business situations (hospitality); he offers drink to others in order
to smooth the acquisition of information (manipulation), and he drinks
alone or gives liquor to others to soothe emotional or physical pain (self-
medication).

There are, however, major differences between Spenser and Marlowe. For instance, Spenser allows himself to be tempted into making love
to both the wife and daughter of his employer and his only sign of compunction on the issue is a reluctance to face the two women together
afterward. This contrasts strongly both with Marlowe's statement to
Vivian Regan that General Sternwood did not hire him to make love to
his daughter and his discomfort at being caught by Mr. Grayle embrac-
ing Mrs. Grayle. For Marlowe, to make love to the daughter or wife of
a man who has provided drink is a violation of hospitality as well as the

relationship between employer and employee. Spenser may sense that this is the case, but does not govern his behavior accordingly.

Secondly, Spenser seems to have no hesitation about drinking with criminals. When he is taken to Joe Broz' office he does not even attempt to turn down the offered drink (94). On the other hand, Lieutenant Quirk's willingness to drink with Spenser does seem to betoken an acceptance of Spenser as being on the side of law and order, despite their differences concerning the handling of the case (125–26, 156).

Spenser does not attempt, at least in this volume, to obtain information by getting an informant drunk. The only incidents involving alcohol that might be considered to fall under this category include buying Terry Orchard a beer with lunch while questioning her about her organization, even after she admits to being underage (17), and treating Iris Milford to lunch and drinks in return for information about campus politics (125).

The use of alcohol as self-medication is more extensive. Spenser expresses amused contempt for Mr. Orchard as he resorts to brandy at about two-thirty in the afternoon after his daughter's arrest: "He handled stress well. I decided what the flush under the tan was" (54). But despite this contempt for Mr. Orchard, Spenser also resorts to alcohol for comfort on several occasions. In some ways he resembles Mike Hammer more than Marlowe as he spends an evening drinking beer while mulling over the case and fixing dinner: "after three or four beers everything began looking better to me" (71). Yet the case has not developed to the point of hopelessness for which excessive drinking could be an antidote. This point does seem to be reached after he is taken to Broz' office and threatened. On his return to the office Spenser helps himself generously to the office bottle of bourbon and eventually muses: "More bourbon. It wasn't really so bad, didn't taste bad at all, made you feel pretty nice in your stomach. Made you feel tough too, and on top of it—whatever it was" (99). Here the medication seems to be for his ego rather than for any real hurt. He has been picked up by hoods and pushed around; even though he got some of his own back by fighting Sonny, he knows that Broz could have had him killed at any point.

The alcohol Spenser administers to Terry after rescuing her from the Ceremony of Moloch is more clearly indicated. Spenser finds her tied to a cross, naked and gagged, about to be raped with a phallic wand. Spenser rescues her from the cult and takes her to his apartment. He ministers to her physical and emotional shock with two shots of bourbon over ice followed by a hot bath and wine with dinner. Then, with his own judgment perhaps impaired by drink, he is persuaded to comfort her with sex as well (115–19).

The Spenser of *The Godwulf Manuscript* is personable and capable, with something of an anti-authoritarian attitude. However, he does not seem to be a fully developed or coherent character. There is none of the discussion of a personal code that becomes so important in later novels, nor does he display any particular self-discipline in terms of exercise or abstinence. Subsequent novels will build on this modest beginning.

The third novel in the series, *Mortal Stakes* (1975), has attracted much critical attention for its extensive discussion of the conflicts between different codes of behavior. Spenser is hired to investigate the possibility that Red Sox star pitcher Marty Rabb is manipulating game scores. He discovers that Rabb is doing so because he is being blackmailed by an anonymous person who has discovered the existence of a pornographic video of his wife, a former prostitute whose past has been kept secret. Spenser eliminates the gamblers who are profiting from the information, but the possessor of the actual video threatens to continue the blackmail. Rabb's wife, Linda, decides to go public about her past, with the help of a friendly journalist lined up by Spenser, thus defusing the threat.

The first extended discussion of ethics in the novel occurs as Spenser explains the situation to Brenda Loring, one of the women he is seeing on a regular basis. Rabb, he tells her, is caught between the code that demands a man protect his family, in this case by keeping his wife's past from becoming publicly known, and the jock ethic: "commitment to play the game as best he can" (105). Or as Linda Rabb summarizes the problem: "We're part of it too, me and the boy—the game and the family. It's all he cares about. That's why it's killing him because he has to screw us or screw the game. Which is like screwing himself" (115).

While Rabb is caught between the conflicting demands the blackmail puts on his loyalties to family and to baseball, Spenser is also put in a situation in which his code seems to fail him. When he is threatened by the gambler who has been profiting from the blackmail he arranges a meeting in a rural area, arrives early enough to see the gambler's henchman set up an ambush, goads the gambler into drawing first and kills both men. In a later confrontation with the team announcer who has the incriminating video he loses his temper and nearly beats the man's bodyguard to death. He discusses both incidents with Silverman, yet curiously seems to feel more guilt for the killings (which were clearly in self-defense) than the beating, even though his actions in the latter case were out of proportion to the threat the man presented. He tells Silverman: "It all seemed to bubble up inside me and explode. It wasn't Lester; it was Doerr and Wally Hogg [the men he killed] and me and the case and the way things worked out so everyone got hurt some. It all just exploded out of me, and I damn near killed the poor creep" (186). Silverman accepts that Doerr and Hogg had to be killed and asks why it matters how it was done. When Spenser calls the question a matter of honor Silverman suggests that Spenser is old and wise enough to know better. This comment leads to a much-cited speech in which Spenser defines the necessity of a code of honor for someone like himself who does not have religion, success, family or patriotism to order his life. "Being a person," he tells her, "is kind of random and arbitrary business.... And you need something to keep it from being too random and arbitrary to handle.... So you accept some system of order, and you stick to it" (187).

Silverman summarizes his code as "never to allow innocents to be victimized and never to kill people except involuntarily," adding that the situation had forced him to violate one and that he "will live a little diminished" because of it (189). Yet this often cited scene seems somehow forced. Spenser has done everything short of letting Doerr fire first, and while one would admire Spenser less if he were casual about killing, even in clear self-defense, his expressions of angst on this occasion seem contrived to give him an opportunity to expound to Silverman.

Curiously, the occasion seems also contrived by Parker to display Silverman in a light that can hardly be called feminist. She calls Spenser "a classic case for the feminist movement. A captive of the male mystique, and all that" (189–90). Her position could be viewed as an example of Freud's assertion that women are incapable of abstract morality, that they care only about the welfare of family and friends regardless of rules of justice. In attributing this trait to women Freud regarded it as a sign of their moral inferiority. The logic of the Spenser series, which requires the reader to admire and identify with Spenser, leads to frustration with Silverman's inability to "get it." A strange dichotomy is built into the structure of the series as Spenser seems to require Silverman's approval of his actions, which she routinely gives despite her continued inability to understand the reasoning behind them.

Spenser's friend Hawk plays a similar role in later novels. Hawk and Spenser became friends when they were both boxers and Spenser helped Hawk fight off a racist gang who jumped him after a match. While Spenser is usually clearly on the side of law and order and works as a licensed private investigator, Hawk is a free-lance enforcer for the underworld, a "leg-breaker" for loan sharks. His own code is strictly practical: do what is necessary to survive. He will not violate his personal loyalties, refusing, for instance, to accept a contract to kill Spenser. He also will not violate his word once it is given. However, he will not let abstract ideas of fair play prevent him from eliminating a potential threat. Hawk is not likely to compare himself to Gary Cooper in *High Noon*, as Spenser does in *Mortal Stakes*, for he is unlikely to allow an armed enemy to approach him while another armed enemy lurks at his back. He will quite casually execute dangerous men Spenser is unable to bring himself to kill. Despite their differences Hawk expresses a reluctant admiration for

Spenser. Root comments that Hawk seems to speak mainly to express admiration for and wonder at Spenser's behavior (28).

The epigraph for *A Catskill Eagle* (1985), from Herman Melville's *Moby-Dick,* sets a high tone:

> And there is a Catskill eagle in some souls that can alike dive down into the blackest gorges, and soar out of them again and become invisible in the sunny spaces. And even if he forever flies within the gorge, that gorge is in the mountain: so that even in his lowest swoop the mountain eagle is still higher than the other birds upon the plain, even though they soar.

This epigraph appears to be intended as a description of Spenser, thus making the claim that Spenser "in his lowest swoop" is still better than other men. The novel gives the superficial impression that it tells the tale of a knightly quest, as Spenser goes forth to rescue first Hawk and then Silverman from the dragon who has made her captive. But a closer examination destroys this impression. Silverman meets Russell Costigan while interning in Washington, D. C. After her graduation from Harvard he convinces her to move to California and take a position in a hospital run by his very wealthy family. Because her relationship with Spenser has been troubled she agrees, although she remains in communication with Spenser and claims to love him. She calls Hawk for help, not because she is held prisoner, but because she is unsure of her feelings; Russell is pressuring her to stay with him and she is "too involved to leave on her own," as Hawk relays to Spenser after his rescue from jail (30). She has been seeing a therapist to help her deal with her conflicted feelings.

When Hawk arrives at the apartment in California there is a confrontation with Russell and his bodyguards, since Russell has bugged Silverman's phone and knows of her desire to leave him. Hawk kills one of the bodyguards while resisting Russell's attempt to force him out, and Silverman sends Spenser a note telling him that Hawk is in jail before leaving with Russell. Informed by a San Francisco lawyer that the town is controlled by Russell's father, Jerry Costigan, and that Hawk is likely to be railroaded, Spenser flies to California and breaks Hawk out of jail. On the run in San Francisco with little money, they pick up two prostitutes, keep them prisoners in their apartment for two days and rob and kill their pimp and his bodyguard when he comes to pick up their earnings. Spenser and Hawk then go to Jerry Costigan's house searching for Silverman. In the process they kill at least four security guards. Told that Russell and Silverman are at the family lodge in Washington, they go there as well and kill several more Costigan employees.

When they return to Boston they are approached by Federal agents who inform them that Jerry Costigan has been selling weapons to proscribed nations, that he may begin dealing in tactical nuclear weapons and that the government can get no firm evidence because agents sent into his operation disappear, presumably killed. Therefore the CIA has decided that assassination is the only option. Hawk and Spenser are offered any help they need to find Silverman and cancellation of the warrants against them if they kill Jerry Costigan. They locate Silverman and Russell and free her, killing more Costigan employees in the process. Then, with Russell's help, Spenser locates and enters Jerry's stronghold and kills him. In a final confrontation Russell has the opportunity to kill Spenser but does not do so because, as he admits, he has already lost Silverman and she would never forgive him if he killed Spenser. Spenser and Silverman then turn to rebuilding their relationship.

Spenser abandons all semblance of his code in this novel. All the killings, thirteen by Eisman's count (111), are rationalized by the overriding need to find Silverman and free her from Russell, even though there is no evidence that she is being held by force or ill-treated in any way. As Russell declares to Spenser, "She was so fucked up she couldn't oppose me alone." Silverman herself admits, after her "rescue," that Russell prevented her trip to New York just by telling her not to go: "I couldn't do something he told me not to" (233). At this point one might expect an outburst of moral indignation from Spenser, who has been turned into a murderer, a fugitive and a pawn of the government merely because Silverman has a problem choosing between two lovers. One might also expect that Silverman, who is portrayed throughout the series as warm, intelligent and concerned, and who is, after all, a mental health professional, would suffer moral revulsion at the carnage Hawk and Spenser have created in their pursuit of her. Yet at no point do either of them face up to the fact that many people have died, not because Silverman was an innocent woman held prisoner by an evil man, but because she is a neurotic held prisoner by her own inability to take responsibility for her decisions. Silverman's failure to confront her accountability for needless deaths would not seem significant, in itself. However, Parker continues to use her character to validate Spenser. In the *Colloquium* interview given shortly after the publication of *A Catskill Eagle* Parker explains the function of the women in Spenser's world.

> They understand the themes important to Spenser—honor and integrity and autonomy.... The reader also perceives Spenser as better ... because these good women do understand him and they explain this understanding to him [Parker and Ponder 200].

An example of this understanding and feedback occurs in the next novel in the series, *Taming a Seahorse* (1986), when Spenser and Silverman discuss the events of *A Catskill Eagle*:

> "Whatever you did, and whoever you killed, and however you feel about it, you have to judge all of that in context. You were doing what you felt you had to do, and you were doing it for love."
>
> "The people I killed are just as dead."
>
> "Yes. It makes no difference to them why you did it. But it makes a difference to me and to you. What we've been through in the last couple of years has produced the relationship we have now, achieved love, maybe" [220–21].
>
> "What makes you so attractive, among other things, is that your capacity for violence is never random, it is rarely self-indulgent, and you don't take it lightly. You make mistakes. But they are mistakes of judgment. They are not mistakes of the heart" [222].

At this point one must agree with Eisman that "only a human can turn love into a blind obsession that mutilates and destroys all that is good in a man; only love can cause a man to sink into the slime of his own ruin and cause that man to lap it all up with relish" (116). Eisman says this of Spenser, but the statement is equally applicable to Silverman.

Parker is by no means finished with the concept of Spenser's code, however. *Potshot* (2001) revisits the subject somewhat obsessively. The plot plays off the western film *The Magnificent Seven*, as Spenser is hired to find the killer of Steve Buckman, a businessman in the town of Potshot, Arizona. Buckman's widow tells Spenser that she is convinced that a gang holed up in a nearby ghost town known as the Dell is responsible, since he refused to pay the protection money they have extorted from other businesses. Spenser assembles a crew composed of men he has met on previous cases, some of them gangsters, others merely dangerous fighters. Hawk, of course, is one. The others are Vinnie, who was formerly an enforcer for Spenser's old opponent Joe Broz; Tedy Sapp, a gay bouncer Spenser met in *Hugger Mugger* (2000); Bernard J. Fortunato, a Las Vegas detective who first appeared in *Chance* (1996); and Chollo and Bobby Horse, Los Angeles gang members who appeared in *Stardust* (1990). The group consensus is that, since they are outnumbered by the inhabitants of the Dell, a sneak attack is the best strategy. Spenser vetoes the idea because he doesn't want a massacre. Eventually interference with their collection of protection money goads the gang into attacking the house in which Spenser's group is staying. The Dell gang is defeated and Spenser's crew sustains some injuries and wounds. In a post-confrontation discussion Hawk explains Spenser's method to the others:

> "It's what makes him different than you, or me or Vinnie or Chollo or Bobby Horse…. The rest of us, we see something that needs to be done, we do it. We don't much care how we do it. Spenser thinks that how you do it is as important as what you do."
>
> "Why?" Bernard said.
>
> Hawk grinned suddenly. "So he be different than us" [285].

Yet there is no real need to treat Spenser's plan as a moral mystery. Even gangsters are capable of understanding the requirement to protect oneself from the repercussions of violating the law. The group has been hired to protect the town by a group of prominent businessmen and can hardly expect their actions to remain secret. While others of the group would be able to fade back into the underworld once the job is done, Spenser, Sapp and Fortunato have livelihoods, which would be lost if they were wanted for murder. Therefore the group must wait to be attacked and be seen to act only in self-defense. The entire debate about going after the Dell seems to have been written only to bolster the mystique that Parker has created, the idea that Spenser's use of violence is somehow set apart from the way others use it. "The fact that Spenser will kill somebody is much less significant than the fact that he won't or that he does so in a controlled, almost civilized fashion. Like Shane, Spenser kills when he must. *Shane* is, in many ways, about how a hero won't kill until he must, and when he must, he does" (Parker and Ponder 199). Yet, unlike Shane, Spenser never lets standing by a matter of principle cause him to be beaten up or forced to back down from a physical confrontation. In his willingness to use violence, Spenser resembles Mike Hammer much more than critics seem to acknowledge.

Although the role of his code in controlling violence has been shown to be problematic in *A Catskill Eagle* and subsequent works, there is an important aspect that remains. Respect for one's pledged word is a virtue that can be found even in men who have few others that conventional society would recognize.

In *Pastime*, Spenser is looking for Paul Giacomin's mother, who has disappeared with a new lover. The lover turns out to have embezzled money from an operation run by Gerry Broz, son of Spenser's old nemesis, Joe Broz. Joe pulls Spenser in to discuss his interference, explaining that Gerry has to be allowed to go after the embezzler if he is to be fit to take over the racket after Joe dies. Spenser makes an agreement: "I find Beaumont, I'll leave him in place and take the woman. I won't hold Beaumont for Gerry, and I won't tell Gerry where he is, but I'll leave him out there for Gerry to hunt" (179–80). As it turns out, Spenser and Gerry find Beaumont at the same time and Gerry and his men end up hunting Spenser through the woods until Spenser manages to capture Gerry and force his men to leave them to walk to the nearest road. Asked why he spared Gerry, who will continue to be a danger, Spenser can only point to the conversation with Joe. He didn't promise Joe not to kill Gerry, but he implied that he would not (272). Later, Joe and Gerry come to Spenser's office. Joe tells Gerry that if he is to inherit he must be able to kill Spenser himself for shaming him in front of his men, not have Vinnie or anyone else do it for him. He must prove himself:

"You want me to take him out," Gerry said. "You're telling me that right in front of him."

"Right in front," Joe said. "So he knows. So there's no back-shooting and sneaking around. You tell him he's gone and then you take him out" [295].

Joe has defined what he sees as the only way to maintain control of a criminal organization, to let the world know that you are good enough and tough enough to kill a man even when he is expecting you to try. Furthermore, a man must keep his word, whether it be to spare a man or to kill him. Later, in *Potshot*, the men Spenser has hired are discussing whether to carry out Spenser's plan of waiting for an attack by the Dell:

"But I got something else," Bernard said. Chollo waited. Loose in his chair. Peaceful.

"We ought to do what he says."

"Because?" Chollo asked.

"Because we said we would."

"And we cannot change our mind?"

"Bernard J. Fortunato's word is good," he said [258].

This settles the argument. Keeping one's word is a value everyone assembled can understand.

Despite Norman's remarks about alcohol use being part of the code, the topic does not seem as important for Parker as for Chandler or Hammett. Control is an issue for Spenser, but he does not feel that he needs to control his alcohol intake at all times. Part of the pleasure of a baseball game is the "tendency to drink six or eight beers" (*Mortal Stakes* 10). On the other hand, Spenser turns down a drink at ten in the morning:

"Why not, tastes just as good...."

"That's what I'm afraid of. I got enough trouble staying sober now" [98].

The remark passes as a casual one designed to take the sting out of the refusal, but there is a kernel of truth, since Spenser spends quite a bit of time in the novel drinking while he thinks about the case. Much of this drinking would come under the category of self-medication as he is confronted by unpalatable alternatives. Hired to discover whether Marty Rabb is throwing Red Sox games, he learns that this is indeed the case. At this point he could consider his job done, take the evidence to the management and watch as Rabb is fired and banned from all association with baseball. But Spenser has learned that Rabb did not act for his own profit, but because he is being blackmailed with the threat that his wife's past as a prostitute will be revealed. Spenser is sympathetic, both because Rabb is acting to protect his family and because Linda Rabb/Donna Burlington is a decent woman who used the only means she had to escape a dirt-poor background. Knowing that the information he has gathered would destroy the Rabbs gives Spenser "a bad taste I want to get rid of and the bourbon is quicker [than beer]" as he tells Lieutenant. Quirk (120). The need to drink is even more clear after the killing of Doerr and Hogg:

> On the way I stopped and bought a quart of Wild Turkey bourbon. Turning off Route 1 toward Smithfield Center, I twisted the top off, took a mouthful, rinsed my mouth, spit out the window, and drank about four ounces from the bottle. My stomach jumped when the booze hit it, but then it steadied and held [161].

He proceeds to Silverman's house and suggests she drink while he tells her what has happened: "It'll be easier to take if you're a little drunk too" (163). Apparently it is, because without even probing for details Silverman offers her reassurance, soon to become standard, that whatever Spenser did must have been right.

In *Valediction* (1984) Spenser endures a severe emotional blow when Silverman announces that she has taken a job in California, that she needs to be alone and desires no contact with him for an unspecified period. Hawk notices that something is wrong and invites him for a drink. As they drink Spenser thinks: "The thing I like about Irish whiskey is that the more you drink the smoother it goes down. Of course that's probably true of anti-freeze as well, but illusion is nearly all we have" (29). Spenser takes on a case, but his evenings are empty except for alcohol: "I had some Irish whiskey for supper and watched the ballgame and when I felt sleepy and dull enough I went to bed and slept badly" (65). Despite starting a relationship with Linda Thomas, Spenser's low level functioning continues as he works on the case. His inattention to detail almost gets him killed, as he fails to realize until she turns a gun on him that the woman he set out to rescue is, in fact, the mastermind of a heroin marketing and money laundering scheme involving a church and a construction company. The excessive drinking could be seen as the cause of his near-fatal lack of acuteness, but it seems to be more a symptom of his lack of interest in his own life. Even after his near death he does not tell Silverman of the incident, and the book ends with her invitation for him to visit her in San Francisco. This work is followed by *A Catskill Eagle*, in which alcohol is not an important issue.

Alcohol use, particularly of hard liquor, also has a role in defining manhood. In *Pastime* Spenser and Silverman are having drinks together when she comments on the fact that he is drinking scotch instead of his usual beer. He replies that he is feeling celebratory because both she and

Paul are in town, and when asked why scotch is a celebratory beverage he tells of the first time he ever had a drink stronger than beer. When he was seventeen he and his father went pheasant hunting in an abandoned apple orchard. They are separated in thick brush when the youthful Spenser encounters a bear, drunk on fermented windfall apples. He knows both that he cannot outrun a bear if it charges and that a shotgun loaded with birdshot is inadequate to stop it. His father arrives after a few minutes, alerted by the barking of their pointer, and the bear eventually moves away:

> "And then my father and I went down to the bar and my father ordered two double scotch whiskies. The bartender looked at me and looked at my father and didn't say anything and brought the whiskey. He put both of them in front of my father and my father pushed one of them over in front of me."
>
> "'Ran into a bear in the woods today,' my father said.... 'Kid stood his ground.'"
>
> "The bartender ... looked at me and nodded ... and my father and I drank the scotch."

•   •   •

> "'That brown liquor,'" Susan said, 'which not women, not boys and children, but only hunters drank.'"
>
> "Faulkner," I said.

•   •   •

> "I had acted like a man, in his view, so he treated me like a man, in his view" [22–24].

The important factor to note here is that drinking hard liquor is not itself a rite of passage, but a celebration of an act that constitutes a rite of passage. The difference is that between a college fraternity prank in which young men attempt to prove their manhood by drinking too much and the celebratory drink that one might be treated to after an onerous task such as completing a marathon, passing the bar exam, or facing down a bear. To drink to prove manhood is to put the symbol in place of the accomplishment. The story is appropriate to this novel because the action centers around Paul's search for his mother and his need to face the fact that she will never be the mother he might have wished for. He must face this reality before he is ready to take the step toward manhood of marrying and preparing to found a family of his own.

Although control of alcohol consumption is at least a minor issue in most of the works discussed it is not the only issue of control in Parker's work. At various times Spenser manipulates his caffeine intake as well, switching from regular coffee to decaffeinated, or even giving up coffee altogether. In *Valediction*, Belson and another officer come to his apartment in the morning to ask about the four men he killed the night before.

Spenser offers them coffee, "Water-decaffeinated ... Mocha almond," from a shop in Cambridge (207). In *Pastime* Hawk gives him some mild ribbing on the subject:

> "I thought you quit coffee," Hawk said.
> "I changed my mind."
> "Couldn't do it, huh?"
> "Decided not to" [114].

Although Spenser may weaken in dietary resolves, Silverman is the epitome of control in terms of food and drink. A typical description of a meal with her includes passages like the following from *Pastime*: "Susan ate a small forkful of chili and nibbled the edge of a small piece of corn bread" (324). Root makes:

> ...a connection between Spenser's ... obsession with looks and Susan's persistent near-anorexia. Yet Spenser admires Susan's food and makeup rituals as though they were *her version of a private moral code* and deserving of his respect for their mystery and their capacity to express her essential nature [33; emphasis added].

The contrast is obvious; Spenser has a code dealing with life and death, truth and honor; Silverman's equivalent deals with being beautiful. No wonder she can never really understand Spenser's actions, but can only offer uncomprehending approval based on her own self-image as someone who would not love Spenser if he were not a good man. In contrast to the respect that Root claims Spenser shows for Silverman's dietary habits, some readers find the constant repetition of her ability to turn one cashew and a sip of white wine into a three-course meal extremely annoying. Perhaps Parker intends us to be annoyed with Silverman, so that any excess of Spenser's seems forgivably human in contrast. Alternately, Parker may be unable to incorporate criticism of Silverman into his view of the series, possibly because she is patterned on his wife.

What is consumed, as well as how much, has significance as well. Spenser tends to be a beer drinker. In the earlier books he prefers imports, such as Heineken or Amstel. In later books he has switched to less common, yet still nationally known, brews such as Rolling Rock and Sam Adams. He also drinks suitable wines with meals and, as we have seen, changes his hard liquor preference from bourbon to Irish whiskey in the course of the series. Hawk is even more of a connoisseur, drinking French champagne by preference, single malt scotch and other costly beverages. These details are in line with Thomas Roberts' "newspaper reality."

In the seventies, when Spenser made his debut, beer was still a working-class beverage and most sales were of light lagers such as Budweiser, Pabst Blue Ribbon, and Miller High Life. A few people had been introduced to other types of beer while on military service overseas, and there was a beginning of beer snobbery based on a preference for imports, which are stronger flavored than most Americans were accustomed to. The late seventies and early eighties saw an increase in imports and the beginning of regional specialty brews. Changes in federal tax laws made brew-pubs and micro-breweries possible, and by the nineties a large supermarket in an urban area would feature dozens of types of beer, both domestic specialty brews and imports. One may note that Parker does not name any brands so obscure that a nationwide audience might be unfamiliar with them. Sam Adams, for instance, sounds as though it might be the name of a Boston area microbrew, but is actually distributed nationally. Similarly, when Spenser drinks bourbon, it is Wild Turkey; when he switches to Irish whiskey, it is to Bushmill's, one of the most widely distributed brands. Spenser, in short, is slightly ahead of the curve in his drinking habits, but not so much so as to seem eccentric.

Parker began his academic career as an expert on Hammett's and Chandler's development of the hard-boiled genre. When he turned to writing the genre rather than studying it, many reviewers hailed him as another Chandler. It is perhaps not surprising that he was allowed to complete "The Poodle Springs Story," which Chandler left unfinished at his death in 1959. Robert Parker gained permission from the Chandler estate to complete the novel and published it as *Poodle Springs* in 1989.

The novel begins as the newly married Philip Marlowe and the former Linda Loring take up residence in Poodle Springs, a thinly disguised Palm Springs. Linda expresses dismay when Marlowe announces his intention of setting up an office and continuing his private investigation practice. He explains that he has no intention of merely living on her money. His first customer is a local club owner, Manny Lipshultz, who sends two gunmen to attempt to compel Marlowe to meet with him. Parker takes Chandler's four chapters and spins a complex tale in which a search for a missing gambler turns up false identities, bigamy, blackmail and murder. Linda becomes increasingly displeased with Marlowe's refusal to settle down to a life of wealthy privilege, especially when his investigation begins to impinge on her social circle. By the end of the novel they have agreed to a divorce, yet clearly will continue to be lovers.

Although some critics feel that Parker captures the Chandler style, there are problems with *Poodle Springs*. Some are minor, as when the wife of the man Marlowe is searching for displays her figure provocatively to emphasize that she is not worried by competition from the models her husband photographs, and Parker's Marlowe responds, "Zowie" (44). This expression is more characteristic of Spenser than of Marlowe. Another point, perhaps not so minor, is that Parker has Marlowe adopt gimlets as his regular drink. But in Chandler's work, gimlets appear only in *The Long Goodbye*, in which Terry Lennox introduces Marlowe to the cocktail. While it is true Marlowe was drinking a gimlet when he first met Linda Loring, this was the commemorative gimlet asked for in Lennox's letter. When Marlowe meets the disguised Lennox, returned to Los Angeles in the guise of Señor Maioranos, he refuses to drink with him, although Lennox admits his identity by saying, "I suppose it's a bit too early for a gimlet" (730). A Marlowe who is sentimental enough to drink the commemorative gimlet when he believes Lennox is physically dead would shun their shared drink after Lennox became dead to him in spirit. Every sip of gin and lime juice would taste of a friendship betrayed.

A more important aspect of Parker's reconstruction of Marlowe in *Poodle Springs* is Marlowe's code. Marlowe agrees to search for a man who owes $100,000 to an illegal gambling casino. It is marginally possible that Marlowe, as Chandler conceived him, would do this since the very nonenforcability of a gambling IOU in court has traditionally made it a debt of honor. Manny Lipshultz tells Marlowe that he will be killed by his employer, Mr. Blackstone, if he does not recover the missing money. But it is utterly incredible that the same Marlowe who refuses to shake hands with Clark Brandon because he "hired a gun" (*Playback* 868) would drink with and accept a retainer from Clayton Blackstone, who is also a retired mobster (158, 225–27). Parker seems to have put all his effort in building Marlowe's character into his principled refusal to quit working and the resultant conflict with Linda. Although Chandler himself expressed doubt over the marriage he had created for Marlowe, it is by no means certain that he intended to make such difficulties the major theme of *Poodle Springs*. In an October 14, 1958 letter to Roger Machell he says:

> My next book is to be laid in Palm Springs with Marlowe having a rather tough time getting along with his wife's ideas of how to live…. She won't like it that he insists on sticking to his own business and modest way of life, … I don't know whether the marriage will last or whether he will walk out of it or get bounced [MacShane, *Selected Letters* 478].

Nor does it read true that Marlowe's pride would allow Linda to discard him as a husband yet keep him as a lover. Parker seems obsessed with giving fictional characters love lives similar to the arrangement he has reached with his own wife, Joan: Spenser and Silverman continue to live apart, though in the same city, and Jesse Stone, Parker's second series character, maintains ties to his ex-wife Jennifer, at least in the first two volumes. It should be noted that under earlier divorce law, a divorce action was canceled if the parties continued to have marital relations, a fact Parker seems to disregard when he has Linda claim that her visit to Marlowe at his apartment has nothing to do with their impending divorce.

Whether or not one accepts Parker's vision of Marlowe, there is little new in terms of development of the detective's code or alcohol consumption. Marlowe encounters the usual range of society lushes, alcoholic nymphomaniacs and sad, older drunks. Spenser writes scenes similar to those Chandler constructed. Marlowe accepts the hospitality of wealthy men who serve good whiskey and is denied the hospitality of rich women who drink in front of him. He drinks with and questions, until she passes out, a regular at a bar who witnessed an argument between the man Marlowe is hunting and the woman the man is suspected of killing. After Linda announces her decision to divorce him, he drinks cheap bourbon alone in his office. Parker does not introduce new themes in this work. Unfortunately, the relations he allows between Marlowe and underworld figures suggest that he has failed to discern the moral limits Chandler put upon his creation.

Parker's career has been uneven. It was marked in the beginning by critical acclaim as Spenser was seen as the new paradigm for the fictional private detective, a type that appeared to have been led into a dead end by such ultra-violent examples as Mike Hammer. As noted, however, some critics took issue both with the characterization of Susan Silverman and with the manner in which the crisis in the relationship between Silverman and Spenser was developed and resolved. Corrigan notes that the novels of the 1990s seemed to be slimmer, less developed (725). Some felt that Parker was tired of the character but trapped (like Chandler's fictional Roger Wade) by the popularity of his work. In any case, *Pastime* was seen as a return to the intensity of the earlier work and Parker continues to produce approximately one Spenser novel each year. Parker's work on *Poodle Springs* is the sort of project one might expect a dedicated fan who is also a writer in the genre to undertake, especially since the last few decades have featured something of a fad of continuing series by dead authors. Sherlock Holmes and James Bond are among the characters given new life in this manner, not to mention attempts to complete such classics as Dickens' *The Mystery of Edwin Drood*. Parker has published only one more Marlowe novel, *Perchance to Dream*, a sequel to *The Big Sleep*. His reasons for discontinuing the effort are unknown, although it could be argued that the critical response and sales figures may have been less than encouraging. In 1997, Parker branched out yet again with the creation of Jesse Stone, who first appears in *Night Passage*. Stone is a former Los Angeles homicide detective who becomes chief of police in a small New England town. He is, therefore, outside a study of the private detective. An even more recent addition to Parker's work is Sunny Randall, a woman detective. Both of these characters are too new to determine whether they will equal or rival Spenser in popularity or in critical attention.

Spenser is cited by many reviewers for his wit, which continues the tradition of the private eye who jokes in the face of danger. Lawrence Block, one of Parker's more gifted contemporaries, has created a private investigator with a much darker view of life. Matthew Scudder is a former police officer who "does favors" for people who cannot afford or would not approach a more conventional detective. Scudder's career is shaped by his denial, recognition and confrontation with alcoholism, a theme that makes him a natural subject for this study.

Lawrence Block

"A Wide-Awake Drunk"

Of the writers examined in this work, Lawrence Block is the most prolific. No one, in fact, is sure exactly how many books and stories he has published, for much of his early production was pseudonymous. He has created four series characters during his career: Evan Tanner, a gentleman adventurer who never sleeps; Chip Harrison, a sexually frustrated teenager who becomes factotum to a would-be Nero Wolfe; Bernie Rhodenbarr, a career burglar who daylights as a bookstore owner; and Matthew Scudder, an alcoholic former police detective. Introduced in 1976 in *The Sins of the Fathers*, Scudder is not technically a private investigator. As he explains to a potential client: "Private detectives are licensed. They tap telephones and follow people, they fill out forms, they keep records, all of that. I don't do those things. Sometimes I do favors for people. They give me gifts" (2). Despite his informal status, Scudder fits the role of the hard-boiled detective, since he does earn his living through investigations in a world in which crime and corruption are ubiquitous, rather than solving crimes out of curiosity, happenstance or to clear himself or an acquaintance of suspicion, as is usually the pattern for the fictional amateur detective. From the beginning of the series it is clear that Scudder is a heavy drinker, and his confrontation with the fact that he is an alcoholic becomes a major theme of the later works, thus making the series an appropriate subject for this study.

Lawrence Block was born June 24, 1938, in Buffalo, New York. He attended Antioch College near Dayton, Ohio, but dropped out before his final year, as he had already established himself as a professional writer, with both novels and short stories published. In 1960 he married Loretta Kallett; they have three daughters and divorced in 1973. In 1983 he married Lynne Wood. He and his second wife live in Greenwich Village, having returned to New York after a few years in Florida.

Block's first publication was a short story, "You Can't Lose," in *Manhunt* (February 1958). His first novel published under his own name was *Mona* (1961). He also wrote erotic novels under various pseudonyms. His first series character was created in 1966 with the publication of *The Thief Who Couldn't Sleep*, featuring Evan Tanner, a man who suffered damage to the sleep center of his brain and has, as a result, more hours per day to devote to various obscure causes, including his personal passion for restoration of the Stuart line to the British throne. The Tanner novels are adventure stories rather than mysteries, though the books, like most of their kind, are marketed and shelved with detective fiction.

A second series character, Chip Harrison, appeared as author as well as protagonist of *No Score* (1970) and *Chip Scores Again* (1971). Only the last two Harrison books, *Make Out With Murder* (1974) and *The Topless Tulip Caper* (1975), are mysteries, and the series has since been reissued under Block's name. In *The St. James Guide to Crime and Mystery Writers*, the bibliography lists Leo Haig, Chip's employer, as the series character, rather than Chip (Gardner 86). As mentioned above, the Matthew Scudder series was inaugurated in 1976. In 1977, *Burglars Can't be Choosers* introduced Bernie Rhodenbarr in a series that can be described as light-hearted or even comic. Block has also published a number of short stories, some of them featuring his series characters, conventional novels, and non-fiction works, as well as a long-running column on the art of writing fiction in *Writer's Digest*.

Block has been the recipient of a number of awards. *Eight Million Ways to Die* (1982) earned the Shamus Award from the Private Eye Writers of America, as did *The Devil Knows You're Dead* (1993). Block received the Edgar Allan Poe Award from the Mystery Writers of America for both *A Dance at the Slaughterhouse* (1991) and *A Long Line of Dead Men* (1994), and for several short stories. In 1980 *The Burglar Who Liked to Quote Kipling* won the Nero Wolfe Award from the international organization of Nero Wolfe fans, and in 1987 and 1991 Japanese fans awarded their Maltese Falcon to *When the Sacred Ginmill Closes* and *A Ticket to the Boneyard*, respectively. Other novels have received nominations for these and other awards, and several of Block's short stories have won prizes as well. In 1994, at the age of fifty-six, Block was the youngest writer to be named a Grand Master by the Mystery Writers of America, according to Charles Ardai in *Mystery and Suspense Writers* (63–66). Notably, the Scudder series has garnered the majority of critical acclaim and award nominations.

Given the depth of detail and the number of pages devoted to the portrayal of Scudder as an alcoholic, most critics assume a connection with Block's own life. Block admits to Ernie Bulow in *After Hours* that he created a character with parallels to his own situation: separated from his wife, and living alone in a studio apartment in the same block on West Fifty-eighth Street on which he situates Scudder's hotel (75). Scudder even drinks in the same bar as his creator, an actual establishment called Armstrong's. Block is reticent on the subject of his alcoholism, telling Bulow that it is not a secret that he formerly drank but has quit. Asked how bad his condition was, Block replies, "Well, if it hadn't gotten bad, I wouldn't have stopped" (39–40). Questioned on whether the stories Scudder hears in AA meetings derive from real life he points out, "they do call it Alcoholics Anonymous, and a part of what's implicit in that is that my characters are not talking about anything outside of the context of fiction. Just as I am disinclined to say whether I am or am not a member of Alcoholics Anonymous because since there is an AA tradition against identifying oneself as a member, I feel that whether I am or am not, that it is certainly in the spirit of that tradition for me not to say" (93–94).

In *Even the Wicked* (1997) Scudder's friend Elaine remarks with implied disapproval that some "Hollywood types go straight from Betty Ford to Barbara Walters" (151). Block also responds to Bulow about the effect of alcohol on the quality of writing, his own and other's: "What it does in so many cases is lead to a certain degree of arrested development. Writers get to a certain level and then they stop evolving, growing—their work doesn't get any better or any deeper because the drink shuts it off. Even if it doesn't deteriorate, it just shuts off. You don't feel like growing" (40). Block's temperance appears to have saved him from this problem, as he continues to create new characters, as well as to develop established ones such as Scudder and Rhodenbarr.

Matthew Scudder makes his first appearance in *The Sins of the Fathers*, written together with the next two volumes, *Time to Murder and Create* and *In the Midst of Death*, in 1974 and published in 1976. Scudder is a former New York City police detective. One day in the unspecified past, he was drinking after work when the bar he was in was held up. The robbers shot the bartender and Scudder pursued them, shooting and killing one and seriously wounding the other. However, one bullet went astray, ricocheted from the pavement and struck seven-year-old Estrellita Rivera in the eye, killing her instantly. Scudder was not blamed for the girl's death, indeed he was commended for apprehending the robbers, but the event precipitates a breakdown in his life. In *The Sins of the Fathers* he tells a potential client, Cale Hanniford, "I lost the faith ... I didn't want to be a cop anymore." He adds to himself, "Or a husband or a father. Or a productive member of society" (10). Scudder lives in a hotel room, eats his meals in bars and coffee shops, and earns enough money from his investigations to maintain himself and to irregularly send money to his ex-wife for his two sons. He also puts ten percent of his earnings into church poor boxes, an impulse he cannot explain, even to himself. He is not religious in any conventional sense, noting only that the Catholics get most of his money because their churches are more likely to be open on weekdays and evenings. He also has a habit, when in a Catholic church, of lighting candles for the victims of whatever crime he is currently investigating, and for Estrellita.

In the course of the novel we learn that Scudder is a fairly constant drinker. He will sit for hours in Armstrong's, a bar near his hotel, drinking coffee with bourbon; seldom drunk, seldom sober. His drinking increases and becomes less controlled when he is under emotional strain, as when he confronts his client about the possibility of an incestuous relationship with the step-daughter whose death Scudder is investigating. In the middle of the conversation he abruptly asks Hanniford whether he has anything to drink in his office, wonders how anyone could not know whether or not he has liquor on hand, and drinks several ounces straight when it is produced (*The Sins of the Fathers* 142). Wendy Hanniford was working as a prostitute and living with Richard Vanderpoel when she was found stabbed to death. Richard was on the street in front of their apartment, raving and covered with blood, and is arrested for the murder. Richard commits suicide in his cell and the police consider the case closed. Cale Hanniford feels guilty that he lost track of his step-daughter after she abruptly left college and wonders whether he is partially responsible for her fate. Scudder surmises that Wendy was working out her feelings about her real father, who died in Korea before she was born, by having sex with older men after her provocative advances to her stepfather were rejected. Scudder also learns that her "boyfriend" was actually homosexual and that they were not lovers. Scudder's investigation leads him to the conclusion that Richard's father, the Reverend Martin Vanderpoel, had actually committed the crime and allowed his son to take the blame. He visits the minister, tells him what he believes happened and points out that if the investigation is reopened the police will undoubtedly discover evidence to support his reconstruction of events. He offers Reverend Vanderpoel the option of committing suicide with Seconal before the police are reintroduced to the case. Scudder has fortified himself for this interview with a half-pint flask of bourbon. He offers a drink to Vanderpoel, who refuses, adding that he doesn't use alcohol or allow it in his home." I thought about that and decided he wasn't in a position to set rules. I took a long drink" (177). Vanderpoel accuses Scudder of forcing him to die. Scudder points out that he is offering a choice, and explains his action by asserting, "It's bad for society when murders remain unpunished" (181).

Scudder's drinking habits remain fairly stable for the next two books, *Time to Murder and Create* (1977) and *In the Midst of Death* (1976). In *A Stab in the Dark* (1981) the drinking increases and becomes less controlled and Scudder almost attends an Alcoholics Anonymous meeting, entering and then leaving abruptly. Near the beginning of *Eight Million Ways to Die* (1982), we learn that Scudder suffered an alcohol-caused seizure and blackout and was released from the detox ward only a week earlier. At the urging of a former lover and drinking partner who is in recovery, he has begun to attend AA meetings, but, as the events of the novel show, he rebels against accepting the definition of himself as an alcoholic and struggles to prove he can get back in control. He is hired by Kim Dakkinen, a call girl, to help her leave her pimp, Chance. Chance assures Scudder that he has no intention of keeping Kim against her will, but is the natural suspect when the woman is found slashed to death in a hotel room. Chance then hires Scudder to find the real killer, knowing that since the police assume that he hired a killer and set up an alibi for himself they will not pursue the case actively.

Another prostitute in his string, Sunny, frightened and depressed by the death of her colleague, commits suicide with sleeping pills and alcohol. A little later a transsexual streetwalker who works without a pimp is found slashed to death in another hotel, leading the police to assume both murders have been committed by a sexual psychopath preying on prostitutes. Scudder eventually solves the case by learning that Kim had a boyfriend, a jewel dealer who had cheated Colombian emerald smugglers. A drug dealer Scudder questioned earlier told him that Colombian criminals have a reputation for killing an entire family rather than just the person who has broken trust. Since the jewel dealer has no wife or children they kill his girlfriend, Kim, and his brother, the transsexual streetwalker.

Scudder and the police set a trap, but Scudder is nearly killed himself when the murderer outmaneuvers the police and manages to hide in his hotel room. Scudder shoots and kills the attacker. In addition to Scudder's detective work two themes are interlaced throughout the story: his struggle with liquor, including drinking, resisting the urge to drink, and attending AA meetings; and accounts of random violence in the city, garnered from the tabloid papers and conversations with other New Yorkers. It is Detective Joe Durkin who recalls the old television series "The Naked City" and its claim that "there are eight million stories in the naked city," converting stories to "ways to die" (122).

Scudder's preoccupation with liquor in *Eight Million Ways to Die* first becomes apparent as he describes Kim entering the room. He notes that her jeans are the color of burgundy, her fur jacket the color of champagne, her nails lacquered the color of tawny port (1–4). Several times in the first few pages of the story Scudder recounts strong urges to drink, but he resists. At one point he ruminates about the role of alcohol in his life, thinking about how alcohol used to fill time, that he used to sit for hours drinking coffee and bourbon, never quite drunk and never quite sober, but that this method of killing time doesn't work for him without the alcohol (52). After Kim's murder he attends an AA meeting, but an anguished internal monologue drowns out the other participants:

> I thought, My name is Matt and I'm an alcoholic and we sit around in these goddamned rooms and say the same damned things all the time and meanwhile out there all the animals are killing each other. We say Don't drink and go to meetings and we say The important thing is you're sober and we say Easy does it and we say One day at a time and while we natter on like brainwashed zombies the world is coming to an end [59].

After the meeting he takes a drink, realizing that it has been over fifteen years since he had gone a full week without one. Over the next few days he constructs elaborate justifications for his behavior, first deciding on a two-drink limit and being pleased that he is able to stick to this limit (67). The next evening he decides that, since his previous drink was over twelve hours earlier, it doesn't count on this day's total and that he is "entitled to another," adding, "I had the sense to realize that it was the number of drinks that was significant, not their size, and then it struck me that I'd cheated myself. My first drink had been a short measure" (68). He drinks several ounces of bourbon in his hotel room, then goes out to a bar. In a stunning rendition of the logic of the addicted mind Scudder tells us:

> I realized something. I'd been controlling my drinking for days now, and before that I'd been off the sauce entirely for over a week and that proved something. Hell, if I could limit myself to two drinks a day that was fairly strong evidence that I didn't *need* [emphasis in original] to limit myself to two drinks a day. I'd had my problems with alcohol in the past, I couldn't very well deny it, but evidently I had outgrown that stage in my life [69].

He orders another drink and wakes up in the hospital after two days of blackout and a grand mal seizure. The attending intern pulls no punches in telling him that continued drinking will put him back in the hospital and eventually kill him. He checks out of the hospital, mortified by thoughts of what he may have done or said during the missing days. He returns to the case, noting that continuing the investigation was something to do instead of drinking (125). Urges to drink come and go, sometimes strong and sometimes fleeting. The strongest comes after he is accosted by a mugger after leaving an uptown bar. He manages to defeat the man and take his gun and considers killing the mugger, but he finally decides to break the criminal's legs to keep him from returning to his profession. After doing so he has the shakes and is desperate for a drink. He almost goes to a bar, but calls his friend Jan, the former drinking companion mentioned above who broke off their connection after joining AA earlier. After he pours out the events of the last several days they begin talking about the AA program and the kind of remarks they have heard at meetings. She mentions a man who said that being sober helped him experience his grief after the death of a family member. Scudder wonders what good it is to do so, then considers how his life might have been different if he had let himself experience his feelings after killing Estrellita instead of dealing with the feelings by "pouring bourbon on them" (191).

Later in the investigation he is depressed by Sunny's suicide and his lack of progress in finding Kim's killer. He tells himself that he would feel better if he drank, although he would regret it in the long run. He recalls a speaker at a meeting who told the group that "Bad feelings won't kill me. Alcohol will..." (233). Once again Scudder resists the urge to drink. We begin to see how AA meetings function, how hearing others' stories of addiction and recovery helps the new member. But the battle is not won. After the case is solved Scudder is feeling good, yet he goes to a bar and orders a double bourbon. "Why? ... I wasn't nervous, I wasn't anxious, I wasn't depressed.... What the hell was the matter with me? If I drank the fucking drink I would end up dead or in the hospital.... I knew that." He leaves the drink on the counter and heads for the nearest AA meeting. There he finally speaks up: "My name is Matt and I'm an alcoholic," and he starts to cry as the novel ends (320–22).

Critics who focus on Block's treatment of alcoholism have taken a variety of approaches to the topic. These approaches are adequate to the treatment of Block in isolation, although the conclusions reached by some writers are debatable. One can link Block's treatment of alcohol in the Scudder series to the patterns already observed in earlier authors in the genre. Understandably, the critics focus on Scudder as an admitted alcoholic, and on the changes he undergoes as he makes the transition from out-of-control drinker to recovering alcoholic, a transition that sets him apart from the typical genre protagonist. The Op, Marlowe, Hammer and Spenser may age and acquire experience, but they do not undergo any major transformation of character. Even Hammer's seven-year drunk is portrayed merely as in interlude in his career. Once the interlude is over the old Hammer is back, with only an occasional pro forma claim that his mental or physical performance has been adversely affected by the abuse to which he has subjected himself. Given this tendency for static characterization in the genre it is to be expected that critics such as Wedge and Ardai would focus on the portrayal of Scudder's recovery.

Other critics, such as Donna R. Casella and Landon C. Burns analyze the reasons for Scudder's alcoholism. These approaches reflect a desire to examine the ways in which Scudder differs from other hardboiled detectives. This study examines both the individuality of the character and the ways in which the series uses some of the same assumptions and patterns as its predecessors in regard to alcohol.

Lawrence Block, James Crumley, and James Lee Burke are three contemporary writers of hard-boiled fiction mentioned by George Wedge in the entry on alcohol in *The Oxford Companion. to Crime and Mystery Writing*. Wedge calls *When the Sacred Ginmill Closes* "the most penetrating study in the twentieth century of the private eye as recovering alcoholic" (*Oxford Companion* 11). Wedge has also written two reviews of the Scudder novels for *Dionysos*, a journal which focuses on intoxication in literature. "An Unlicensed PI in AA" reviews the Scudder novels through *A Ticket to the Boneyard*. Wedge notes that Scudder hit bottom in *A Stab in the Dark* (1981), the fourth in the series. Wedge concludes that there are two major tensions, in addition to the detection of the killer, in the next volume, *Eight Million Ways to Die* (1982). Both tensions concern the transformation of character: the question of whether the cultured and sensitive Chance will continue as a pimp or find a more suitable way of life, and the question of whether Scudder will admit that he is an alcoholic and begin the process of recovery ("Unlicensed" 25).

In respect to both questions we are given only a glimpse of the future, as Chance considers using his personal collection of African art to begin a career as an art dealer, and Scudder admits his alcoholism for the first time at an AA meeting and breaks into tears. In *A Ticket to the Boneyard* Wedge sees Scudder forced to confront questionable actions he took during his drinking past when a killer is released from prison. Because Scudder had been unable to discover enough admissible evidence of the crimes he knew the man had committed, he framed him for something he had not done. The ex-convict sets out to punish Scudder for having set him up by killing any woman he has had a connection with. As Wedge puts it, "drinking life has come home to roost, the life in which expediency justified bad means to a good end." Speaking of *Eight Million Ways to Die*, *When the Sacred Ginmill Closes*, *Out on the Cutting Edge*, and *A Ticket to the Boneyard*, Wedge calls them "essays at a mid-life *bildungsroman*, for alcoholics are often seen as cases of arrested development" ("Unlicensed" 29–30).

In a later article in *Dionysos*, Wedge reviews *A Dance at the Slaughterhouse*, *A Walk Among the Tombstones* and some short stories. In these books he finds "'tenderness,' Matt's sad but dogged devotion to what is right, and his perplexed, meditative attempts to figure out, in difficult circumstances, just what right may be" (30). For instance, is it right to use the resourcefulness of TJ, the black street kid, in ways that may endanger him? Is it right to use the hacking skills of the two computer whiz kids known as the Kongs when they set up free long distance service on his phone? Is it right to work for a known drug dealer whose wife has been murdered? Is it right to let the dealer's brother, an alcoholic and heroin addict, live with despair that leads him to suicide? Wedge comments that Scudder's frequent recourse to AA meetings is not mere interlude, but necessary regeneration as Scudder works on such issues. Wedge summarizes, "these novels are about growth in recovery, the things that change and the things that stay the same when a detective ... becomes sober" ("Matt Scudder: Fighting the Good Fight" 32).

David Geherin, in *The American Private Eye*, notes that alcohol is never used for comic effect in the Scudder novels and that Scudder's drinking becomes increasingly serious as the series progresses, with the detective awakening after binges to find that he has lost memories to alcoholic blackouts (192). In *The Sins of the Fathers*, Geherin finds a contrast between Scudder's excessive drinking and the hypocrisy of the Reverend Vanderpoel, who is a teetotaler but who has committed the worse sins of murder and disloyalty (81). Similarly, Barry Gardner, in an entry in the *St. James Guide to Crime and Mystery Writers*, notes of the later novels that Scudder "never forgets (nor are readers allowed to) that the central fact of his existence is alcohol and its daily absence" (87).

While AA is, in fact, mentioned in every Scudder novel, including the most recent, *Hope to Die* (2001), the theme is not stressed as much in this book as in earlier works. Only once does Scudder feel a sudden strong urge for a drink, when he meets his grown sons at a bar after the funeral of his ex-wife, whom he has not seen for years (30). We learn that he continues to attend AA meetings, though not as regularly as in the past, and that he has not sought out a replacement for his sponsor, who was murdered in an earlier episode (19). But Scudder's exposition of his daily life, with concerts, dining out, quiet evenings with his wife Elaine, and continued interaction with his surrogate son TJ, makes it clear that his life has achieved a greater breadth than Gardner's comment would suggest.

Donna R. Casella, writing in *Clues*, "The Matt Scudder Series: the Saga of an Alcoholic Hardboiled Detective," takes a psychological approach to Scudder's problems. She cites the Jungian view that alcoholism results from a search for wholeness, an attempt to reconcile sides of one's personality not fully acknowledged. Casella also sees an interaction between the hard-boiled settings of the novels and Scudder's alcohol use. The hard-boiled world is one of bars, cheap hotels and sordid crimes. It is the world that makes Scudder wonder why anyone would want to stay sober in New York. There is a sense in which this gloom drives the detective to drink. But drink is also his entree into the hard-boiled world; the people who hire Scudder and the people he needs to talk to in order to solve crimes are often to be found in bars. An example Casella could have given is that one of Matt's main informants through the years has been Danny Boy Bell, an albino African-American who can only be located sitting in a favorite club, drinking ice-cold imported vodka and retailing information. Casella seems uncertain whether to regard Scudder's environment as a causal factor in his drinking or as what dependency professionals call an "alcoholic alibi." Interestingly, Block mentions the concept of an alcoholic alibi, although without the label, when he discusses with Bulow the supposed relationship between drink and the writing profession. When Bulow gives the argument that writers may be prone to alcoholism because the profession is a lonely one, Block suggests that the excuse is just that:

> LB   I've heard a variety of people from various occupations talk about how this applies to them. A house painter says, "Of course house painters have to drink. It's part of the job description." You know—but, of course, librarians have to drink.
> EB   Cops. Any stressful occupation, I suppose.
> LB   Yeah, right. Or non-stress [Block and Bulow 41].

Casella refers repeatedly to the idea that Scudder drinks because he is questioning his role as a hard-boiled detective. However, her reading seems to betray a lack of background in the genre when she says, "Unlike other hardboiled detectives, he doesn't perceive his role as fixing society's moral fabric" (37). Yet it is a given of the genre that the hard-boiled detective can never mend society, that the problems he confronts are too deeply rooted and too comprehensive for any one man (or woman) to fix. Or, as Scudder explains to Willa Rossiter in *Out on the Cutting Edge*, that most wrongs are never righted, that the dragons are the ones in the castles and that he can't get close enough to slay them (120). The hard-boiled detective can only apply his own code to the situations he confronts, discover some criminals, exonerate some innocents and hope that his actions serve justice in the isolated instances that constitute his cases. Casella asserts:

> The detective's relationship to the code is an attempt at personality wholeness; it also helps the reader define and understand the hardboiled detective. Scudder has no such set of rules governing his behavior, because his relationship with alcoholism replaces a relationship with the code. He is playing in a hardboiled world without a code and that bothers him; so he wonders about what is right and wrong and who he is in terms of those questions [39].

She cites dependency counselor Jean Fortune in giving a list of personality traits common in alcoholics: anxiousness, impulsiveness, negative mental outlook, low tolerance level, defiance, grandiosity, perfectionism (39–40). Casella refers to scenes from the novels in which Scudder uses alcohol to assuage a generalized anxiety and other instances in which grandiosity and perfectionism lead him to feelings of moral superiority over criminals. For instance, she maintains that there was no need for Scudder to force suicide on Reverend Vanderpoel in *The Sins of the Fathers*, since the law would have taken care of him. She attributes Scudder's action in this case as well as his punishment of a young mugger by breaking his fingers to "the intensity of his superiority and his own physical aggressiveness" (Casella 42).

While it is easy to accept that the maiming of the mugger is a product of aggression, one can interpret Scudder's action toward the Vanderpoel in a more charitable light. If the police investigate and confirm that Vanderpoel killed Wendy Hanniford, his entire life will be made a mockery. He has been a respected minister, but will be revealed as having carried on a sexual liaison with the woman he believed to be his son's lover and as having been unable to remove himself from this relationship without killing her. Further, the world, including his congregation, will learn that he is a coward who let his son take the blame for his crime, leading the young man to self-destruction. Scudder offers him the choice of dying privately with his sins left secret, and he takes advantage of that offer, apparently coming to agree that he would be extremely foolish not to (*The Sins of the Fathers* 183).

While Casella raises interesting points about alcoholic traits in Scudder's personality, her analysis seems confused. Speaking of the now sober Scudder of *When the Sacred Ginmill Closes*, she claims: "His struggle to find and understand whether he has a moral code is gone." But she later asserts that "He is no longer violent, angry or morally superior; he is not confused over a moral code because he has found one" (47–48). Yet in this novel Scudder is specifically recounting events of ten years in the past. Even without the process of recovery from alcohol, it would not be surprising if he had gained a detachment from the events and an ability to question his past actions.

Casella published "The Matt Scudder Series" in 1993, but she treats no works beyond *When the Sacred Ginmill Closes*, published in 1986. She apparently feels that the Scudder of this volume is the Scudder who will continue to appear. However, *A Dance at the Slaughterhouse* disabuses readers of the notion that a sober Scudder has left violence, anger, and moral superiority behind. In this novel Scudder discovers the identities of a man and wife who are thrill killers. They have killed at least five people and will probably kill again. Yet he cannot provide enough evidence to even bring the police into the investigation of the snuff film that initiated his search. His solution is to ally himself with Irish gangster Mick Ballou in a raid on the couple's hidden stronghold, telling Ballou that there will be at least $50,000 on the premises. Scudder participates in the raid, shooting the woman three times after Ballou has killed the man with a cleaver. Scudder later explains his actions to his AA sponsor, Jim Faber: "Because I just plain wanted them dead, ... and I just flat out wanted to be the sonofabitch who did it to them" (203). These are hardly the words or deeds of a man who has left violence behind, although he assures Faber that he does not intend to make a habit of it and is as good as his word in the next volume, *A Walk Among the Tombstones*, when he refuses to participate in the execution of another two sexual predators.

Landon C. Burns argues in "Matthew Scudder's Moral Ambiguity" that Casella reverses cause and effect in her argument that Scudder cannot develop a code because of his alcoholism. Burns maintains that "Scudder is an alcoholic because he lives in a world that makes a mockery of any code that could be devised" (23). Burns calls the "random and unjustified death" of Estrellita Rivera "an objective correlative for Scudder's sense of an existential world where nothing is certain, where society is powerless to stem the rising flood of violence, where the best intentions end in totally unpredictable bad results" (20–21). In the absence of a code Scudder must wrestle with each moral issue as it comes up, devising ad hoc solutions to the quandaries presented by his cases. Burns sees two levels to Scudder's moral ambiguity. First, there is his willingness to transgress conventional ideas of right and wrong, for instance in bribing police officer friends for access to confidential files, or in having an outlaw for a best friend, a teenage Times Square hustler for an assistant, and a call girl for a lover (and later wife). His choice of clients also displays an ambiguous attitude about who is deserving of help, including "blackmailers, pimps, and drug dealers. In each of these cases, however, there has been something that overrides his distaste for the man's vocation—although he says, in fact, he prefers to take money from people he doesn't like" (25–26).

Burns is disturbed by the instances in which Scudder seems to be playing god, using the end to justify the means. Like Casella, he finds one such instance in Scudder's treatment of Reverend Vanderpoel. He also cites the similar action taken against an ambitious political figure in *Time to Murder and Create*. Concluding that one of Huysendahl's staff killed the man who was blackmailing him, like the knights who killed Thomas Beckett, Scudder threatens to turn over the blackmail material (photos of Huysendahl engaged in sex with boys) to the press unless Huysendahl renounces his plans to run for governor. And, in *When the Sacred Ginmill Closes*, Scudder plants evidence to convict Tom Tillary of a murder he did not commit. Burns sees such "violations of the most basic tenets of traditional moral philosophy" as evidence that Scudder lives in an existential world, a godless world like that of Camus' *The Plague*. Burns concedes that neither Vanderpoel nor Huysendahl was forced to do as Scudder suggests; they could have taken their chances with the police and public opinion. Burns finds the case of Tillary more problematic. Scudder discovers that Tillary, whom he has helped clear of suspicion that he murdered his wife, had actually committed the crime, but he has no evidence that would stand up in court and the police regard the case as closed. So when Tillary's girlfriend calls Scudder to tell him that she is committing suicide because Tillary has dumped her and had her fired from her job, Scudder goes to her apartment, makes the suicide look like homicide and frames Tillary for the crime. Burns maintains that the fact that Scudder recalls and recounts the case shows that he is still bothered by his actions. A much firmer case for Scudder's regret over past actions is made in the examination of *A Ticket to the Boneyard*. In this case Scudder admits that not having played by the rules in getting Leo Motley sent to prison is the cause of Motley's vengeance campaign once he is released. Burns concludes his analysis of Scudder's moral ambiguity by calling Block's theme "the fragility, absurdity and moral uncertainty of the age" and claiming that his novels are "about the plight of a courageous man in an existential world" (30).

Charles Ardai, in his article on Block in *Mystery and Suspense Writers*, sees the chronicle of Scudder's career as composed of five periods. Dealing with the works up to *A Long Line of Dead Men* (1994), the twelfth book in the series, Ardai divides the novels into four trilogies and one book that does not fit into a group. The first trilogy—*The Sins of the Fathers, Time to Murder and Create*, and *In the Midst of Death*—presents a ragged anti-hero traumatized by encounters with the "arbitrary hurtful nature of Block's universe." Scudder has abandoned family, career, home and sobriety and "plays God in a world desperately lacking God's attention" (76). The second trilogy, written after Block quit drinking, is composed of *A Stab in the Dark, Eight Million Ways to Die* and *When the Sacred Ginmill Closes*. In *A Stab in the Dark* Scudder attends his first AA meeting, but flees before it gets underway. In *Eight Million Ways to Die*, he attends more meetings before being able, finally, to speak aloud of his alcoholism and begin the road to recovery. In *When the Sacred Ginmill Closes* Scudder is sober, looking back on an earlier period of his life with a clarity he was incapable of at the time. *Out on the Cutting Edge* is the first account of a case undertaken after Scudder is sober and Ardai finds it not of a piece with others before or after (77). In the third trilogy Block turns to a new type of villain, the serial sex sadist, and Scudder confronts his own taste for violence and appetite for blood. In *A Dance at the Slaugh-*

terhouse he eagerly embraces the role of executioner. In *A Walk Among the Tombstones*, he retreats from the role. He helps rescue a kidnapped girl from the killers but leaves their execution to the husband of an earlier victim. Ardai defines the fourth trilogy as a period of gradual recovery. *A Long Line of Dead Men*, *The Devil Knows You're Dead* and *Even the Wicked* tell of Scudder's marriage to Elaine, his acquisition of a private investigator's license, his continued relationship with TJ, and even the surrender of his hotel room. The "theme of this trilogy," says Ardia, "is how one confronts mortality and prepares for death" (78). Ardai's analysis was published in 1998 and therefore does not deal with *Everybody Dies* and *Hope to Die*, the most recent books in the series. While his analysis of the first three trilogies seems well supported, the final trilogy is not so much a preparation for death as for life. Scudder formalizes his long term relationship with Elaine Mardell, the former call girl who re-entered his life in *A Ticket to the Boneyard*. Together they serve as surrogate parents to TJ, who works for Elaine in her antique shop when he is not doing investigative chores for Scudder. And by making a gift of his hotel room to TJ, Scudder closes a door on the isolated person he had become while in the grip of alcohol, fully committing himself to his life with Elaine.

The question of whether alcohol affects Scudder's adherence to the hard-boiled code can only be determined in association with an analysis of the form the code takes for Scudder. Casella sees an absence: "What is missing in Scudder is a hardboiled code, a set of rules based on what is perceived as right or wrong." Moreover, as cited above, she blames this lack on Scudder's alcoholism, stating that the relationship with alcoholism replaces one with the code (38–39). In a somewhat similar vein, Gardner claims: "The capacity for passing moral judgments upon his fellow human beings has been lost or discarded by Scudder somewhere along the way; his best friend is a murderous criminal, his lady a one-time call girl" (87). Geherin notes that Scudder is cynical and non-idealistic, particularly with regard to police work, and that as a police officer he took his share of graft. Scudder does, however, adhere to the principle that murder is wrong and that society suffers if it is not punished. This principle sometimes leads him to the conclusion that it is permissible to do the wrong thing for the right reason, as when he will frame for another crime a person guilty of an unprovable murder (*American Private Eye* 193–94). Wedge has a more charitable view of Scudder, calling him "not a hero, just a good guy with a sometimes dirty job to do" ("Good Fight" 29).

Block himself comments on the idea that the detective is a man with a code. After mentioning a fictional detective who talks with his girlfriend about the code he follows, Block tells Bulow:

the idea is clear that the private detective has his particular morality all worked out, and that way he knows what he likes and doesn't like and what he'll do and won't do.... I don't know a lot of people with a clear code like that—of any sort. Scudder makes it up as he goes along. That's what I do. That's what most of the people I know do, one way or another. There may be some underlying precepts there, but figuring out what to do next is the chief challenge we're given in this life. So I think Scudder makes it up as he goes along and he isn't necessarily bothered by the things we're brought up to be bothered by [Block and Bulow 82].

Here Block seems to be disclaiming the sort of self-consciousness about behavior displayed by Parker writing about Spenser. In contrast to Spenser's explanations to Susan either of why his code required that he take a particular course of action or his concern that his actions have violated the code, Scudder's discussions tend to take the form of reminiscing to a companion about a past action that he cannot clearly justify and still questions. For example, in *The Sins of the Fathers* he tells a woman friend about a case, when he was still a policeman, in which he and his partner were sure that a man had committed a murder but could not prove it since the polygraph the suspect failed was not admissible in court. Because the man has a history of violence toward women, the partners believe he will eventually kill again and debate ways to prevent this. Scudder's solution is to borrow narcotics from a friend on the vice squad and frame the man for drug possession. He muses:

"Did we have a right to set him up? I couldn't see letting him walk around free, and what other way was there to nail him? But if we couldn't do that, did we have right to put him in a river? That's a harder one for me to answer. I have a lot of trouble with that one. There must be a line there somewhere, and it's hard to know just where to draw it" [159].

Scudder's moral quandaries usually revolve around a conflict between law and justice; not necessarily between justice and the way the law is written, but the way it works in practice, as when a criminal goes free because key evidence is ruled inadmissible or a witness refuses to testify. His solutions are, as Burns says, "ad hoc" in nature, although this author does not believe that Scudder's world is as existential as Burns believes it to be.

Scudder's code of ethics is extremely personal. As Geherin states, Scudder accepted a certain amount of corruption when he was on the police force—such as free drinks or meals at establishments that welcome an unofficial police presence. He also takes for granted that favors must be paid for. Whenever he needs access to police resources he suggests that a friend on the force needs a new hat, code for twenty-five dollars, or a new suit, code for one hundred dollars.

In *A Walk Among the Tombstones*, Scudder jokes with his friend Joe Durkin about committing a class D felony, and even cites the code section for bribery in the third degree (62). In exchange for these bribes he may get the opportunity to browse through a case file, check the stolen automobile list for a license plate he is trying to trace or learn the physical location of a particular telephone number. For the later purpose he will sometimes use his knowledge of police procedure to obtain the information from a telephone operator by using a false name and badge number. However, he will seldom, if ever, pose as a police officer in person, though he may not go out of his way to correct a witness who merely assumes that his inquiries are official. We are never told explicitly why he makes this distinction, but we may assume that it is self-protective. The telephone is anonymous (or was before the advent of caller ID) and he is unlikely to be charged with the crime of impersonating an officer, whereas to do so in person would be much more risky. Recalling his terminology in explaining himself to Hanniford as one who is like a priest who has lost the faith, Scudder perhaps finds something a little sacrilegious in claiming a form of respect to which he is no longer entitled.

Scudder explains part of his logic concerning accepting money and favors in *The Sins of the Fathers*. He has just interviewed Lewis Pankow, the young officer who arrested Richard Vanderpoel, probing for details that were not in the official report. Pankow is hesitant to take the twenty-five dollars Scudder is offering him, and Scudder admonishes him:

> "Stupid. This isn't graft. It's clean money. You did somebody a favor and made a couple of bucks for it.... Listen to me.... Nobody's going to want you in a car with him if you've got the wrong kind of reputation.... If you don't take money when someone puts it in your hand you're going to make a lot of people very nervous. You don't have to be a crook. Certain kinds of money you can turn down. And you don't have to walk the streets with your hand out. But you've got to play the game with the cards they give" [30].

Later in the same novel Scudder expresses surprise that Rick's sleeping pills are still in the apartment, remarking that "Cops are apt to pocket them, and men who would not take loose cash from the dead have trouble resisting the little pills that pick you up or settle you down (78). On the other hand, Scudder tells an acquaintance in *Eight Million Ways to Die* of his first experience responding to a death in a SRO hotel:

> "...my partner went though the dead man's belongings, scooping up the little cash he had to his name, counting it deliberately and dividing it with me.... 'What do you think happens to it otherwise? Somebody else takes it. Or it goes to the state.' ... Later on, I was the one who ... counted and divided their leavings" [144].

We also learn that Scudder has occasionally turned a blind eye to low-level criminal activity. As he tells Jacob "Spinner" Jablon, a small-time grifter in *Time to Murder and Create*, "You know I used to take. I let you buy your way out of a collar or two, for Christ's sake" (15). For Scudder, the line between clean graft and dirty graft seems to resemble that between victim and victimless crime. No one is hurt if a bartender gives a police officer a free beer after work. Equally, no one, except the perpetrator, is hurt if Scudder views a crime file or checks the stolen car list and gets a lead that helps solve the case, especially since he usually takes a completed case to the police in charge of the investigation so that they can make the arrest and have the credit for clearing a case.

When police officers like the young Scudder and his partner have the unsavory task of removing a decomposing corpse from a hotel room, there is no harm done if they divide the small amount of cash left by the deceased, who is unlikely to have heirs. They know that anything left behind in the room will probably be seized by the building management or whoever else enters next, and if the money is turned over to the authorities, it goes to the state, an abstract concept to the men who are doing the state's dirty work. In other words, clean graft does not interfere in any substantial way with the duty of the police to protect the public.

If Ardai sees *Out on the Cutting Edge* as not of a piece with the works before or after it, perhaps it is because Scudder is much harder on his past in this volume than in others. In contrast to the cleaned up view of his police history offered in both earlier and later volumes, Scudder admits to a fellow AA member that he was a dirty cop:

> "I didn't actually shake people down and I didn't overlook homicides, but I took money and that's not what they hired me to do. It was illegal. It was crooked.
>
> "And I did other things. For Christ's sake, I was a thief. I stole. One time I was investigating a break-in and there was a cigar box next to the cash register that the burglar had somehow missed, and there was close to a thousand dollars in it. I took it and put it in my pocket. I figured the owner'd be covered by insurance, or else it was money he was skimming, in which case I was just stealing from a thief. I had it rationalized, but you can't get around the fact that I was taking money that wasn't mine" [70].

Scudder continues in this vein, mentioning the actions such as taking money from the dead and sending people to prison for crimes they did not commit that are also discussed in other books. Significantly, Eddie, the small-time criminal to whom Scudder is explaining the AA Fifth Step (moral inventory), is unsurprised by his revelations and responds, "Cops do that kind of shit all the time" (70).

The New York of *Out on the Cutting Edge* seems almost like a third world country. Scudder describes a beggar who "looked as though she belonged in Calcutta" (69). Later, when he is checking government records for evidence that Willa owns the buildings she manages, he comments:

> I had to shell out a few dollars here and there in order to get my hands on it. New York is like that, and a sizable percentage of the people who work for the local government regard their salaries as a sort of base they get in return for reporting to work every morning. If they actually do anything, they expect to be paid extra for it.... It must baffle people from out of town, although those who've lived in Arab countries probably find it familiar and comprehensible [228–29].

Scudder even tells a cover story for Paula Hoeldtke's death that sounds like something that would happen abroad. Unwilling to tell her parents the truth, that a gangster she had been involved with killed her and fed her body to the hogs on Mick Ballou's farm, he constructs a tale of her boating with friends when drug runners kill them and steal the boat to use in smuggling. He even adds that this new piracy is a big problem in the Caribbean.

Out on the Cutting Edge is also the book in which Scudder begins his curious relationship with Mick Ballou, a relationship that originates with his suspicions that Ballou had ordered Eddie Dunphy killed before he could reveal anything about Ballou's operations to an outsider. Instead Ballou solves Paula's disappearance and kills the man responsible.

Scudder's initial relationship with Elaine Mardell was also based on what most would regard as police corruption:

> I did for her the things a cop could do for someone in her position—warned off a predatory pimp, put the fear of God into a drunk client who was giving her a hard time, and, when another client was ungracious enough to drop dead in her bed, I dumped the body where it could do no harm to his reputation, or to hers. I did cop things for her and she did call-girl things for me [*A Dance at the Slaughterhouse* 52].

Although he never says so in so many words, Scudder treats prostitution as a victimless crime. There will always be customers, there will always be women ready to supply the service. As Chance remarks in reference to Kim's desire to leave the business, "If she had any notion how easily she can be replaced she'd most likely hang herself" (*Eight Million Ways to Die* 39).

There are forms of corruption beyond the pale for Scudder. He would not take drug money when on the force and continues to display a distaste for the business. In *A Walk Among the Tombstones* he agrees to work for drug dealer Kenan Khoury, whose wife has been kidnapped, killed, and dismembered, largely because his belief that murder should be punished overrides his disgust concerning drug trafficking. However, he draws a clear line, telling Kenan, "I can't work for you or with you as far as your profession is concerned" (199).

Since Scudder regards murder as the most serious of crimes, he is livid at the idea that a killer could buy off detectives investigating homicide. In *Time to Murder and Create*, Scudder searches for the killer of a blackmailer who has his own idea of fair-dealing. Spinner is collecting from three victims and fears one is trying to kill him. If he is killed he believes the other two victims should be off the hook and their secrets remain concealed, because they have held to the agreement they made with him. This would not happen if the police did the investigation. Not only is there the general possibility of leaks to the press inherent in any public investigation, there is also the possibility that a corrupt policeman would use the evidence Spinner has collected to set himself up as the blackmailer. Therefore, Spinner hires Scudder and gives him an envelope to be opened only in case of his unexplained death. When Spinner is found dead in the river Scudder decides to flush out the killer by letting each blackmail victim think that he has taken over the operation. When the former boyfriend of one of the victims tries to kill Scudder, he concludes that the same man had also killed Spinner in collusion with the victim, who is now married to a wealthy man. Scudder is outraged when the investigating officer tells him there is no basis on which to hold the woman: "What did it cost her to buy out of a murder charge? I always heard you could wash homicide if you had enough cash." The officer is equally angry at the accusation but acknowledges that "you would have to figure it that way" before explaining that the boyfriend had an alibi for the time of Spinner's death: he was in jail in California (171–72). The entire exchange, as well as Scudder's willingness to make himself a target to find a murderer, confirms Spinner's intuition in selecting Scudder for his avenger: "there's always the chance you'll just put it [a $3000 payment] in your pocket and shitcan the rest of the stuff, which if it happens I'll be dead and won't know about it. Why I think you'll follow though is something I noticed about you a long time ago, namely that you happen to think there is a difference between murder and other crimes" (27). And true to Spinner's intuition, Scudder is the only person to care, for his police contact comments, "who wants to bust their balls finding out what happened to an asshole like the Spinner. So he's dead, so nobody's gonna cry for him.... He was a cheap little crook. Whoever bumped him did the world a favor" (21). As it turns out, Scudder is unable to locate and punish the actual killer, but he does insure that the man on whose behalf the killing was done does not benefit.

Scudder's concern that murder be punished is not logical, as Reverend Vanderpoel points out in *The Sins of the Fathers*. Told by Scudder that if he does not commit suicide the evidence that he killed Wendy Hanniford will be turned over to the police, Vanderpoel asserts that since he will never kill anyone again he does not constitute a danger to society. Scudder replies, "It's bad for society when murders remain unpunished." Vanderpoel objects that no one will know that he committed suicide because of his guilt. Scudder responds that he will know (181). Similarly, no one other than Scudder will ever know that Tillary was punished for the cold-blooded murder of his wife rather than the supposed lover's-quarrel killing of his girlfriend for which he is convicted of manslaughter. Nor will the public know that a popular political figure who seemed to be on the fast track for the governor's office dropped his ambitions because a staff member believed those ambitions were more important than the life of a blackmailer and Scudder decides that threatening to use the blackmail materials to put an end to those ambitions is a just punishment for a man who can inspire such a belief in his followers.

In none of these cases can Scudder claim that he is protecting the public from further violence by dissuading others from doing likewise. Nor is he preventing further crimes by these particular persons. Reverend Vanderpoel is not likely to become a scourge of the underworld, slashing to death randomly chosen prostitutes in a fit of religious mania. Nor is Tommy Tillary likely to kill again; his wife is dead and he has the money for which he killed her. And Huysendahl is not a demagogue planning to send black-shirted staff members into the streets to pave the way for his political ambitions. It is an abstract idea of justice that is being served.

If the conviction that murder is a crime that cries out for punishment is one of Scudder's virtues, tenacity is another. Several times in the series others comment that he hangs onto a case like a bulldog, that he just keeps picking away until he finds something, and that once he gets his teeth in a problem he won't let go. In *Even the Wicked*, Adrian Whitfield, a lawyer friend of Scudder's, apparently relies on this quality. Whitfield is dying of cancer. A popular newspaper columnist has bemoaned the release of a child killer whose trial was beset by evidence ruled inadmissible and whose partner, the sole witness against him, committed suicide before testifying. Whitfield first writes an anonymous letter to the columnist stating that the "will of the people" will serve as a backup for a defective justice system, then kills the man. Then he denounces and kills several other people who have gained notoriety by beating the system: a Mafia don who is accused of many crimes but never convicted, and an anti-abortion activist whose rhetoric encourages the murder of doctors but who carefully disclaims any intent to incite such crimes. A black racist also on his list is killed by one of his own followers for adultery with the man's wife. Finally, Whitfield addresses an accusatory letter to himself and enlists Scudder to protect him. Scudder advises him to hire a security firm, which he does. He then commits suicide by poison, in a locked room alone with his bodyguard, letting it appear that the vigilante killer has reached him despite all precautions.

The autopsy reveals the cancer and his personal physician confirms that he had been told that he had less than a year to live. Scudder continues to investigate and eventually determines that Whitfield committed the earlier murders. Scudder concludes that, since Whitfield was obviously not in real fear of becoming a victim of murder, he must have hired him with the intention that the truth eventually be revealed. Scudder muses to Elaine, "He alluded to my tendency to stay with a case. Stubbornness, you could call it." Elaine concludes: "He wanted you to solve it. He didn't want to leave loose ends. He wanted to baffle everybody, he wanted the audience holding its breath when the curtain went down. But then, after a decent interval, he wants a chance to come out and take a bow. And that's where you come in" (205). Scudder is not convinced that the explanation makes sense, but it seems that Block expects the reader to agree with Elaine.

Allied to this stubbornness is an unwillingness to give less than full value to a client, even one like Spinner who will not benefit in any real way. Scudder occasionally claims that it is easier to take money from someone he doesn't like: "I had no reason to dislike this man [Hanniford]. I have always felt more comfortable taking money from men I dislike" (*The Sins of the Fathers* 4).

The implication is that he will then not feel badly about doing a poor job, but in fact he gives full value to every client. Ironically, this sometimes works to the disadvantage of the client, as when Tommy Tillary makes the mistake of hiring Scudder to help establish his innocence when he is actually guilty. The case is closed, because one suspect is dead, the other has accepted a plea bargain, and there is no concrete evidence. When Scudder presents his suspicions to the police he is told that even if Tillary is guilty no one has the time or the desire to reopen a case that will be too complex to present to a jury. Confronted with Scudder's deductions and after virtually admitting that they are correct, Tillary tells him, "All we got tonight is booze talking, your booze and my booze, two bottles of whiskey talkin' to each other. That's all. Morning comes, we can forget everything was said here tonight. I didn't kill anybody, you didn't say I did, everything's cool, we're still buddies. Right? Right?" (*When the Sacred Ginmill Closes* 250). But Scudder does not forget, and when the opportunity is presented by the suicide of Tillary's callously discarded girlfriend he sets Tillary up for a manslaughter charge. Tillary is sent to prison and killed later by another inmate, so justice is served indirectly (259).

Examinations of Scudder's ethics in the later books inevitably lead to discussions of his unlikely friendship with Mick Ballou. Ballou, the son of an Irish woman and a French father, owns and operates a bar called Grogan's Open House. His actual source of income, however, is a variety of criminal enterprises: hijacking truckloads of valuable merchandise, operating as a loan shark, and occasionally robbing other criminals, such as drug dealers, who have the advantage as victims that they cannot go to the police. Scudder and Ballou seem very unlike, but a relationship develops in which they occasionally spend a night sitting in the closed bar exchanging stories as Ballou drinks fine Irish whiskey and Scudder matches him with coffee or Coke. Scudder's AA sponsor is concerned that he spends time so close to the temptation offered by a bar; his police friends do not understand how he can be friends with a known criminal "an animal oughta be in a cage," as Joe Durkin says (*Out on the Cutting Edge* 192). Scudder himself regards it as one of those inexplicable relations between people.

Ballou and Scudder do share some qualities. Ballou despises drugs and refuses to sell them even if they fall into his hands as part of another crime. He has killed, and does not conceal the fact, even admitting a certain joy in such acts. "But you don't kill for no good reason. You don't make up reasons to give yourself an excuse to shed blood," he tells Scudder, explaining his anger with his bartender Neil for Paula's murder. Paula overheard details of a job Ballou's gang had carried out and Ballou told Neil to send her home to Indiana, where no one would find an opportunity to question her. But Neil used the excuse to kill her instead, first making love to her, then knifing her in cold blood. This is the sort of thrill killing for which Ballou has no tolerance (*Out on the Cutting Edge* 224). He has his own code of ethics as well, telling Scudder in *A Dance at the Slaughterhouse* of a time he prevented an employee from raping a woman they had come to kill. He understands that the man thought it was a shame to waste an opportunity, but he rebels at the idea, cynically adding, "why not roast her liver and eat it, why let the flesh go to waste?" He and Scudder share a certain dark view of life, the major difference being that Scudder has abandoned the alcohol that Ballou finds necessary: "I don't know how you get through it on fucking coffee, I swear I don't" (169–170).

As in the scene cited above, Ballou appears to be a character who treats alcohol as a form of self-medication for the ills of the world. In a later passage he compares whiskey to the smoked glass necessary to look at the sun during an eclipse: "Isn't it as dangerous to see life straight on? And don't you need this smoky stuff to make it safe to look at?" (176). Scudder's police acquaintances also use alcohol to numb themselves on occasion. In *Eight Million Ways to Die* Scudder and Detective Joe Durkin go to a bar to discuss the dead-end investigation of Kim's murder. Durkin orders a double vodka, drinks part of it and says, "Aw, Jesus, that helps. It really helps" (111). They sit for several hours discussing the increasing level of violence in the city and the inability of the police to stem the tide. Eventually Durkin becomes angry with Scudder for not drinking, accusing him of feeling superior (123). Years later in *A Dance at the Slaughterhouse* Scudder and Durkin meet again in a bar to discuss a case gone wrong. Durkin has viewed the tape of the snuff film that started Scudder on an investigation of the Stettners. But since the figures are hooded and masked on the tape and the identity of the victim is unknown, the district attorney's office declares there is no case, not even cause for further investigation. Reminded by Scudder that they have "a visual record of two people committing murder," Durkin replies, "Right. That's what I saw and that's what I can't get out of my fucking head and that's why I'm drinking bad whiskey in the worst shithole in town" (242).

It would be easy to assume that Scudder's abuse of alcohol began as self-medication for the pain of having killed Estrellita. But evidence suggests that he was already a problem drinker before the crucial incident. In *Eight Million Ways to Die* he meditates that it has been fifteen to twenty years since he went as much as a week without drinking (61). This predates by many years the bar robbery in which Estrellita was killed. In addition, the fact that he was drinking in a bar after work instead of going home to his family in Long Island suggests a pre-existing problem. After Scudder becomes sober, alcohol for self-medication is ruled out. Instead he attends AA meetings. As late as *Even the Wicked*, when he has been sober about fifteen years, he comments:

> My attendance at AA wanes and waxes with the tides in my life. I go less often when I'm busier with other things, and seem to add meetings automatically in response to the promptings of stress, which I may or may not consciously feel…. The thought did come to me that I'd been sober for too many years to need so many meetings and I told the thought to go to hell. The fucking disease almost killed me, and the last thing I ever want to do is give it another chance [139].

Clearly AA meetings have taken over the self-medication function in Scudder's life.

Scudder does not often set out to use alcohol to coerce information from people. However, he is not above taking advantage when the opportunity is afforded. For instance, in *A Dance at the Slaughterhouse* he has been following Richard Thurman on the suspicion that Thurman helped kill his wife, rather than being the innocent victim of an interrupted burglary turned to rape and homicide. Alerted that Thurman is at a nearby bar he casually makes his acquaintance, pretending to be drinking to fit the mood of the already intoxicated Thurman. Although nothing comes directly from that meeting it leads to another in which Thurman admits the killing and discloses his fear that the Stettners, who urged him to kill his wife and helped in the commission of the crime, are now planning to eliminate him. In any such session before he became sober Scudder was likely to be drinking as much as his informants, and though he may have benefited from their loss of inhibition the situation would not have been as calculated as when the Continental Op feels glad that Brand has missed the table with her glass or when Marlowe brings a bottle to Florian's house.

Hospitality is less of an issue with Block than it is for Chandler. Since Scudder usually meets clients in a bar or coffee shop the issue of being offered a drink is often moot. Either party can wave down a waitress or walk to the bar for a refill. In a courtesy that may be allied with hospitality, those who know he is abstinent sometimes ask permission before drinking in front of him, as Khoury does in *A Walk Among the Tombstones* (32), and he routinely gives permission. Scudder does refuse any refreshment from those whom he visits with an ultimatum. Reverend Vanderpoel offers Scudder coffee at his second visit, but Scudder, who is about to accuse Vanderpoel of the murder of Wendy Hanniford, declines. Similarly, when Scudder returns to Huysendahl's office to tell him that he has deduced that a member of Huysendahl's staff was responsible for Spinner's murder he refuses a drink, even though he is still drinking at this point in his life. Since he intends to use the blackmail materials to pressure Huysendahl to end his political career, it would be inappropriate to accept the man's hospitality.

On a slightly different note in *When the Sacred Ginmill Closes*, Scudder is drinking with Tillary when he comes to the realization that Tillary is really guilty of the murder of his wife: "I picked up my glass. Then I remembered he had bought the drink, and I started to put it down. I decided that was ridiculous. Just as money knows no owner, whiskey never remembers who paid for it" (248). Of course, this is the actively alcoholic Scudder speaking, not the sober Scudder who recalls the incident. The hospitality-related issue of giving offense by refusing to drink with a man arises during Scudder's first meeting with Ballou. Ballou asks, "You don't drink at all, or you don't drink with me?" and is mollified when Scudder replies that he doesn't drink at all (*Out on the Cutting Edge* 178). Since Scudder has already asked for coffee or a Coke, it is clear that it is specifically the refusal to drink alcohol with a companion that is seen as potentially insulting.

The fact that Scudder is unlicensed for most of the series means that he has a different range of clients than a detective such as the Continental Op, who works for a large agency, or Marlowe and Spenser, who have offices and telephone listings. Some of his clients are referred by former co-workers on the NYPD who will give his name to distraught relatives dissatisfied with the official investigation. Other clients, like Spinner

Jablon, Kim Dakkinen, and Chance, are denizens of the underworld themselves, people who would never contact a regular private investigator. After he joins AA some cases result from members approaching him with a problem or referring a friend or relative to him.

Although not the most recent of the fifteen books in the Scudder series, *A Dance at the Slaughterhouse* contains many of the continuing themes of the series. As in many hard-boiled detective stories, two seemingly separate cases turn out to be intertwined. The novel begins with Scudder investigating the death of Amanda Thurman. According to the version accepted by the police, Amanda and her husband Richard were returning to their apartment from a party when they interrupted a burglary on the floor below theirs. The burglars tied them up, raped and killed Amanda and left Richard unconscious. He eventually came to, rubbed the tape from his mouth and called for help. However, Lyman Warriner, Amanda's brother, doubts the story and hires Scudder to search for evidence that Richard was involved. Earlier, in a unconnected incident, a fellow AA member brings Scudder a rented video tape which has a homemade video recorded over the middle portion. The added material shows a young man being sexually used, then tortured and killed by a man and a woman. Both figures are masked and Scudder's efforts to discover anything further about the source of the film are fruitless. Thurman is a cable television producer, and when Scudder goes to see him at work at a local boxing arena he notices a man and boy in the crowd. A few days later Scudder suddenly realizes that a gesture the man used reminds him of the killer on the tape. He then renews his investigation of the tape and attempts to identify the unknown man at the arena. In the course of these investigations he becomes steeped in the tawdry world of the sex shops of Times Square and meets TJ, a young black street hustler whose wit and obvious intelligence inspire Scudder to ask for help in contacting street kids who would never speak to a middle-aged white man who still looks like the cop he once was.

Scudder also spends a few evenings with Ballou, trading stories and discussing the dark underside of New York. Scudder learns that the man in the video is Bergan Stettner, who is connected with the company financing the cable company that employs Thurman. When he meets Thurman in a bar he lets him know he is investigating Stettner, and the next day Thurman meets with him and tells the whole story. Stettner and his wife, Olga, had ensnared Thurman with a combination of sexual adventure and Nietzschean philosophy and gradually brought him over to a plan to kill his wife for her money, first involving him in the killing of the cameraman who filmed their video and has been blackmailing them with a copy (the one that fell into Scudder's hands). Now Thurman fears they plan to kill him. Scudder goes to the police with the story and is set up with a wire for the next meeting, but Thurman does not show and his body is found below his apartment window. Without his testimony there is no case, as Joe Durkin tells Scudder. Scudder contacts the Stettners with the information that he has their missing tape, offering to sell it to them for fifty thousand dollars. Scudder then goes to Ballou, tells him that he can set him up for a robbery that will net at least fifty thousand, probably more, since Stettner is also laundering money for Iranians in California. Ballou assumes Scudder wants the five percent he has been told is standard payment for such information and is surprised when Scudder asks to go in as part of the team. The invasion is a bloody one, with one of Ballou's men wounded by Stettner's guards. They force Bergan to open his safe, from which he pulls a gun. Ballou kills Bergan with his meat cleaver and Scudder shoots Olga.

The major theme of this novel is Scudder's experiment in being an active agent in eliminating a villain, rather than employing misdirection as he has in the past. The volume also introduces TJ, who becomes a regular character, and is one of several that feature serial killers. As in other novels in the series Scudder continues to live and work in an environment in which most of the people he meets in the course of a case drink, some heavily. As demonstrated above, in some instances drinking is a form of self-medication, in others it is one of the trappings of hospitality expected in our culture, or a means of easing the transfer of information. Despite his stubbornness in remaining in this alcohol steeped milieu Scudder is able to continue his recovery process, attending meetings and refraining from alcohol, even when in the company of drinkers, thus maintaining a central theme of the series.

For anyone confronting the issue of excessive alcohol use, choice is a major issue. The AA program is based on the belief that the alcoholic can, one day at a time, make the conscious choice to refrain from drinking. Further, the program assumes that the temptation will never go away, that no alcoholic is ever cured, only recovering. The program is partly spiritual, with prayer, references to a Higher Power and a program of personal regeneration, including the Fifth Step of confessing one's faults. It also has a practical component: a support network of people who have confronted the same problem, sponsors to call when tempted to drink and the advice to stay away from circumstances that might lead to an impulse to drink. Scudder's business puts him in many circumstances that he could use as an excuse to return to drinking.

For instance, in *Out on the Cutting Edge* he is listening to Ballou explain that Paula's body cannot be returned to her parents because Neil fed it to the hogs: "I wanted a drink. There are a hundred reasons why a man will want a drink, but I wanted one now for the most elementary reason of all. I didn't want to feel what I was feeling, and a voice within was telling me that I needed the drink, that I couldn't bear it without it" (223). In other books he is tempted to drink because of the tension of knowing someone is trying to kill him or people close to him. But he is able to resist. Similarly, in *A Walk Among the Tombstones* Peter Khoury is tempted to return to heroin use after his sister-in-law is kidnapped and killed. This book contains an even more interesting commentary on the role of choice in addiction when Scudder confronts Callander, the serial killer who killed Khoury's wife and several other women. Scudder asks him why he does what he does and whether he has a choice about doing it:

> "But do I have a choice? I *think* I do [emphasis in original]. It's not as though I'm driven to act out every time the moon is full. I always have a choice, and I can choose not to do anything, and I do choose not to, and then one day I choose the other way.
>
> "So what kind of choice is it, really? I can postpone it, but then the time comes when I don't want to postpone it any longer. And postponing just makes it sweeter, anyway" [261].

Taken out of context this could almost be a discussion of whether to yield to the temptation of an ice cream sundae, a day of gambling, a visit to a pornographic Website, or any other behavior of the type sometimes labeled addictive. The scene is ambiguous. Are we meant to believe with Callander that he does have a choice and then despise him for exercising it? Or are we meant to see his belief that he has a choice about whether or not he kills as the pathetic illusion of a madman? Block makes a more prolonged attempt to display the mind of a killer in his most recent book, *Hope to Die*, in which about a quarter of the text is given from the killer's point of view. However, in *Hope to Die* as in *A Walk Among the Tombstones* the motives for murder include material gain. Block seems to have a difficult time confronting the idea of a killer who kills only for pleasure and not for any practical purpose.

Matthew Scudder grows and changes in ways that the other characters we have dealt with do not. This is possible, in part, because the series is comprised of more volumes than those devoted to the Continental Op, Philip Marlowe or Mike Hammer. However, sheer quantity does not guarantee character development, as demonstrated by the dead-end into which Parker seems to have written Spenser, in which glib discussions of masculine codes substitute for deeper confrontations with moral issues. It may be that Scudder's depth reflects his creator's confrontation with alcohol dependency, just as the facile shallowness of Nick Charles reflects Hammett's inability to confront his own problems. One hesitates to embrace a crude biographical determinism, but the fascinating connections between Block's and his character's histories are deeply embedded in this impressive fictional series.

All of the works treated so far have been written by and about men. The world of the fictional PI has been so exclusively masculine that some would argue that any change in the formula violates the genre boundaries. However, starting in the early 1980s a new generation of female writers created female detectives. Their adventures are a new chapter in the development of the detective code.

"Groomed to This End for Years"

The Rise of the Woman PI

Up to this point the detective has been consistently referred to as *he*, for no female detectives appeared in the early period of the hard-boiled genre. The rise of the fictional female PI is usually seen as beginning in the late 1970s with the publication of Marcia Muller's *Edwin of the Iron Shoes*, which features San Francisco detective Sharon McCone. McCone's few predecessors are frequently ignored by historians of the genre. In 1939 Erle Stanley Gardner, writing as A. A. Fair, introduced Bertha Cool, a woman detective, and her assistant, Donald Lam who did most of the footwork in the investigations. The series was successful but did not generate imitators ("Gardner," Lachman 174–75). G. G. Fickling introduced Honey West, "the sexiest private eye ever to pull a trigger," in 1957. Honey West was successful on television as well, in a series starring Anne Francis (Heising, *Detecting Women* 93–94). Yet as Hans Bertens and Theo D'haen comment in *Contemporary American Crime Fiction*, "Gardner's Bertha Cool and G. G. Fickling's Honey West are equally implausible, even if they could not be more different" (13). This very implausibility keeps these anomalous examples from being considered as part of the mainstream of the genre.

It would have been unrealistic for authors to introduce female private detectives when no such persons were likely to be found in real life. Even within police forces women were confined, until recently, to the role of matron, dealing with children and female prisoners. As Maureen Reddy explains in "The Female Detective From Nancy Drew to Sue Grafton," mystery fiction is "rooted ... in realist traditions" and "tends to reflect prevailing social conditions and to present at least a surface verisimilitude ... hence the scarcity of female police or private investigators before women moved into a broad range of occupations in the 1970s and thereafter" (1049). As women became police officers and lawyers it became possible to imagine a woman with the background to work as a PI. An audience for such characters was also in place, for as Reddy notes, women who had read and enjoyed Nancy Drew mysteries as young women grew to adulthood eager to continue reading mysteries with female protagonists (1048).

Nevertheless, there is more to the problem of the female PI in fiction than the existence of prototypes in the working world, for private eye novels are not documentaries on the field of private investigation. The ideal of a man with a code that compels him to risk his all in a quixotic effort to achieve justice in an unjust world is, as established earlier, a literary convention. The mutation of this convention to allow female protagonists raises questions, not of verisimilitude but of adherence to the literary formula. Some critics seem to feel that the formula lacks the flexibility to admit women. Bertens and D'haen call "private eye fiction, a field whose tough guy masculinity seemed almost designed to keep out female writers, let alone female protagonists" (10). They seem set on supporting their assertion by calling the early McCone "too tame to qualify as a tough investigator" then criticizing Muller for turning the later McCone "into a sort of international crusader and one-woman rescue team" (23). But male critics are not alone in feeling that women have difficulty fitting the genre conventions. Kathleen Gregory Klein, in *The Woman Detective: Gender and Genre*, claims that the "genre defines its parameters to exclude female characters, confidently rejecting them as inadequate women or inadequate detectives" (223). This is hardly an argument about whether women can actually perform jobs such as police officer, soldier or private investigator. That question is being settled by real women on real streets. The question is one of ideology, for it is largely feminist critics who have analyzed these works, with the result that the issue becomes not whether a female character can function convincingly as a detective but whether a female detective can function as a feminist. Priscilla L. Walton and Manina Jones summarize the conflict between different definitions of feminism in *Detective Agency* (88) citing critics such as Rosalind Coward and Linda Semple who feel that the hard-boiled genre is unsusceptible to feminist interpretation because of the "extreme individualism, violence and outrageous social attitudes toward women and other minority groups" displayed by writers such as Hammett, Chandler and Spillane (Coward and Semple 46). Such critics appear to believe that the only legitimate reason to write women into the traditionally male genre is to advance the feminist cause. Further, they define feminist as anti-maculinist. Therefore, to be seen as feminist, the protagonist must reverse the values labeled masculine by these critics. But to do so would be to transform the hard-boiled novel into something else. Since writers such as Sue Grafton and Sara Paretsky have not performed this transformation, the feminism of their works is questioned, for if the female detective performs like her male counterpart she is deemed to lack feminist credibility. Of course this form of analysis ignores the fact that mass market fiction must satisfy an audience and that the audience does not necessarily define feminism in the same terms as academics and theoreticians. An essay by Alison Littler aptly sums up the problem:

> How the term "feminist" is defined, of course, will be crucial to the kind of answers that are offered. If, for example, "feminist" is used in a liberal-humanist-independent-career-woman-in-control-of-her-own-life sense, then most certainly the recent series of women private eyes are feminist. If, however, "feminist' refers to a woman deconstructing phallocentric ideologies wherever they are naturalized and structured into social, cultural and political practices, then a feminist private eye is a contradiction in terms. She is a man in woman's clothing—or is it a woman in man's clothing? [133]

As Bertens and D'haen put it: "Female investigators give no indication of having read Derrida or Lecan or of seeing the true phallocentric nature of things" (15). Yet, it seems curious to define the traditional values of the PI: loyalty, persistence, courage, devotion to justice, and ability to work autonomously, as masculine rather than as traits available to both women and men.

The question of whether works featuring women PIs are feminist is not to be determined here. Despite the concerns of feminists and the quibbles of some critics the addition of women protagonists to the genre has been embraced by the reading public. *Detecting Women* lists over 100 current series featuring women investigators who fall, at least roughly, into the category of PI (Heising 300–302). Presumably these books are finding a market and must, therefore, satisfy the expectations of fans.

Among the qualities that readers expect is that the detective's behavior has boundaries. However, these boundaries do not necessarily coincide with those of the law. As we have seen, fictional PIs will conceal evidence, refuse to cooperate with police, break and enter, and threaten or even assault witnesses to solve a case. These behaviors are accepted by the reader so long as they serve the greater good of bringing a perpetrator to justice or protecting a potential victim.

In the hard-boiled genre the detective's willingness to violate the law is usually justified by the portrayal of society as corrupt. The criminal may be protected by wealth or political power or the police may be seen as ineffective, either because they are understaffed or hampered by "technicalities," or because they are corrupt. Or the court system may have acted in error, freeing a guilty person or convicting an innocent one, leaving the injustice to be corrected by the PI. In return for the latitude given the PI in regard to the law, the genre conventions require a fearless pursuit of the truth, protection of innocents and loyalty to friends. Of course these traits can be found in the protagonists of the classic mystery as well, however the amateur detective seldom becomes directly involved in violence, whereas the option of direct attacks on the detective or other uses of violence remain more open to the author of hard-boiled fiction. It is perhaps the tendency to judge all violence, especially killing, as a part of a masculine value system that leads certain feminist critics to see the hard-boiled genre as inherently masculinist.

If one accepts that the female PI can be considered as subject to the same codes as the male, the question arises of whether her relationship with alcohol has the same meanings as have been found in novels with male heroes. Will alcohol be treated realistically, or will an element of fantasy in the support of "toughness" creep in, as has been demonstrated in some of the works of male authors? Will women detectives use alcohol in ways similar to males? If they do not, what are the reasons? Will the use of alcohol be a key to judging the moral worth of other characters? We already have established that society views drinking by women in a different light than drinking by men, especially in terms of greater disapproval of female drunkenness, and that in America the influence of the female dominated temperance movement meant that fewer women than men drink. Women are also more likely to drink wine than beer or hard liquor and more likely to consume cocktails than hard liquor straight or on the rocks. We may expect these matters of taste and custom to be reflected in the "newspaper reality" of the works we examine.

However, by the late 1970s Prohibition was only a memory. The emotional charge it held for the generation that created the hard-boiled genre was gone and for most American adults drinking was a matter of personal choice, influenced by family background, religious beliefs and class. Drinking among American women had jumped from 45 percent in 1939 to 66 percent in 1978 (Barr 154). This growth was partly propelled by the marketing of lighter tasting drinks, such as vodka and light rum, fruity wine coolers and smooth wines, such as white zinfandel. On the other hand, as society became more open (one might almost say compulsive) about discussing problems that had formerly been kept as personal or family secrets, the public became more aware of the scope of alcoholism and related problems.

Alcoholism in women had been greatly underestimated, both because women tended to drink alone at home and because families were more likely to deny the problem or protect wives and mothers from public scrutiny. Both the relaxation of earlier attitudes about women and drink, and the concerns of the late 1970s and 1980s will be found reflected in detective fiction of this era.

As noted already, the history of contemporary female PIs in America begins with Marcia Muller's creation of Sharon McCone in 1977. But it was not until 1982 that the hard-boiled novel with a female protagonist took off with the publication of a second McCone adventure and the introduction of Sue Grafton's Kinsey Milhone and Sara Paretsky's V. I. Warshawski. The number of series grew though the 1980s and 1990s and new authors enter the field on a regular basis. Muller, Grafton and Paretsky have shared the majority of critical attention, Muller because of her position as the first acknowledged contender in the field and Grafton and Paretsky because of their prominence in the market. This chapter will deal with Muller and Grafton, and with a somewhat lesser known writer, Karen Kijewski, who was chosen because both the author and her PI, Kat Colorado, are former bartenders, and drinking is fairly prominent in the series.

According to Bonnie C. Plummer's biographical notes in *Great Women Mystery Writers*, Marcia Muller was born in 1944 in Detroit, Michigan. She received a B.A. in English from the University of Michigan at Ann Arbor in 1966 and an M.A. in Journalism in 1971. She was married to Frederick T. Gilson in 1967, a marriage that lasted until 1981. In 1992 she remarried to Bill Pronzini, a fellow mystery writer, and lives with him in Northern California. Although Sharon McCone was introduced in 1977, Muller did not become a full-time writer until 1983 (Plummer 244). That year she introduced a second series character, Elena Oliverez, a Mexican arts museum curator based in Santa Barbara. In 1986 Muller created a third series, featuring Joanna Stark, an international art investigator living in the Napa Valley of California. While there are currently 23 titles in the McCone series, both Stark and Oliverez appear to have been abandoned, with no new titles appearing since the late 80s. Muller has also produced volumes of short stories and has collaborated with her husband on novels, reference guides and anthologies.

The McCone series has received several nominations and one major award. *The Shape of Dread* (1989), *Where Echoes Live* (1991), and *Wolf in the Shadows* (1993) have been nominated for the Shamus, awarded by the Private Eye Writers of America. *Wolf in the Shadows* was also nominated for the Edgar, awarded by the Mystery Writers of America and won the Anthony, awarded by fans at the Bouchercon each year. *A Wild and Lonely Place* (1995) was nominated for the Macavity by the Mystery Readers International. (Heising 200–201)

In an article about McCone's character in *Mystery Scene*, Muller comments that she was "fascinated by detectives who, unhampered by regulation and procedure, would set off down the mean streets to right wrongs, strong and unafraid." However she determined not to conform her character to the "stereotype of the hard-bitten loner with a whiskey bottle in the desk drawer." Muller tells how she decided to create a woman character because she felt she didn't know about being a man. However she did not want the character to be autobiographical, so McCone is taller and thinner than Muller, a native Californian from a large blue-collar family who worked her way through the University of California at Berkeley, and has Native American features and long black hair that mark her as throwback to her family's 1/8 Shoshone blood (Muller "Partners" 26). In *Edwin of the Iron Shoes* we learn that McCone is almost thirty, lives in a studio apartment in the Mission District of San Francisco, earned a degree in sociology and was introduced to the investigative field by working department store security. She is a licensed PI who works for All Souls Legal Collective, which is housed in a Victorian house in Bernal Heights. Later in the novel a call to her family in San Diego reveals that her father is a retired Navy Chief, her mother presumably a housewife, and that she has at least two brothers and two sisters. (*Edwin of the Iron Shoes* 22–28, 193–94)

Traditional motifs of the hard-boiled genre appear early in the story. Lt. Gregory Marcus, the homicide detective assigned to the murder of an antique dealer warns McCone not to interfere with the case. He also expresses scorn for PIs in general. McCone divulges that she was fired from the first company she worked for because she refused an assignment to entrap a man for a divorce case (25), harkening back both to Marlowe's refusal to handle divorces and to the theme of independence and insubordination that is characteristic of many fictional PIs. McCone is also determined to investigate the murder of Joan Albritton, even when she learns that the Salem Street Merchants Association, which originally hired her through All Souls to investigate arson and vandalism against members involved in real estate redevelopment plans, has not voted to employ her. She continues the investigation under the cover of doing an inventory of the dead woman's store and discovers a ring of art smugglers. She is putting together the final clues when the murderer appears, searching for the last painting of a set, and confesses when confronted by McCone. In this first effort Muller has included several elements of the formula: conflict between the PI and the police; a detective who refuses cases based on ethical judgments, and a detective who pursues a case in the face of opposition from both police and client.

Muller's treatment of alcohol is not exceptional. McCone drinks in the course of the story, as do other characters. Charlie Cornish, the antique store owner who discovered the first victim, is a long-time alcoholic who may have been responsible for the fire that killed his wife and child years earlier. McCone describes her apartment manager as a habitual drinker who passes out each afternoon after a day spent drinking beer.

In describing these characters Muller manifests the dichotomy shown by other authors in that the effect of alcohol on secondary characters seems more realistically depicted than the effect on her protagonist. For example, when McCone attends a private real estate meeting in hopes of questioning Cara Ingalls she has three drinks before being discovered and ejected. The first could be justified, although McCone does not bother to, as necessary camouflage for infiltrating a cocktail meeting. The second two are for "fortification" as McCone reacts to the conversations going on around her about the Yerba Buena Convention Center, a project that was opposed by many liberals because it eliminated low cost housing and small businesses in the area south of Market Street (44–45). But nothing is said of the effect of these drinks, and McCone does not hesitate to drive across town to visit Cornish. When she reaches his shop she finds that he has been drinking, starting with martinis and descending to straight gin from smeared glasses. The effects are apparent: bleary eyes, slack mouth, and morose and maudlin conversation followed by unexplained belligerence. Cornish even admits the effects, stating that he will have a terrible hangover in the morning and that if he tries to sleep now all he will get is "the whirlies" (52–57). In the final chapter McCone and her boss Hank Zahn, joined by Cornish, drink cheap red wine while McCone explains the outcome of the case. Although Muller throws in the occasional descriptive phrase such as "Hank and I nodded in drunken agreement" (209), the surrounding conversation has none of the irrational leaps, incoherence or repetition that Hammett so brilliantly portrayed in *Red Harvest*.

Alcohol plays a more dominant role in the second McCone novel, *Ask the Cards a Question* (1982). Linnea Carraway, a friend whose marriage has fallen apart, is staying with McCone. She is drinking heavily, to the point of suffering blackouts. When a neighbor is killed with a piece of rope that matches McCone's new drapery cord she fears that Carraway may be involved. McCone also displays ambivalence about supplying her friend, on one hand recognizing that Carraway will buy her own liquor if none is in the house, on the other hand deciding not to bring home a bottle of wine she has purchased earlier: "Linnea was starting on her second stinger; by the time she got home, she'd be ready to drink all night, and I didn't want the wine there to tempt her" (59). By the time the case is resolved Carraway has come to terms with her divorce and stopped drinking. We last see her sipping Perrier, declaring that she wants her children to see her sober when she returns (206). Like Spillane,

Muller depicts excessive drinking as a response to stress, a mode of self-medication that can be easily abandoned once the situation is resolved.

Ask the Cards a Question continues the conflict between McCone and Marcus, as she follows the hard-boiled pattern by withholding evidence out of loyalty to her friend, and fails to report a second murder because she does not want to be questioned by police before she has a chance to follow her own hunches. Muller also continues the pattern of describing the drunken behavior of supporting characters in detail while glossing over the effect of alcohol on the protagonist. At one point McCone sits up drinking brandy with Zahn, going over ideas in the case. She crashes on the office sofa, but the worst effect we are told of is that she oversleeps, her face is pasty, her hair is snarled and a couple of aspirin would be welcome (150–51).

McCone does not remain a static character as the series develops. She begins and ends romantic involvements, takes on an assistant at All Souls and develops more sophisticated tastes. In *There's Something on a Sunday* (1993) she tells us of a new taste in wine: "I'd recently started drinking the good stuff—the varieties with corks—rather than the jug brands that had been a staple of my youth" (123). In the same book we find something of a twist on the use of liquor to loosen up a witness. McCone dines with Zahn, who drinks wine steadily through the meal and after it. McCone senses "that he might be getting ready to discuss what was really bothering him" (149).

By 1999 Muller seems more able to be frank about the effect of alcohol on her protagonist as well as on her other characters. In *A Walk Through the Fire* McCone is working on a case and having problems in her relationship with Hy Ripinsky. After a confrontation with him she fixes a "gin and tonic that was mostly gin" thinking that "If I was to spend the night holding inane conversations with myself, I might as well do it drunk." A little later she wonders about the wisdom of freshening the drink but decides "The hell with it." However, a little later in the evening a conversation that reminds her of her family brings back a memory of a family gathering that ended when McCone, "who had been known to defensively tipple at family gatherings, got rip-roaring drunk and ended up in our tree house singing dirty songs with Pa at three in the morning … the memory of the monumental hangover I'd suffered quelled my desire for more gin" (157–59).

Earlier in this novel we have had an example of the contrast between the way women and men are regarded in respect to alcoholic excess. McCone is helping a friend, Glenna Stanleigh, who is disturbed by suspicious accidents on the sets of the film she is making about a prominent Hawaiian writer who disappeared some years earlier. When McCone and Ripinsky arrive they are invited to stay with the son who is Glenna's partner. Before leaving for a family party Peter Wainwright suggests they have a few drinks first and explains that his mother will be so "smashed" that she will not remember that she does not already know them. McCone is nonplused, thinking, "What do you say when someone you've just met comes out and tells you his mother's a drunk?" Peter reacts somewhat defensively to their surprised silence, adding that "it's no secret about my mother" (32). Yet much less is made of the several male characters who are known to drink excessively. And even when she learns that Peter's younger brother is a drug user McCone does not find the information as embarrassing as the comment about Mrs. Wainright.

Muller may be the originator of the female PI, but Sue Grafton is probably currently the best known practitioner, credited by Jean Swanson with transforming the American mystery (439). Her alphabet series has currently reached "Q" and is so familiar to genre fans that Lawrence Block can have his character, Bernie Rhodenbarr, joke about it. She has been the recipient of numerous awards: "*A" is for Alibi* (1982) won the Anthony; "*B" is for Burglar* (1985) the Anthony and the Shamus; "*C" is for Corpse* (1986), the Anthony; "*G" is for Gumshoe* (1990) also the Anthony and Shamus; and "*K" is for Killer* (1994) the Shamus. She has been a nominee for these and other awards as well (Heising 108–09). Grafton herself was a professional writer before beginning the series, working as a film and television screenwriter. She also wrote two non-mystery novels, *Keziah Dave* in 1967 and *The Lolly Madonna Wars* in 1969, before turning to the genre. Sue Grafton was born in 1940 in Louisville, Kentucky to Vivian Harnsberger, a high school chemistry teacher, and Chip W. Grafton, a lawyer who also wrote mysteries. She obtained her B.A. in English from the University of Louisville in 1961 and like her character, Kinsey, has been divorced twice, runs for fitness and lives in Santa Barbara. She married Steven F. Humphrey in 1978 and has three children. (Hoyser 134) (Taylor 5) Natalie Kaufman and Carol Kay published a biography, "*G" is for Grafton*, in 1997 which reveals that Grafton's parents were alcoholics. Although her father was functional in that he was able to work, her mother drank and "went to sleep on the couch." Grafton is quoted as stating that "children of alcoholics are always very rules-governed" (282–83). It is easy to suspect that Grafton finds an outlet in her protagonist, who is driven to help enforce the law, yet delights in such violations of the rules as lying and breaking and entering. In an interview with Bruce Taylor, Grafton describes Kinsey as "a stripped down version of me ... the person I would have been had I not married young and had children. She'll always be thinner and younger and braver, ... our sensibilities are identical" (10).

Kinsey Milhone is thirty-two in the opening book of the series. She ages one year for each two and-a-half books and will be about forty when

"Z" is reached (Heising 108). She is twice divorced and lives alone in a converted garage rented by Henry Pitts, a retired baker in his eighties. She is a former police officer for the fictional city of Santa Theresa, who, like many of her PI predecessors, has opted for the independence of a private practice. She uses office space in a building occupied by California Fidelity, an insurance company, in exchange for investigating claims. Milhone is an orphan whose parents were killed when their car was buried in a land slide, leaving five-year-old Kinsey trapped for several hours with her dead and dying parents. Adopted by her maternal aunt, who has also died, she grows up believing she has no other relatives. It is not until *"J" is for Judgment* (1993) that she learns that members of her mother's family live in nearby Lompoc. In *"Q" is for Quarry* (2002)she is still dealing with the implications.

The fact that the female PI tends to be a loner has drawn comment. Reddy states: "In their solitariness—parentless, spouseless, childless— these detectives resemble their male counterparts, but that similarity serves to throw profound differences into sharper relief ... solitary woman is ... 'unwomanly' while the solitary man's maleness is affirmed." She notes that Muller allows on-going romantic involvements to McCone while both Sara Paretsky and Grafton produce heroines who value their independence and seem to regard romance as a threat. (1054–56) Only Milhone's continued relationship with her landlord, who provides both food in the form of fresh-baked treats and a sympathetic ear, and Rosie, the imperious owner of a local restaurant who feeds her complex eastern European meals, with desert only if she finishes, provide a surrogate family.

While an average number of problem drinkers appear as characters in the series Milhone herself is a moderate, but regular drinker. She drinks white wine, chilled or over ice, or beer from the bottle. When she eats at Rosie's she drinks whatever wine the eccentric and dictatorial Rosie produces with the meal, or helps herself to the cheap Chablis kept behind the bar. Chablis, a better grade which requires a corkscrew, also stocks her office refrigerator. Milhone's attitude is demonstrated in this early scene from *"A" is for Alibi*, which occurs after a difficult meeting with the police detective who handled the case she has been hired to reopen.

> ... it was 4:15 and I needed a drink. ... I propped myself up on the waist-high ledge and sipped my wine. I could smell the ocean and I let my mind go blank, watching the pedestrians down below. I already knew that I would go to work for Nikki but I needed just these few moments for myself before I turned my attention to the job to be done [13].

This is not the only occasion in the novel in which she "needs" a drink, usually after a long day, as she works up her notes from the day's work.

In this first novel, Milhone is hired by a woman, convicted of killing her husband, who has served her time and wants the real killer found. Milhone sets out to interview the associates of the dead Lawrence Fife, including his law partner, Charlie Scorsoni. Milhone is attracted to Scorsoni, against her better judgment. He takes her out to an incredibly seductive dinner, preceded by a delicate wine "pale and cool" (145). They become lovers, but further into the case Milhone regains her caution and asks him to put the relationship on hold until she finishes the investigation. She then discovers evidence that he is the killer, not of his partner, who was killed by his ex-wife, Gwen, but of the accountant who had discovered he was embezzling and of two others since Milhone reopened the case. When he discovers her suspicions, Charlie pursues Milhone along the beach. He has discovered her hiding in a trash bin and is threatening her with a butcher knife when, as Milhone tells us, "I blew him away" (214).

Drinking does not play a major role in this novel, although there are several characters who had or have problems with alcohol. The first is Gwen Fife, the dead man's first wife, who remarks that she had given up drinking but that before the divorce she was "knocking back a *lot* of scotch" (53). As she delves into the case Milhone discovers that Fife had had an affair with Charlotte Mercer, the wife of a local judge. When she goes to interview Charlotte she finds her drinking. "I wondered if she used it [Lemon Pledge] to disguise the mild scent of bourbon on the rocks that wafted after her." As they talk Milhone notes that Mercer is "repeating herself. It was the second hint I had that she wasn't as sober as she should have been, even at that hour of the day [after 6 P.M.]." Mercer does not attempt to conceal her problem, explaining that no one would believe her opinion about the murder because: "I'm just your Mrs. Loud-Mouth Drunk. What does she know?" She fills Milhone in on other women in Fife's life, but Milhone does not take everything at face value, thinking, "Charlotte Mercer was shrewd and perhaps not above using her drunkenness for its effect," a potential case of the drunk manipulating the detective rather than the more common pattern of a PI using drink to loosen a witness's tongue. (59–62) Another character who had problems with drink is Garry Steinberg, who employed the accountant killed at the same time as Fife. With Steinberg, however, the problem is not loss of control but weight. He has lost ninety-four pounds and admits that giving up alcohol is the hard part of the diet, estimating that at least fifty pounds of his shed weight was from quitting (24).

Given the end of the novel, *"A" is for Alibi* certainly seems like a hard-boiled novel but the question of whether Milhone fits the pattern of the hard-boiled detective is a complex one. Panek, feels that "Sue Grafton is not really a hard-boiled writer" since her plots frequently

involve a fairly closed family setting rather than the wider ranging corruption of society found in the more typical works of the genre. In addition he mentions her use of the Had-I-But-Known formula, more typical
of the classical mystery (*New Hard-Boiled Writers* 97–98). Kaufman and
Kay do not seem to take a position on the topic, though they quote Grafton's comments on the reasons she is attracted to the genre: "'He [the
hard-boiled PI] smoked too much, drank too much, screwed and punched
his way through molls and mobsters with devastating effect. In short, he
kicked ass'" (321). Rachel Schaffer, writing in *The Armchair Detective*,
examines Milhone's black humor as a means to cope with danger and
achieve emotional distance (322), while Scott Christianson reminds us
in "Talkin' Trash and Kickin' Butt" that tough talk is a prominent feature of the genre, and wisecracks are a way to show that the PI doesn't
respect convention or authority, adding that Milhone backs up her talk
with a willingness to use violence (130–32). The question of adherence
to a code of behavior is less clear. The critics do not seem to focus on it,
except, as above, in discussions of whether the masculinist code of the
genre can be adapted to feminist purposes. Milhone does not discuss the
idea of a code, indeed her most common comments on her own behavior are statements of how she enjoys the challenge of lying and the thrill
of breaking in.

In a later novel, "*K*" *is for Killer* (1994) Milhone muses that she is
haunted by unsolved homicides, thinking of the victims as caught in a
limbo, whispering in the wind. "I can sometimes hear them murmuring.
They mourn themselves. They sing a lullaby of the murdered. They whis-
per the names of their attackers (1–2). This soliloquy is reminiscent of
Marlowe's "voices in the night" speech, both in its romanticism and in
that it seems to assign to the PI a role that the police are unable to fill.
Against her better judgment Milhone is talked into investigating the death
of a young woman whose body was too decomposed when discovered
to determine cause of death. Lorna's mother, however, is convinced that
her daughter was murdered. Milhone discovers that Lorna worked a day
job at a water treatment plant but made much better money in her second career as a call girl. The investigation leads her into the night time
world of prostitution and pornography and late night clubbing. She
becomes friendly with Danielle, another young prostitute, a friend of the
victim. She also learns that Lorna was engaged to an underworld figure.
A mysterious man in a limousine gives Milhone a phone number to call
if she finds out more about Lorna's death. Milhone does learn who the
killer was, but there is not enough evidence for an arrest. When she hears
that Danielle has died after an attack presumed to have been committed
by Lorna's killer, she calls the anonymous number and gives the murderer's name. With a sudden change of heart she goes to warn Lorna's

former boss, but he paralyzes her with a Taser gun before she can speak
and leaves with a stranger. He is never seen again. Milhone is left with
the question: "Having strayed into the shadows, can I find my way back?"
(292)

Overall, alcohol does not seem to bear much symbolic weight for
Grafton. This is, perhaps, surprising considering her background as the
child of alcoholic parents and her clear identification with her protagonist. However, it seems to be the case that food is actually a stronger motif
in defining Milhone's character. She does not cook, except hard-boiled
egg sandwiches, and she can be absent minded about eating, especially
when busy on a case. But when she does eat she is sometimes embar-
rassed by her own response, moaning or whimpering with pleasure when
eating something particularly appealing. She also expresses guilt about
her favorite meal-on-the-run, "a Quarter Pounder with cheese, fries and
a Coke. It's filling, fast, and cheap—all great values for a PI who just needs
to refuel and get back to work (Kaufman and Kay 76–79). This particular dietary sin is expiated with extra jogging, as Hoyser observes (136),
part of the greater realism of the 1980s in which authors recognize that
their characters cannot be expected to be believably tough unless they
have a fitness routine. Both Schaffer, in an essay on Sue Grafton's black
humor, and Kaufman and Kay, comment on Milhone's use of food imagery.
Schaffer views this use of images relating to traditional female interests
as a means of coping with danger by achieving emotional distance (322).
Kaufman and Kay see some images involving food as appropriately cozy,
such as comparing a house to a wedding cake or a smooth voice to fudge.
But some images they find grotesque, such as describing hair rollers as
resembling chicken bones or a corpse in storage as feeling like a package
of raw chicken breasts (298–99).

Karen Kijewski entered the PI field in 1989 with *Katwalk*, a novel
featuring Kathy [Kat] Colorado. *Katwalk* won The St. Martin's Press
PWA award for best first private eye novel, the Anthony and the Shamus.
The series is set in Sacramento, California, with Colorado working out
of an office in downtown Sacramento and living in the suburb of Orangevale. Colorado's cases take her to neighboring areas as well, the Gold
Country, the Sacramento Delta and even Las Vegas. The series, which
features nine books from 1989 to 1998, has received little critical attention (Heising, *Detecting Women* 150). But the role that alcohol plays in
the novels call for Kijewski's inclusion in this study.

Karen Kijewski was born in Berkeley, California in 1943. She earned
both her B.A. and M.A. in English from the University of California at
Berkeley and taught high school English in Massachusetts before mov-
ing to Sacramento in 1982. (Oser 179–80, Heising, *Detecting Women* 150).
Kijewski worked as a bartender from 1980–1991 and told an reviewer for

Macleans that the experience of listening to people contributed to her fiction (49). The experience also seems to have contributed to her descriptions of bars and of drinking behavior.

At first Kat Colorado seems to fall into the loner category of detective. She lives alone, although she does have a dog, and later a kitten. Her mother is dead, she never knew her father and her younger sister died when only three. But she has acquired a surrogate family. A neighbor, Alma, takes her under her wing and functions as an adopted grandmother, and Colorado is fiercely loyal to her and to her friends. Like her creator, Colorado worked as a bartender, a background that is put to use in the fourth novel, *Copy Kat* (1992).

Katwalk introduces Kat Colorado and her friend Charity Collins, who is an advice columnist for a local paper and in the midst of a bitter divorce. She asks Colorado to trace $200,000 that her husband, Sam, claims to have lost in Las Vegas, but that she believes has been diverted to investments. Colorado is reluctant: "I don't like working for friends—the complications are endless" (2). But her ingrained loyalty to friends persuades her to take the job against her better judgment. Leaving the Las Vegas airport she encounters another friend, one she hasn't seen since they grew up together in Sacramento. She soon realizes that Deck Hamilton is involved in shady business, but is reluctant to hurt his feelings because he had defended her from bullies when she was a child (10). Although Deck works for the man who turns out to be her opponent, and later admits that their meeting was not accidental, he repays her loyalty by trying to rescue her when she walks into a trap set by his employer, Don Blackford, who is engineering a crooked real estate deal. Deck is killed by the backup men sent by Blackford and Colorado pays a sympathy visit to his mother after the case is concluded, assuring her that though her son had gone astray, he had died attempting to save her.

In the course of the investigation Colorado meets Hank Parker, a Las Vegas police officer who intervenes when she is hassled by drunks outside a bar. They eventually become lovers. He shares with her the pain of being a widower; his wife was killed by a car bomb intended for him. She shares her background, an alcoholic mother who named her Colorado because the man who may have been her father said he was from that state. Her mother neglected both Colorado and her younger sister, who died of untreated pneumonia. Colorado tells Parker, "I begged her to call the doctor but she was drunk and paid me no mind," and "Ma missed the funeral. She was drunk. of course. I never forgave her for that, not that she noticed" (63–64). The neglect continued into her teen years, for Colorado's mother skips her high school graduation and is found that evening at the foot of the stairs, dead from a drunken fall.

Interestingly, this background of alcohol related abuse does not turn

Colorado against alcohol. Indeed, alcohol fulfills the familiar trio of roles in the series. Colorado shares drinks with most of the people with whom she interacts: Collins, who is a close enough friend to help herself to Colorado's wine when she comes by for help; Joe Rider, a reporter who shares information about corruption in Las Vegas; his wife Betty; and Hank Parker. For women, part of establishing independence is not to become solely a recipient of hospitality. When Colorado and Rider meet for dinner she tries to pay for the after-dinner drinks. But Rider prevails by pointing out that he can put the tab on his expense account, since they are discussing a potential story (40). This turns the meal from personal hospitality to a business meeting, although Rider then invites her to a dinner at his home. Colorado meets Parker later the same evening. After running off the men who were hassling her he suggests they return to the bar for a drink. She assumes he is intends to take advantage of the situation by making advances and objects that "Just because you're a cop … doesn't mean I have to have a drink with you." He explains that her assailant and his friends are known trouble makers who might follow her to her hotel, "And if they stopped by, it wouldn't be to offer you a drink." She capitulates, but continues "I had my money out right away. 'First one's on me'" (44).

Although Parker was being genuinely helpful, not all proffered hospitality is untainted. After Hamilton is killed, Blackford has Colorado brought to his house, where he intends to break her spirit and turn her into a sexual slave, as he has already done to a woman named Carmelita. Blackford has renamed Carmelita, submerging her personality by erasing her independent identity, but Colorado recruits her as an ally by repeatedly calling her by her real given name. Although she eats with Blackford and sips some of the wine he offers, at one point Colorado throws a glass against the wall to demonstrate her unwillingness to cooperate and drinks only water during the meal. Eventually Carmelita is goaded into stabbing Blackford and the two women are rescued from Blackford's guarded mansion by Las Vegas police (212–21).

Blackford's attempt on Colorado blends coercion and a perverted hospitality. Colorado herself does not seem to use alcohol deliberately to coerce witnesses, although she does meet some informants at bars and restaurants and drinks with them. But there are no scenes, in the novels under consideration, in which she takes advantage of someone obviously unable to control their drinking.

The use of alcohol as self-medication is assumed throughout the novel. Charity Collins drinks Colorado's wine while she expresses her outrage over Sam's diversion of money that should be part of their community property (2). When Colorado goes to a casino with Hamilton she discovers a recently murdered woman in the rest room. After being questioned by police she tells Hamilton that she needs a drink. "One look at my face convinced him." He orders a couple of shots of brandy for her, then she switches to wine, and after she rejects the idea of dinner Hamilton cautions her to slow down on the wine (24–26). Hamilton also comforts Colorado after his aborted attack on her by offering cognac from his hip flask (193). And finally, although Colorado has refused the cognac that Blackford offers while she is captive, as soon as he is dead she retrieves the bottle and pours a double shot for Carmelita (221).

Kijewski does not dwell on the effects of alcohol on her characters, except for the unredeemed, disapproving portrayal of Colorado's alcoholic mother. The only mention of negative effects on Colorado herself occurs the morning after her first evening in Las Vegas. She oversleeps, admitting that she was "still a little sideways from the wine" and can't eat breakfast (29). On another occasion, later in the case, she mentions deciding "to call it a day" rather than have another drink (79). Although she does not expand on the effects of drinking Kijewski does discuss the conventions of alcohol use. As Colorado explains:

> There's an art to behaving well in a bar and its not as easy as falling off a log—or a bar stool in this case. Most people, women especially, are clueless about it. After my time as a bartender (seven years, two months, and three days, but who's counting?), I ought to give a class in it. Adult Education 101 "Drinking With Style" [34].

In a later meeting with Charity she comments on her friend's choice of a strawberry daiquiri: "I haven't been able to break her of the frou-frou drink habit" (73). Don Blackford is a drinker who orders to display his wealth rather than his taste, the type described by Andrew Barr as ordering Dom Perignon because it is reputed to be exclusive, and therefore expensive. Barr notes that nearly a million bottles a year are actually sold in the United States, at prices ranging from $120 retail to $250 in restaurants (Barr 398). When he meets Colorado for lunch Blackford waves aside her order of white wine and calls for Dom Perignon. But his pretense of elegant living is betrayed by the fact that, "He drank deeply and ignored his food. It was a wine for savoring, but he tossed it down" (120–22). These details demonstrate that Blackford is a person who can use his ill-gotten riches to buy expensive food and drink, the company of beautiful women, a large and elegant house, but not class.

Copy Kat (1992) give Kijewski more scope to discuss alcohol. Colorado goes undercover as a bartender to investigate the death of Deidre Durkin, whose husband owns and runs a bar in the California Gold Country. When she arrives at the Pioneer bar, Colorado admits to feeling like she has come home, but when a rowdy customer breaks a glass she muses that "this part of it was depressingly familiar" (30). When she meets the rest of Deirdre's family, her sister Chivogny is "getting sloshed" on vodka gimlets. When she makes a scene Colorado comments that "Drunks prattle the obvious as though it were a brand-new insight ... it was drunken logic, thoughts strung together on an emotional line like lights on a Christmas wire" (62). Meeting Chivogny later at the gift shop she runs, Colorado thinks:

> I recognized that oh. It was the I-had-too-much-to-drink-and-said-things-I-shouldn't-have oh. The kind of oh that remembered that while she was drunk I had been sober, and although she might have forgotten what transpired I wouldn't have [81].

Kijewski also gives us a reminder that women who drink may be judged by different standards when Chivogny announces that she is pregnant; Colorado's reaction is puzzlement at the fact that only the day before "she sat all night drinking steadily and heavily" (132).

The damage that alcohol can do to lives may be reflected in the locations in which they drink. Colorado describes another bar she enters during her investigation:

> There are bars like the Amble Inn all across the country and they fit a generic description. They are dives: long, narrow, smoky, dusty, dirty and with the sour smell of alcohol, of spills not quite wiped up, urine, things gone rotten, hopes gone bad.
>
> •　•　•
>
> Bars that open at eight or ten in the morning make no pretense. They are bars for losers, losers who have admitted it, who no longer try to hide it. They are what they are. They are drinking at eight in the morning drunk at eleven, drunker still at four [227].

We are reminded of Chandler's sad man in every quiet bar, but without the glamour of Terry Lennox's description of the first drink in the evening.

In *Honky Tonk Kat* (1996) Colorado is protecting another friend from the old neighborhood, Dakota Jones, who has become a country music star. Jones reminds Colorado of seeing her after her shift as a bartender smashing empty liquor bottles into the dumpster. Colorado explains: "I didn't want to take it home with me; the anger and hatred and disgust and other things that alcohol releases that it is better not to name (103). Later she recalls the days when she and Jones hung out together: "It was Friday night in Rio Linda and people were here to get drunk and happy, drunk and stupid, or drunk and laid, depending" (321).

Colorado's evaluation of her own and other's drinking seems to have no particular relation to her code of ethics, which includes loyalty to friends, giving good value and independence. In *Katwalk* she expounds:

> I like my job. I like the notion of pulling some kind of order out of confu-
> sion or ignorance or malfeasance. I only work for people who appeal to
> me and I like that too. The idea of being a good guy, working for good
> guys, tipping the cosmic scale a little in the right direction [118].

Like other female detectives she feels she must guard her independence
from well meaning men: "I didn't want to fight with Hank but neither
did I want him telling me how to handle my job" (58). She also worries
about some aspects of the job, as when Sam Collins is killed after she
talked with him about the kind of enterprise he has been investing in.
She believes he confronted Blackford with her suspicions and was killed
to keep him from going to the authorities. "Maybe if it weren't for me
he'd be alive" (94). And in *Copy Kat* she feels ashamed of the lying and
snooping she does as part of the investigation, mockingly labeling herself "slime" (117) and musing: "Did caring about a little boy help make
up for it?" (120).

McCone, Milhone and Colorado have in common that they are
women in a job previously defined in masculine terms. Each of these
characters drinks, usually in moderation, and, in line with the habits of
the 1980s and 1990s, frequently white wine. Each of them drinks, at least
occasionally, for self-medication, to ease the tension of a difficult case or
the pain of an investigation that has gone wrong. And each of them interacts with characters who drink, frequently to excess. It is impossible to
generalize about so many works by three different authors. Nevertheless
there are some comments that can be made. For Muller, drunkenness by
women seems to pose a greater threat than that of men. Compare the
anxiety and distaste McCone feels for her friend Linnea Carraway in *Ask
the Cards a Question* with the pity she displays toward Charlie Cornish
in *Edwin of the Iron Shoes*. Grafton gives Milhone an office bottle, though
it is of wine rather than whiskey, which combines with her wise-cracking
style to make her seem more an exemplar of the hard-bitten male detective. Milhone does not seem to have strong feelings about alcohol, using
and observing its use as part of the social landscape. Kijewski perceives
the negative aspects of alcohol use clearly, as one might expect from a former bartender, and gives her protagonist a similar background. Colorado,
does not extrapolate from the personal pain of an alcoholic, neglectful
mother to judge all drinkers. Her most vivid comments on alcohol are in
the descriptions of low-end bars with their "loser" clientele. At least for
these writers alcohol does not seem to bear a heavy symbolic load.

Conclusion

This study began with the premise that the hard-boiled detective genre consistently features protagonists who live by a set of rules, a code of behavior that governs the type of case they undertake, how they set out to solve it and how they will relate to the people they meet. This code is personal and may be cited as the reason they are unable to serve an organization, even one such as the police or district attorney's office, supposedly dedicated to the cause of justice. But even those detectives who, like the Continental Op, work for an organization reserve the option of putting their own moral standards ahead of the rules of the organization. Further, in a society in which official corruption or obstructionism may stand in the way of justice the detectives are frequently called upon to break the law in order to serve a client or their own sense of what is right. Sometimes they will even go against the wishes of a client in order to seek the full truth. In examining this idea of the detective code and the relationship between the treatment of alcohol and the exposition of the code, eight major writers in the genre, novelists whose writing careers range from 1929 to the present have been analyzed.

Dashiell Hammett, the acknowledged originator of the hard-boiled detective novel, is the natural author with whom to begin such an examination, particularly as his career began during Prohibition, an era that both reflected and shaped the peculiarly American ambivalence about the role of alcohol in society. Inspired by Hammett, Raymond Chandler is, for many, the established master of the genre. Chandler's Philip Marlowe became the prototype of the private eye as modern knight. However, there is much in Chandler's work to suggest that his private struggles with alcohol helped shape his creation of Marlowe and other significant characters. This influence reaches its zenith in *The Long Goodbye*, a book that can be seen as a quasi-apology, quasi-explanation to his dying wife for the role of alcohol in his own life.

Mickey Spillane will probably never appear on any list of the classics of the genre, since many critics seem to regard his work as almost sub-literary. However, his popularity, especially in the 1950s, exceeded that of any other writer of PI novels and his character, Mike Hammer, is known world-wide. Spillane may not have originated the trench-coat-wearing PI with the office bottle close at hand, but he certainly helped reinforce the archetype.

Robert B. Parker has the reputation of having created a new kind of PI, a man capable of expressing his feelings rather than drowning them in booze, a detective with an ability to seek new solutions to problems, as when he refers a teen prostitute to an ethical and accomplished madam rather than fruitlessly trying to talk her out of prostitution. However, much of this critical acclaim can be reduced to "Wow, he cooks," for the idea of a tough guy who prepares meals rather than living from greasy spoons or expecting a woman to feed him seems to have struck critics as revolutionary. Close examination reveals that Spenser is more violent than Marlowe, as violent as Hammer and differs little from either in his drinking habits.

More recently, Lawrence Block created a detective who moves from hard-drinking alcoholic to sober AA member while continuing to do investigations as "favors" for people. The success of the Matthew Scudder series reflects a society increasingly aware of alcohol-related problems and able to accept an author who deals with the subject with honesty.

The 1980s saw the entry of many women writers to the hard-boiled field. Of these Marcia Muller may be counted as first, Sue Grafton as among the best known, with Karen Kijewski well received, but less well known. Their protagonists work cases with the same independence, determination and dedication to righting wrongs as the male characters examined here. Their drinking habits reflect the society of the time, with wine or beer a more likely choice than rye whiskey or bourbon.

Dashiell Hammett created novels featuring three different private investigators with different attitudes toward detection. The Continental Op, as his lack of a personal name implies, is very much a company man. He does not choose his own cases, but sets out to do his best on whatever assignment he is given, whether it is investigating corruption in a mining town, solving a diamond theft, protecting an heiress or guarding a gathering of the rich. He seldom lets his own emotions affect the job and cannot be bought off by offers of money or sexual favors. Alcoholic drink is an everyday part of his life, as it is for the members of the underworld in which he must move to do his work. Despite Prohibition, it is also part of the lives of the supposedly law-abiding middle- and upper-class clients for whom he works. This in itself says much about the failure of prohibition. But it does not mean that everyone in America was ignoring the law; the statistics do not bear out that supposition. However, the temperance supporters who had campaigned for the law and the type of quiet citizen who would obey the law whether or not they agreed with it were not likely to loom large in the world of the PI. As shown in *Red Harvest* and *The Dain Curse*, the role of alcohol and other drugs in these novels centers on the issue of self-control. When necessary the Op will take advantage of others' lack of self-control to discover needed information. When he loses his objectivity and turns an effort to clean up the town into a private vendetta against the police chief who has tried to have him killed, he is sufficiently disturbed by his actions to sacrifice his own self-control to the temporary oblivion of alcohol and drugs, then must spend the rest of the novel regaining control of the situation. In *The Dain Curse* he successfully maintains control of himself when drugged against his will and then proceeds to help Gabrielle Leggett reclaim her life from the addiction that had been forced on her. In both novels the issues surrounding alcohol and drugs are largely of self-restraint and self-respect.

In *The Maltese Falcon* Hammett turns to a protagonist whose problems with self-restraint tend to be sexual rather than related to alcohol. Sam Spade's affair with his partner's wife leaves him in an equivocal position when that partner is killed, and his affair with Brigid O'Shaughnessy forces him to choose between love and self-preservation when he discovers that she murdered his partner and has been manipulating him throughout the case. Like the Continental Op, Spade takes liquor for granted as a part of his world, drinking on his own when upset, serving liquor to those he wishes to put at ease and accepting liquor from those who seek to put him at his ease. Nick Charles, in *The Thin Man*, is a detective who has abandoned detection for a life of leisured wealth and who shows little interest in any pursuit other than drinking and socializing. His wife pressures him into working on a case, which he does end up solving, but, as discussed earlier, the depiction of alcohol use has moved into the realm of fantasy, a fantasy in which one can drink from noon to dawn, day after day, without becoming incapacitated. Hammett's failure to continue his writing has been attributed by some to his own problems with alcohol, but the evidence in this regard is inconclusive. It does seem, however, that Hammett lost his ability or his desire to write honestly about alcohol use, a loss that would have affected his ability to continue in a genre which is supposed to reveal the ugly underside of life rather than gloss it over.

Raymond Chandler had a longer career as writer than Hammett, and concentrated his novelistic skills on one protagonist, Philip Marlowe. Marlowe was seen by his creator as a man of honor in a corrupt world.

It is in Chandler that we first find the full pattern of situations in which the discussion of alcohol is deployed in the service of character development. Hospitality, given or withheld, accepted or rejected, is one means by which Chandler defines relations between Marlowe and the people he encounters in the course of his investigations. When Marlowe shares alcohol with potential informants it can be in a quasi-hospitable fashion, as when he questions the room clerk in *Playback*, or the alcohol can have a coercive function, as when he plies the drunken Jessie Florian with liquor to get her to reveal more than she wishes about Velma. Marlowe feels some shame when he takes advantage of drunken individuals in this way. The hard-boiled genre is one in which cases frequently do not go well. Sometimes the investigation sets off a series of murders, sometimes the culprit escapes justice, sometimes the detective is simply overwhelmed by the layers of corruption he discovers, the seemingly respectable people with sordid secrets, the people who prey on the helpless. It is at such times that the detective is most likely to seek alcohol for self-medication, to cushion the ugliness of reality. However, if he is to be effective, he cannot resort to alcohol too frequently and must not let it distort his actions in ways that violate his values. Several Marlowe novels end with him drinking and meditating on the unsatisfactory conditions of his life. But the next case finds him ready once more to do his job.

Like Hammett, Chandler was known to have personal problems with alcohol. These problems did not end his writing career; indeed, he was working on a new Marlowe novel when he died. However, his private quandary concerning the question of whether he should be considered an alcoholic seems to be reflected in *The Long Goodbye*, a novel in which two characters struggle with alcohol and in which Marlowe responds to these struggles. The central question of the book seems to be whether alcoholism is to be defined purely by the amount of alcohol consumed, by how one behaves when drunk, or by other criteria. The question is not finally resolved and Chandler returned to more conventional mystery themes in his last novel, *Playback*.

Few critics would place Mickey Spillane in the same company with Hammett and Chandler. However, Mike Hammer is a detective who became very much part of the image of the PI. Those who have not read the novels have been exposed to the trench-coated, hard-drinking tough guy personified by Hammer on television, movies and beer advertisements. Prominent critics treat Hammer as a violent goon barely distinguishable from the criminals he fights, but criminals, by definition, lack the social consciousness to live by a code. Even the Mafia code of silence amounts only to self-protection. Hammer, however, does live by a code; loyalty to friends, protection of the innocent, patriotism, courage, and vengeance are some of its elements. And although Hammer drinks heavily, especially in the earlier works, he seldom lets drinking interfere with his pursuit of a villain. Like Chandler, Spillane explicitly explores the subject of alcoholism, but this exploration is unrealistic. The symptoms may be real, as when Hammer has lost weight and is hallucinatory after a seven-year drunk in *The Girl Hunters*. But the portrayal of his recovery is fantastic. He simply quits drinking, with no relapses, and regains his mental acuity and physical health in a matter of days with no treatment other than soup and vitamins. The recovery of Dr. Morgan in *Black Alley* is equally unrealistic. In both cases alcoholism is treated as a chosen retreat from an unsatisfactory life situation rather than as an addiction with long-lasting physical consequences.

Robert B. Parker's Spenser seems at first to be the very antithesis of Mike Hammer and has been hailed as part of a new generation of detectives. His code, which he explicates frequently, emphasizes preventing harm to innocents and refraining from killing except in self-defense or to protect others. But his actions turn out to be almost as violent as Hammer's. Spenser has acquired a reputation among critics as a feminist because of his ongoing relationship with Susan Silverman, who is an independent professional, and as something of a New Age sensitive man because he cooks for himself, has a best friend who is black, and relates well to homosexual men and women. However, his dependence on the relationship with Susan, who is constantly called upon to validate his sense of himself, is so great that when it is threatened he abandons his code and kills almost indiscriminately in a quest to recover her. Spenser's relationship with alcohol is not as patterned as Marlowe's. In earlier works he has resorted to the office bottle mainly when a case is going poorly but he teeters on the edge of out-of-control drinking when Susan leaves him. In addition, various alcoholic beverages play a strong role in creating the "newspaper reality" of the series as Spenser's drinking preferences reflect changes in national taste.

Lawrence Block is another author who is known to have had problems with alcohol. His detective, Matthew Scudder, has in common with Marlowe and Spenser a background in law enforcement, but whereas we are led to believe that Marlowe and Spenser were reluctant to stay in official employment because they disdained the compromises made necessary by political pressure and corruption, Scudder freely admits to having been part of the corruption. The picture he paints of the police is one in which some cops will finish taking what the burglar left, will pocket money or drugs left in a dead man's room, will accept bribes to overlook crime and expect a certain number of free meals and drinks from local businesses as perks of office. Despite these breaches of faith as a police officer, Scudder has a code that functions even when he is an out-of-control alcoholic. That code will not allow him to overlook murder or to abandon a case once he starts it. His relationship with alcohol changes in the course of the series. For the first several volumes he regularly resorts to self-medication, using alcohol to soothe his boredom when unoccupied and to drown negative feelings engendered by a life that has gone seriously wrong. After he joins AA drink becomes his enemy and situations which would have sent him to a bar or a bottle earlier now send him to an AA meeting or to call his sponsor. But even as Scudder regains control of his life, the society in which he lives is depicted as growing more dangerous and unpredictable.

While critics debate whether women can be hard-boiled the public seems to have accepted the entrance of female protagonists to the field. Those who produce these works are too numerous to list, however Marcia Muller, Sue Grafton and Karen Kijewski are each authors of long-running series. Marcia Muller deliberately avoided the stereotype of the PI as a hard-drinking loner when creating her Sharon McCone. McCone has a family with whom she remains in contact, co-workers and friends with whom she has regular interaction. This interaction may include drinking, indeed many cases include sessions over a bottle of red wine with her boss, Hank Zahn. While drink does not play a central role in the series Muller does betray some discomfort with the idea of women as heavy drinkers, even as she minimizes the effects of consumption on her protagonist. None of the biographical material available suggests that Muller herself is a problem drinker, so this discomfort may reflect societal expectations of women rather than a personal aversion. Sue Grafton, the best known of the three authors treated here, does have a background as the child of alcoholic parents. She does not, however, extend this background to her protagonist, Kinsey Milhone. Milhone is more socially isolated than McCone, orphaned thrice, first by the deaths of both parents in an automobile accident when she was five, later by the death of the maternal aunt who raised her. She is also twice divorced and works alone, rather than in an office with others. She does exchange occasional chat with the secretary of the insurance company from which she rents office space, but her main social contacts are Henry Pitts, her landlord, and Rosie the owner of a local bar where she takes many meals. Milhone does have an office bottle, of white wine, and often drinks while working up notes or otherwise thinking over a case. Alcohol does not seem to be a problem for her however, nor does it figure more strongly in the series than would be expected in the social milieu described. Karen Kijewski spent several years working as a bartender and extends this experience to her detective, Kat Colorado. She also gives Colorado a hard luck life history, with an unknown father and an alcoholic mother, and an only sibling lost to neglect in early childhood. Despite this, Colorado is able to form strong attachments to those who have befriended her and to those she befriends. She drinks in moderation but is clearly aware that many of life's failures are caused by drink or drugs. These three authors may not, of course, be representative of the range of attitudes possible in regard to women and alcohol. One might guess that readers who prefer not to read about women who drink may avoid the hard-boiled genre. The fact that these series do sell well suggests that the attitudes and habits displayed by the protagonists are acceptable to the fans and reflective of contemporary attitudes in general.

The authors treated here are not the only writers whose work features alcohol use as a strong plot component or definer of character. There are a number of contemporary authors who could be considered for a more extended study of the topic. James Lee Burke, for example, writes novels set in Louisiana centered on the character of Dave Robicheaux, who is, like Scudder, a recovering alcoholic. These works are somewhat peripheral to the genre, since Robicheaux is a police officer or deputy sheriff for major parts of the series. However, he often works against orders or on his own time in ways that make him function like a PI. An author from the Northwest, James Crumley, has created two detectives who suffer from substance abuse, Milo Milodragovitch and C. W. Sughrue. Their adventures take them on extended tours of bars and roadhouses, mostly in the West and Northwest, an environment rather different from the urban settings of most hard-boiled fiction. In *Detecting Men* (1st edition, 1998), Willetta Heising lists at least five detectives identified as alcoholic, recovering alcoholic or teetotaler, out of over 235 series featuring PIs. Interestingly, there is only one woman PI so identified in *Detecting Women* (200). This one is Lynda La Plante's Lorraine Page, described as a "Sober ex-cop turned private eye" (301). It is hard to know whether this is because few authors have created women PI characters who can be described as alcoholic, or because Heising chooses not to mention that characteristic in her brief descriptions.

Heising's work certainly illustrates that the hard-boiled genre shows no signs of disappearing. With 235 current fictional PIs created by men and over 100 created by woman the variety offered by contemporary practitioners of the genre is considerable. Heising's thumbnail sketches of these PIs illustrate this variety. For example, we have Paul Bishop's Ian Chapel, a "one-eyed pro soccer goalie turned P.I."; Dan Kavanagh's Nick Duffy, a "bisexual ex-cop P.I."; William Sanders' Taggart Roper, a "Cherokee writer and private eye"; and Don Winslow's Neal Carey, a "youthful pickpocket turned P.I.," to name only a few (Heising, *Detecting Men* 271–75).

Another dimension in the hard-boiled genre has been opened by the introduction of female protagonists. Marcia Muller is credited by some as having created the first fictional woman PI, Sharon McCone, in 1977.

Somewhat better known are Sara Paretsky's V. I. Warshawski, who first appeared in 1982, and Sue Grafton's Kinsey Milhone, who was also introduced in 1982 in the first of Grafton's alphabet series, *"A" is for Alibi*. Although women PIs are not as plentiful as males, in fiction or in reality, the backgrounds of the fictional ones have nearly as great a variety as their male counterparts, including Winona Sullivan's Sister Cecile Buddenbrooks, a "licensed P.I. nun"; several lesbian PIs; Dana Stablenow's Kate Shugak, a "native Alaskan ex–D. A. investigator," and Abrigal Padgett's Barbara Joan "Bo" Bradley, a "child abuse investigator" (Heising, *Detecting Women*, 300–302).

The continued popularity of the hard-boiled genre suggests that a portion of the reading public harbors some degree of cynicism regarding the function of the justice system in our society. Some may feel that police corruption is the problem, that criminals themselves can buy off police, as was the case in *Red Harvest*, in which Chief Noonan is obviously a tool of the bootleggers who control the town. Nor is this a problem of the past, for the war on drugs has produced well-financed criminal gangs in virtually every area of the nation. Other interested parties may be seen as influencing investigations, as when Harlen Potter uses his financial clout to derail the investigation of his daughter's murder in *The Long Goodbye*. Others may blame the tendency for any bureaucracy to seek the easy answer, the one that makes officials look good. Why reopen a case if the solution seems to have been found, as when Scudder tries to convince the police that Tommy Tillary did, after all, kill his wife in *When the Sacred Ginmill Closes*? Or the problem may be seen as understaffing, when there are too few detectives and too much crime, resources must be concentrated on high profile cases or on cases that seem the likeliest to be solved quickly. And, even if an investigation is successful and an arrest is made, procedural problems may free the culprit, or a jury may be swayed by a skilled defense attorney, as Mike Hammer fears will happen in *I, the Jury* if the killer of his best friend is arrested and brought to trial. None of these fears is entirely without foundation, although they may be exaggerated in fiction to provide a rationale for the actions of the PI as protagonist. In reality, private investigators are more likely to investigate erring spouses, fraudulent accident victims, employee theft and other non-violent crime than to discover murderers. But there is comfort in the fantasy that the ultimate crime will be avenged by a tireless and incorruptible man or woman who can be trusted with pursuit of the truth even if it is necessary to break laws, and who often can and will mete out justice to those who cannot be touched by the official enforcers of the law.

A protagonist who is to be entrusted by readers with such responsibilities must be described in such a fashion as to gain the reader's trust and sympathy. The convention of the detective code is one means that has been used to this end by authors in the genre. Detectives may cheat on their spouses, lie to the police, conceal evidence, break and enter to obtain evidence, threaten witnesses or commit any number of other offenses against law and conventional notions of decent behavior. But so long as the reader remains convinced that the detective's goal is to discover the truth about a crime and to bring the perpetrator to justice, much can be forgiven. Obviously the fact that some detective series are more popular than others suggests that authors are not equally successful in creating detectives who can retain reader sympathy while behaving in ways that would be unacceptable in real life. In addition to concern over failures in the system of justice, many feel concern about new types of crime. Urban youth gangs are no longer armed with the switchblades and zip-guns of *West Side Story*. Profits from illicit drug sales enable gang members to buy Uzis and Glocks, and stiff competition for territories encourages the use of such weapons. Innocent bystanders have become the new urban victim. Because of certain highly publicized cases and the popularity of fictional depictions of similar cases, the public is also newly aware of the sexually psychopathic serial killer who may leave a string of victims across several states. And, of course, terrorism is yet another source of social tension and fear. While these types of crimes are more likely to be the subject of police procedural novels, suspense thrillers or espionage tales, they can also be the subject of the hard-boiled novel. For instance, in *Double Deuce* Spenser and Hawk confront youth gangs in the Boston projects and in *Walk Among the Tombstones* Scudder helps stop two serial killers who prey on victims whose relatives are unlikely to seek help from the police because they are criminals themselves.

As we have seen, alcohol use has been a highly controversial area of behavior for most of American history. What a man drinks and who he drinks with indicates class, education, profession, and character. What, or even whether, a woman drinks has equal weight. Yet the use of alcoholic beverages is such an ingrained part of Western culture that it can serve as a useful marker of character in almost any form of popular fiction. It also serves as a useful marker of newspaper reality. As tastes in alcohol change through the years some beverages decline in popularity, others are introduced, or old stand-bys are adapted by a new generation. Martinis, for example, were thought of by most Baby Boomers as the drink of their parents' generation. But martinis have recently been revived, both in the original gin-and-vermouth version and in many flavored variations. In the Spenser novels, Spenser's favored beer brands have steadily changed as the American beer market has evolved toward greater variety and emphasis on more strongly flavored beers. Similar markers of changes in tastes and drinking habits can be found in other books, as when

Scudder comments that Long Island Iced Tea, a mixed drink ordered by one of his sons in *Hope to Die*, had not been invented at the time he quit drinking. These are the sort of details that assure readers the author is accurately describing the world in which they live.

More important for the issue of character are changes in the attitudes about alcohol consumption and alcohol dependency and its treatment. The temperance movement in America never really died, and there are large sections of the nation with local prohibition or restrictive liquor laws which reflect at least an official disapproval of drink in general. There are also religious groups with substantial memberships that either forbid or discourage alcohol consumption by their members. While, for the most part, Americans accept alcohol as part of the social scene, the past few decades have seen increasing concern for safety and the health consequences of drinking. The campaign against drunk driving, for instance, has greatly increased in intensity since the formation of Mothers Against Drunk Driving in 1980. Concepts such as the "Designated Driver" and slogans such as "Friends Don't Let Friends Drive Drunk" are part of the social landscape that would have been completely foreign to readers of earlier decades. Mike Hammer expresses no qualms about driving across New York state after an evening of drinking beer, yet an author would find great difficulty in justifying a similar action by a contemporary protagonist. Similarly, concerns about the health effects of drinking, even in moderation, have surfaced in the popular press, spurred by conflicting medical studies. Drinking may be good for your heart, but increase the risks of some cancers, not to mention the ever-present consciousness of the possibility of becoming an alcoholic. Food is also a matter of modern concern. Marlowe worried only about whether a coffee shop hamburger would give him indigestion; Kinsey Milhone eats McDonalds, but treats the craving as a character flaw, to be compensated for by extra jogging. This is not to imply that the newer detectives are uniformly interested in health and clean living, but an awareness of health issues concerning alcohol and fast food is part of the general social climate and may be reflected in the characterization of the PI as either a consistently self-disciplined person or as a person who lets alcohol or unhealthy eating habits serve as self-medication for the stresses of the profession.

Contemporary literature may also be expected to reflect the fact that the available options have changed for those who realize they have become addicted to alcohol. When Hammett and Chandler were writing there was little medical consensus on the subject. The acute alcoholic in treatment could be given sedatives to protect the body from the possibly fatal effects of sudden detoxification. However, there was then, and there is still no long-term medical solution. Whether such a solution potentially exists depends on whether alcoholism is actually a disease or a personal or social problem. According to Andrew Barr, the commonly accepted theory that excessive drinking is a disease is unproven and has been accepted by many doctors largely for the practical reason that treatment for a disease will be covered by health insurance, whereas treatment for a character flaw (the traditional view of habitual drunkenness) will not. The disease theory was publicized widely by the National Council for Education on Alcohol, an organization established for that purpose by the founders of AA. Alcoholics Anonymous itself was founded in 1935. In the 1940s only one-fifth of those polled believed that alcoholics were sick, but by the early 1960s nearly two-thirds of Americans interviewed accepted the idea, probably as a result of widespread publicity about the theory and increasing public knowledge about AA methods. As the AA program became widely known it became accepted as the best approach to the problem, and criminals with drinking problems are sometimes referred to Twelve Step groups as a condition of probation. In fact, according to Barr, there is evidence that criminals will sometimes claim to have been drunk when they were not in expectation of more sympathetic treatment (20–21). If *The Long Goodbye* had been written more recently, Marlowe might be expected to spend some time encouraging Lennox or Wade to join AA or to go into a rehabilitation program that incorporated the same principles.

The perception of alcohol as a disease and acceptance of the AA program of absolute abstinence as the only treatment obviously has effects on the three types of depiction of alcohol use discussed throughout this study. Alcoholism, as we have seen when Scudder refuses whiskey from Ballou in *Out on the Cutting Edge*, provides an acceptable reason for refusing a drink, even in situations where such a refusal would have been seen as a deadly insult by earlier audiences. On the other hand, offering or pressing alcohol on someone who has refused it may seem like an act of aggression rather than hospitality, while a consistent refusal to serve alcohol may be perceived as a principled stand rather than a failure of hospitality. Further, using the offer of alcohol to get information or other forms of cooperation from someone becomes despicable rather than merely distasteful if that person is seen as diseased rather than merely weak-willed. Such actions become truly a form of coercion, almost like bribing a starving person with food. Finally, self-medication with alcohol may come to be regarded by readers as recklessly irresponsible behavior, particularly if a character drinks frequently or to the point of blacking out, as does Scudder before he quits drinking. And a first-person narrator who describes such behavior yet claims not to have a problem will probably be considered to be in a state of denial by readers familiar with the concept. An earlier generation could agree with a character who felt that strength of mind would protect a person from becoming a drunk, but an audience taught to believe that alcoholism is a disease that can attack anyone might feel that such as attitude is dangerously naive. In any case, these changes in public perception of the nature of alcohol abuse affect both the portrayal of alcohol use in fiction and the reception of these portrayals by readers.

As demonstrated, the depiction of the drinking habits of characters in hard-boiled detective fiction is more than mere window-dressing, mimetic detail designed to enforce the realism of the genre. Details of specific beverages, including brand names, do contribute to the contemporary feel of a work. However, other questions arise when characters consume alcohol. Under what circumstances do they drink? What and how much? Does the author fully and truthfully portray the physical and mental effects of the drinks? Is the protagonist portrayed differently than other characters in these respects? Such details reinforce characterization, especially the characterization of the detective as a person who exemplifies certain standards of behavior that can be regarded as heroic. Since one of the conventions of the hard-boiled detective genre is that the protagonist is justified in defying law and authority in pursuit of truth and justice, it is necessary to use devices to assure the reader that the protagonist meets certain standards of integrity that go beyond mere obedience to the law. The detective's stance toward drink is such a device, one that resonates strongly for a nation with an extended history of ambiguity toward alcohol.

Bibliography

Primary Sources

Block, Lawrence. *The Sins of the Fathers*. 1976. New York: Avon, 1991.

_____. *Time to Murder and Create*. New York: Dell, 1977.

_____. *Eight Million Ways to Die*. New York: Morrow, 1982. New York, Avon, 1993.

_____. *When the Sacred Ginmill Closes*. New York: Arbor, 1986. New York: Charter, 1987.

_____. *Out on the Cutting Edge*. New York: Morrow, 1989.

_____. *A Dance at the Slaughterhouse*. 1992. New York: Avon, 2000.

_____. *A Walk Among the Tombstones*. New York: Morrow, 1992. New York: Avon, 2000.

_____. *Even the Wicked*. New York: Morrow, 1997.

_____. *Hope to Die*. New York: Morrow, 2001.

Chandler, Raymond. *The Big Sleep*. 1939. Knopf. *Raymond Chandler: Stories and Early Novels*. Ed. Frank MacShane. New York: Library of America, 1995. 587–764.

_____. *Farewell, My Lovely*. 1940. Knopf. *Raymond Chandler: Stories and Early Novels*. Ed. Frank MacShane. New York: Library of America, 1995. 765–984.

_____. *The High Window*. 1942. Knopf. *Raymond Chandler: Stories and Early Novels*. Ed. Frank MacShane. New York: Library of America, 1995. 985–1177.

_____. *The Lady in the Lake*. 1943. Knopf. *Raymond Chandler: Later Novels and Other Writings*. Ed. Frank MacShane. New York: Library of America, 1995. 3–200.

_____. *The Little Sister*. 1949. Knopf. *Raymond Chandler: Later Novels and Other Writings*. Ed. Frank MacShane. New York: Library of America, 1995. 201–416.

_____. *The Long Goodbye*. 1953. Knopf. *Raymond Chandler: Later Novels and Other Writings*. Ed. Frank MacShane. New York: Library of America, 1995. 417–734.

_____. *Playback*. 1958. Knopf. *Raymond Chandler: Later Novels and Other Writings*. Ed. Frank MacShane. New York: Library of America, 1995. 735–871.

Chandler, Raymond and Robert B. Parker. *Poodle Springs*. New York: Putnam, 1989.

Hammett, Dashiell. *Red Harvest*. New York: Knopf, 1929. New York: Vintage-Random, 1992.

_____. *The Dain Curse*. New York: Knopf, 1929. New York: Vintage-Random, 1972.

_____. *The Maltese Falcon*. New York: Knopf, 1929. San Francisco: North Point, 1984.

_____. *The Thin Man*. New York: Knopf, 1933. New York: Vintage-Random, 1972.

Grafton, Sue. *"A" is for Alibi*. 1982. New York: Bantam, 1987.

_____. *"K" is for Killer*. 1994. New York: Ballantine, 1995.

Kijewski, Karen. *Katwalk*. New York: St. Martins, 1989.

_____. *Copy Kat*. New York: Doubleday, 1992.

_____. *Honky Tonk Kat*. 1996. New York: Berkeley, 1997.

_____. *Stray Kat Waltz*. New York: Putnam, 1998.

Muller, Marcia. *Edwin of the Iron Shoes*. 1977. New York: Mysterious Press, 1993.

_____. *Ask the Cards a Question*. 1982. New York: Mysterious Press, 1993.

_____. *There's Something in a Sunday*. 1989. New York: Mysterious Press, 1993.

_____. *A Walk Through the Fire*. New York: Mysterious Press, 1999.

Parker, Robert. *The Godwulf Manuscript*. New York: Delacorte, 1973. New York: Dell, 1987.

_____. *Mortal Stakes*. 1975. New York: Dell, 1984.

_____. *Ceremony*. New York: Delacorte, 1982.

_____. *Valediction*. New York: Delacorte, 1984. New York: Dell, 1988.

_____. *A Catskill Eagle*. New York: Delacorte, 1985.

_____. *Taming a Sea-Horse*. New York: Delacorte, 1986.

_____. *Stardust*. New York: Putnam, 1990.

_____. *Pastime*. New York: Putnam, 1991. New York; Berkeley, 1991.

_____. *Perchance to Dream: Robert B. Parker's Sequel to Raymond Chandler's* The Big Sleep. New York: Putnam, 1991.

_____. *Night Passage*. New York: Putnam, 1997. New York: Jove, 1998.

_____. *Hush Money*. New York: Putnam, 1999.

_____. *Hugger Mugger*. New York: Putnam, 2000.

_____. *Potshot*. New York: Putnam, 2001.

Spillane, Mickey. *I the Jury*. New York: Dutton, 1947. New York: Signet, 1975.

_____. *One Lonely Night*. New York: Dutton, 1951. Fortieth Anniversary ed. New York: Signet, 1991.

_____. *Kiss Me, Deadly*. New York: Dutton, 1952. New York: Signet, n.d.

_____. *The Girl Hunters*. New York: Dutton, 1962. New York: Signet, 1963.

_____. *The Twisted Thing*. New York: Dutton, 1966. New York: Signet, 1966.

_____. *Survival ... Zero*. New York: Dutton, 1970. Lg. prt ed. Thorndike, ME: Hall, 1999.

_____. *The Killing Man*. New York: Dutton, 1989. New York: Signet, 1990.

_____. *Black Alley*. New York: Dutton, 1996. New York: Signet, 1997.

Critical Sources

Ardai, Charles. "Lawrence Block." Winks and Corrigan 63–81.

Auden, W. H. "The Guilty Vicarage." *The Dyer's Hand and Other Essays.* 1948. New York: Random, 1962. 146–58.

Barr, Andrew. *Drink: A Social History of America.* New York: Carroll & Graf, 1999.

Baumgold, Julie. "A Wild Man Proper." *Esquire* Aug. 1995: 132(2).

Bertens, Hans and Theo D'haen. *Contemporary American Crime Fiction.* Crime Files Series. Clive Bloom, ed. Houndmills, England: Palgrave, 2001.

Binyon, T. J. "Private Eye." Herbert 354–55.

Bleiler, Richard. "Formula: Character." Herbert 165–66.

Block, Lawrence and Ernie Bulow. *After Hours: Conversations With Lawrence Block.* Albuquerque, NM: U New Mexico P, 1995.

Britannica 2002 Book of the Year. Chicago: Britannica, 2002.

Burns, Landon C. "Matthew Scudder's Moral Ambiguity." *Clues* 17.2 (1996): 19–31.

Carr, Helen ed. *Genre and Women's Writing in the Postmodern World.* London: Pandora, 1989.

Carter, Steven. "Spenserian Ethics: the Unconventional Morality of Robert B. Parker's Traditional American Hero." *Clues* 1.2 (1980): 109–118.

Casella, Donna R. "The Matt Scudder Series: the Saga of an Alcoholic Hard-boiled Detective." *Clues* 14.2 (1993): 31–49.

Cawelti, John G. *Adventure, Mystery, and Romance: Formula Stories as Art and Popular Culture.* Chicago: U Chicago P, 1976.

Chandler, Raymond. "The Simple Art of Murder." *Atlantic Monthly* 1944. *Raymond Chandler: Later Novels and Other Writings.* Ed. Frank MacShane. New York: Library of America, 1995. 977–992.

Charles, Kate, and Lucy Walker. "Chivalry, Code of." Herbert 67–68.

Christianson, Scott. "Talkin' Trash and Kickin' Butt: Sue Grafton's Hard-Boiled Feminism." Irons 127–47.

Cohen, Michael. *Murder Most Fair: the Appeal of Mystery Fiction.* Madison, WI: Fairleigh Dickinson UP, 2000.

Collins, Max Allan. Introduction. *Tomorrow I Die.* By Mickey Spillane. New York: Mysterious P, 1984. vii–xv.

Collins, Max Allan and James L. Traylor. *One Lonely Knight: Mickey Spillane's Mike Hammer.* Bowling Green, OH: Bowling Green State U Popular P, 1984.

Corrigan, Maureen. "Robert B. Parker." Winks and Corrigan 715–732.

Coward, Rosalind and Linda Semple. "Tracking Down the Past: Women and Detective Fiction." Carr 39–57.

Dardis, Tom. *The Thirsty Muse: Alcohol and the American Writer.* New York: Ticknor & Fields, 1989.

Dooley, Dennis. *Dashiell Hammett.* New York: Frederick Ungar, 1984.

Eames, Hugh. *Sleuths, Inc.: Studies of Problem Solvers.* Philadelphia: J B Lipponcott, 1978.

Eisman, Gregory. "The Catskill Eagle Crashed: the Moral Demise of Spenser in Robert B. Parker's *A Catskill Eagle.*" *Clues.* 11.1: (1990): 107–117.

Fackler, Herbert V. "Spenser's New England Conscience." *Colby Library Quarterly* 34.3 (1998): 253–60.

Filloy, Richard. A. "Of Drink and Detectives: the Genesis and Function of a Literary Convention." *Contemporary Drug Problems* 13:2 (1986) 249–71.

Franklin, Benjamin. *The Autobiography and Other Writings*. Ed. Kenneth Silverman. New York: Penguin, 1986.

Gardner, Berry W. "Lawrence Block." Pederson 86–88.

Gawain Poet, *The Complete Works of the Gawain Poet*. Trans. John Gardner. Chicago: U Chicago P, 1967.

Geherin, David. *Sons of Sam Spade: the Private Eye Novel in the 70s*. Recognitions. New York: Frederick Ungar, 1980.

_____. *The American Private Eye: the Image in Fiction*. New York: Frederick Ungar, 1985.

Gilmore, Thomas B. *Equivocal Spirits: Alcoholism and Drinking in Twentieth-Century Literature*. Chapel Hill, NC: U North Carolina P, 1987.

Gregory, Sinda. *Private Investigations: the Novels of Dashiell Hammett*. Carbondale, IL: Southern Illinois UP, 1985.

Greiner, Donald J. "Robert B. Parker and the Jock of the Mean Streets." *Critique: Studies in Contemporary Fiction* 26.1 (1984) 36–44.

Grella, George. "Murder and Manners: the Formal Detective Novel." Landrum et al. 35–57.

_____. "The Hard-Boiled Detective Novel." Winks. *Detective Fiction* 103–120. Rpt. of "Murder and the Mean Streets: The Hard-Boiled Detective Novel." *Contempora* March 1970. 6–15.

Gross, Miriam, ed. *The World of Raymond Chandler*. New York: A & W, 1978.

Hartman, Geoffrey H. "Literature High and Low: the Case of the Mystery Story." Most and Stone 210–29.

Heising, Willetta L. *Detecting Women: a Reader's Guide and Checklist for Mystery Series Written by Women*. 3rd ed. Dearborn, MI: Purple Moon, 2000.

_____. *Detecting Men: a Reader's Guide and Checklist for Mystery Series Written by Men*. Dearborn, MI, Purple Moon: 1998.

Herbert, Rosemary, ed. *The Oxford Companion to Crime and Mystery Writing*. New York: Oxford UP, 1999.

Hiney, Tom. *Raymond Chandler: a Biography*. New York: Atlantic Monthly P, 1997.

Houseman, John. "Lost Fortnight." Gross 53–66.

Hoyser, Catherine Elizabeth. "Sue Grafton." Klein. *Great Women Mystery Writers*. 134–37.

Irons, Glenwood. ed. *Feminism In Women's Detective Fiction*. Toronto: U. Toronto P, 1995.

Johnson, Diane. *Dashiell Hammett: a Life*. New York: Random House, 1983.

Kaufman, Natalie H. and Carol M. Kay. *"G" is for Grafton: the World of Kinsey Milhone*. New York: Henry Holt, 1997.

Klein, Kathleen Gregory. *The Woman Detective: Gender and Genre*. Urbana: U. Illinois P, 1988.

_____. *Great Women Mystery Writers: Classic to Contemporary*. Westport CT: Greenwood, 1994.

Labianca, Dominick A. and William. J. Reeves. "Dashiell Hammett and Raymond Chandler: Down on Drugs." *Clues* 5:2 (1984): 66–71.

Lachman, Marvin. "Gardner, Erle Stanley." Herbert 174–75.

Landrum, Larry N., Pat Browne and Ray Browne. *Dimensions of Detective Fiction*. Bowling Green, OH: Popular P, 1976.

Lender, Mark Edward and James Kirby Martin. *Drinking in America: A History*. New York: Free Press, 1982.

Lennon, Peter. "The Hardest Jehovah's Witness ..." *Guardian* 23 July, 1999: S2(2).

Lid, R. W. "Philip Marlowe Speaking." Van Dover. *Critical Response*. 43–63.

Lipman, Elinor. "Building Character at the Table." *Gourmet* Jan. 2000: 106.

Littler, Alison. "Marele Day's 'Cold Hard Bitch': The Masculinist Imperative of the Private-Eye Genre." *Journal of Narrative Technique* 21 (1991): 121–35.

Macleans. "Cops and Barhoppers" 28 Mar. 1994: 49.

MacShane, Frank. *The Life of Raymond Chandler*. New York: Dutton, 1976.

MacShane, Frank. ed. *Selected Letters of Raymond Chandler*. New York: Columbia UP, 1981.

McDowell, Edwin. "Drinking Habits: on Literary Symbolism and Mickey Spillane." *New York Times Book Review* 27 Dec. 1981: 16(1).

Meroney, John. "Man of Mysteries." *Washington Post* 22 Aug. 2001: C1.

Most, Glenn W. and William W. Stone, eds. *The Poetics of Murder: Detective Fiction and Literary Theory*. New York: Harcourt Brace, 1983.

Muller, Marcia. "Partners in Crime: Developing a Series Character." *Mystery Scene* 69 (2000) 26+.

Nolan, William F. *Hammett: a Life at the Edge*. New York: Congdon & Weed, 1983.

Norman, Geoffrey. "Still for Hire." *American Way* 15 March 1999: 56+.

Oser, Kathleen. "Karen Kijewski." Klein. *Great Women Detectives*. 179–81.

Panek, Leroy Lad. *An Introduction to the Detective Story*. Bowling Green, OH: Bowling Green State U Popular P, 1987.

_____. *Probable Cause: Crime Fiction in America*. Bowling Green, OH: Bowling Green State U Popular P, 1990.

_____. *New Hard-Boiled Writers: 1970s–1990s*. Bowling Green OH: Bowling Green State U Popular P, 2000.

Parker, Robert B. *The Private Eye in Hammett and Chandler*. Northridge, CA: Lord John, 1984.

Parker, Robert B. and Anne Ponder. "What I Know About Writing Spenser Novels." Winks. *Colloquium on Crime*. 189–203.

Pederson, Jay P. ed. *St. James Guide to Crime and Mystery Writers*. Detroit: St. James, 1996.

Penzler, Otto. *Mickey Spillane*. New York: Mysterious P, 1999.

Plummer, Bonnie C. "Marcia Muller." Klein. *Great Women Detectives*. 244–247.

Porter, Dennis. "Detection and Ethics: The Case of P. D. James." Rader and Zettler. 11–18.

Pyrhönen, Heta. *Murder From an Academic Angle: An Introduction to the Study of the Detective Narrative*. Columbia, SC: Camden House, 1994.

Rader, Barbara A. and Howard G. Zettler. *The Sleuth and the Scholar: Origins,*

Evolution and Current Trends in Detective Fiction. New York: Greenwood P,
  1988.
Reddy, Maureen T. "The Female Detective From Nancy Drew to Sue Grafton."
  Winks. *Mystery and Suspense*. 1047–1067.
Reilly, John M. "Hard-boiled Sleuth." Herbert 201–03.
Roberts, Thomas John. *An Aesthetics of Junk Fiction*. Athens, GA: U Georgia P,
  1990.
Robinson, Doug. *No Less a Man: Masculist Art in a Feminist Age*. Bowling Green,
  OH: Popular P, 1994.
Root, Christina. "Silence of the Other: Women in Robert Parker's Spenser
  Series." *Clues* 19.1 (1998): 25–38.
Ruehlmann, William. *Saint With a Gun: the Unlawful American Private Eye*. New
  York: New York UP, 1974.
Saylor, Louise V. "The Private Eye and His Victuals." *Clues* 5.2 (1984): 111–18.
Schaffer, Rachel. "Armed (with Wit) and Dangerous: Sue Grafton's Sense of
  Black Humor." *The Armchair Detective*. 30:3 (1997) 316–22.
Smith, Johanna M. "Raymond Chandler and the Business of Literature." Van
  Dover. *Critical Response*. 183–201.
Spender, Natasha. "His Own Long Goodbye." Gross 127–58.
Symons, Julian. *Bloody Murder: From the Detective Story to the Crime Novel: a
  History*. New York: Viking, 1985.
Swanson, Jean. "Sue Grafton." Winks and Corrigan 439–448.
Tate, J. O. "The Longest Goodbye: Raymond Chandler and the Poetry of Alco-
  hol." *The Armchair Detective*. 18.4 (1985): 392–406.
Taylor, Bruce. "G" is for (Sue) Grafton". *The Armchair Detective*. 22:1 (1989):
  4–13.
Traylor, James L. and Max Allan Collins. "Spillane, Mickey." Herbert 422–23.
Van Dover, J. Kenneth. *Murder in the Millions: Erle Stanley Gardner, Mickey
  Spillane, Ian Fleming*. New York: Frederick Ungar, 1984.
Van Dover, J. K[enneth] ed. *Critical Response*. Critical Responses in Arts and
  Letters. 18. Westport, CT: Greenwood, 1995.
Walton, Priscilla L. and Manina Jones. *Detective Agency: Women Rewriting the
  Hard-Boiled Tradition*. Berkeley: U California P, 1999.
Watchtower. 2000. Assembly of Jehovah's Witnesses. 7 Oct. 2002 <http://www.
  watchtower.org/library/rg/article_10htm>
Wedge, George F. "Alcohol and Alcoholism." Herbert 10–11.
_____. "An Unlicensed PI in AA: the Matt Scudder Novels." *Dionysos* 3.1 (1991):
  24–31.
_____. "Matt Scudder: Fighting the Good Fight Against Crime and Booze."
  Dionysos 5.1 (1993): 29–32.
Weibel, Kay. "Mickey Spillane as a Fifties Phenomenon." Landrum, et al. 114–23.
Winks, Robin W. *Modus Operandi: an Excursion into Detective Fiction*. Boston:
  David R. Godine, 1982.
Winks, Robin. W. ed. *Colloquium on Crime: Eleven Renowned Mystery Writers Dis-
  cuss Their Work*. New York: Charles Scribner, 1986.
_____. ed. *Detective Fiction: a Collection of Critical Essays*. Englewood Cliffs, NJ:
  Prentice, 1980.

Winks, Robin, and Maureen Corrigan eds. *Mystery and Suspense Writers: Literature of Crime, Detection and Espionage.* New York: Charles Scribner's, 1998.

Wolfe, Peter. *Beams Falling: the Art of Dashiell Hammett.* Bowling Green, OH: Bowling Green State U Popular P, 1980.

_____. *Something More Than Night: The Case of Raymond Chandler.* Bowling Green, OH: Bowling Green State U Popular P, 1985.

Zalewski, James W. and Lawrence B. Rosenfield. "Rules for the Game: the Mysteries of Robert B. Parker and Dick Francis." *Clues* 5.2 (1984): 72–81.

Index